CONTENTS

		Page
Introduction		**v**
1.	**Strategic Setting and Early History**	**1**
2.	**Inverness in the Middle Ages**	**11**
3.	**Inverness in the Seventeenth Century**	**24**
4.	**Inverness and the Jacobites**	**44**
5.	**Inverness Before the Railways**	**63**
6.	**Late Victorian Growth and Development**	**93**
7.	**Some Victorian Notables**	**112**
8.	**The Townscape of Inverness**	**130**
9.	**Inverness in the 20th Century, 1900–1950**	**150**
10.	**Inverness and the Millennium, 1950–2000**	**166**
	Conclusion	**187**
	Further Reading	**195**
	Index	**199**

The Life and Times of Inverness

NORMAN S NEWTON

JOHN DONALD PUBLISHERS LTD
EDINBURGH

ISBN 0 85976 442 7

British Library Cataloguing in Publication Data.

A catalogue record for this book is available
from the British Library.

PostScript Typesetting & Origination by Brinnoven, Livingston.
Printed & bound in Great Britain by Bell & Bain Ltd, Glasgow.

INTRODUCTION

This book is about the people of Inverness over the centuries. It is primarily about their daily life and preoccupations, and less about the architecture of the buildings of the town, or the politics of the ruling elite. Before the middle of the eighteenth century we are forced to rely mainly on inference, or extrapolation, for a reconstruction of local events and their influence on the population, although we are fortunate in having the two volumes of the *Records of Inverness* which reprint some of the Burgh Court Records and Town Council Minutes up to 1688. After 1809, we are fortunate in having the first local newspaper, the *Inverness Journal*, to give us a real insight into real people, and real lives. Later in the nineteenth century other local papers, notably the *Inverness Courier* (from 1817 and still going strong), the *Inverness Advertiser* (1849–85), the *Northern Chronicle* (1881–1969), the *Highland News* (from 1883 and still publishing), John Murdoch's radical newspaper *The Highlander* (1873–82), and Alexander Mackenzie's radical successor *The Scottish Highlander* (1885–98). There were other minor aspirants to the ranks of the fourth estate in the Highlands which lasted a few months, or years.

In Inverness Public Library, card indexes compiled in the 1980s are a treasure trove of information on the people of Inverness and indeed much further afield. Anybody mentioned in the pages of the indexed papers is listed on to an index card, so it is a source of inestimable importance to genealogists and family history buffs, as well as social historians. Of even greater importance are the subject index cards, covering everything from public health and local organisations to emigrations, court cases, accidents and transport — dozens of subject headings comprising a resource of more than local interest, crying out to be computerised and made available to a wider audience.

In common with other Scottish burghs, Inverness in the nine-teenth century produced a plethora of local antiquarians prepared to rummage in the byways of their local history, with the local newspapers providing an opportunity for publication, initially in their weekly columns and eventually in book or booklet form. The Barron dynasty, still extant, and Charles Fraser Mackintosh, MP, were the most active, but several others contributed material which is still of great interest; indeed, some of it has been deservedly reprinted.

In the 1970s, Edward Meldrum contributed an excellent series of booklets on the history of Inverness and surrounding areas, densely packed with well-researched facts and dates, each booklet a mine of basic information, to which all future researchers are indebted. At about the same time, Gerald Pollitt was researching and writing his book *Historic Inverness*, published in 1981; originally a Lancastrian, he served on the Inverness Town Council from 1954 until local government reorganisation in 1975. The first two chapters of *Historic Inverness*, on the buildings and streets of the town, when used alongside the section on Inverness in John Gifford's *Highlands and Islands* in the *Buildings of Scotland* series (Penguin, 1992), give an account of the architectural history and growth of the town which, while leaving some gaps, will stand for many years.

In more recent times, the publications of the Inverness Field Club and the emergence of the Inverness Local History Forum have served notice that there is a revival of interest in local history in the community, which is being harnessed and channelled in a variety of ways. A particular success has been the 'Inverness Remembered' project, focusing on the history of Inverness in the twentieth century, especially in recording and preserving the memories of older residents. Community history has also been encouraged by the support of the Aberdeen University Centre for Continuing Education for local history events and lectures, while local history courses throughout Inverness run by the Workers' Educational Association have done much to stimulate interest in local history and to encourage communities to reclaim their own past. In many ways the innovative Merkinch Project paved the way and showed just what local people can accomplish, using locally available resources. In local secondary schools, reforms in the curriculum over recent years have had the effect of encouraging youngsters to undertake local history investigations, providing an opportunity to explore local history of which their parents' generation was sadly deprived. The excellent series of booklets prepared by Mrs Eileen MacAskill and her team for School Libraries at the Educational Resource Centre have been the first introduction to the riches of historical research for many young Inverness scholars.

One particular tome, edited by Mrs Loraine Maclean of

Dochgarroch for the Inverness Field Club, and published by them in 1975 as their centenary volume, deserves mention, and recognition, as being far more wide-ranging, comprehensive and scholarly than the present volume. Written by experts in their fields, the numerous chapters on the geology and natural environment, archaeology, history, architecture, industry, commerce, agriculture, education, transport, folklore, churches, place-names, people of importance, conservation, newspapers, and much more besides, makes *The Hub of the Highlands: the Book of Inverness and District*, a landmark volume.

So, there is no shortage of material for a history of Inverness, which would, however, require a volume approximately ten times the length of this one! Much research remains to be done, and while paying tribute to previous generations of antiquarians, much reinterpretation and questioning of their work must be carried on. This present volume will focus on the *people* of Inverness, tracing in outline the history of the burgh over the years, covering the major happenings in the history of the town, but detouring into the lives of the people, and describing some of the events which they lived through: the Jacobite occupation and Culloden, public hangings, election meetings, public funerals, royal visits, sporting triumphs and disasters, the coming of the railway, the impact of two world wars and the effect of two reorganisations of local government in the last twenty-one years.

We pay tribute to all who helped and encouraged the writing of this book: the staff of Inverness Library, the staff of Highland Archives, the students of WEA local history classes, the editorial staff of John Donald and especially Mrs Eileen MacAskill, who helped with the selection of illustrations and drew attention to some people and events worthy of inclusion. Any opinions expressed in this book are the responsibility of the author, as are any errors and omissions.

We are all too aware that there has not been room enough in this volume to do justice to many aspects of the local history of Inverness which are deserving of a fuller treatment, but we hope that we have been able to do justice to the people of the town, over the centuries, through our selection of material to illustrate their way of life. Most of all, we hope that we have shown enough of the riches of the vast amount of local history material available to inspire others to explore the sources for themselves.

CHAPTER 1

STRATEGIC SETTING AND EARLY HISTORY

Inverness: the crossroads of the Highlands. Since earliest times Inverness has been the site of a settlement of strategic importance in the north of Scotland. It lies tucked away in the corner of the Moray Firth, funnelling trade and traffic into and out of the Great Glen, that natural geological wonder that we all take for granted and which splits Scotland in half from east to west.

Geology

The Great Glen is a rift valley, a massive geological fault line along which, geological eons ago, a large chunk of land slipped laterally. Geological maps show how rocks on each side would have matched up before the earth movements which split the earth's surface and created the landscape which eventually evolved into what we see today.

This fault line is geologically ancient, and relatively inactive, though from time to time earth tremors are felt in Inverness, and very occasionally stronger earthquakes shake the town. The earthquake felt all over Scotland on 13 August 1816 damaged the steeple of the Tolbooth, twisting it out of alignment; it was not repaired until 1828, by which time it had become an object of curiosity, compared to the leaning tower of Pisa. The steeple which survives today, amidst the excrescences of Bridge Street, was nearly demolished in the 1950s as part of a traffic improvement scheme. Fortunately, the present traffic system, which has closed off the access from Church Street to High Street, has reprieved the historic Tolbooth — all that survives of the original Court House and adjoining prison.

Archaeology

Because the Great Glen is steep-sided, and flat-bottomed, and runs from coast to coast, it has been a natural route for human communication as long as there have been humans about — that is, since the end of the last Ice Age. Starting some 10,000 years ago, the first hunter-gatherers moved up the west coast of Scotland, living mainly on the shore line, on fish, shellfish, birds and sea mammals, feasting seasonally on berries, and moving inland to hunt deer and other land animals. From about 3,500 BC onwards, the first farmers arrived and began to tame and settle the landscape. They built massive communal burial places, chambered tombs, of which the complex just outside Inverness, at Clava, is one of the most important surviving Neolithic cemeteries in Scotland, a ritual landscape of chambered cairns and standing stones, used for many centuries, perhaps for two thousand years, up to the end of the Bronze Age, around 1,200 BC.

Within Inverness itself, building work has revealed occasional traces of early settlement, in the form of burial cists (stone-lined graves with capstones) and stray finds of prehistoric objects. In prehistoric times, much of what we think of as Inverness would have been boggy land, subject to regular flooding; settlement would have been on the fringes of the flood plain of the River Ness, and on the slopes and higher ground to the west and east.

Just to the north-east of Raigmore Hospital, in what in ten years time will be regarded as the centre of Inverness, there is the remains of a circular cairn. It is not in its original position: when the new A9 road was being aimed like a concrete arrow at the new Kessock Bridge, the cairn was moved from the path of the advancing highway to save it from obliteration, and re-erected 3km to the south in its present location. It narrowly missed a similar fate a century earlier, when the railway line into Inverness passed within 1 km to the north-east. Excavations carried out in 1972–3 revealed that underneath the circular cairn, of Clava type, there had been a rectangular timber building, 9.5m long, with a central stone hearth. Only the stone kerb of the cairn itself survived; massive, tapering boulders, which give some idea, with the eye of faith, of a once impressive monument, the body of the cairn having been robbed away long ago for use as building stone in field dykes and farm buildings, probably between 1824 and 1900.

When it was on its original site, the Raigmore cairn was known as the Stoneyfield (or Achnaclach) stone circle. Inside it were cremated burials, in urns and pits, and sherds of Neolithic pottery (grooved ware) dating from 2,300–2,000BC. The underlying structure was dated at 3,000–2,500BC. Unfortunately the full report of the excavation, which took place over two years under the

The distinctive profile of Craig Phadrig hill-fort, with Inverness High School in the foreground.

direction of D D A Simpson, has never been published, so we must await more details of the context in which a sherd of Roman pottery and an enamelled Roman brooch of the second-century AD were discovered.

There is scant evidence of later prehistoric occupation in and around Inverness — most of it probably destroyed in building operations, but from the evidence of surrounding areas we can be confident that this was a busy crossroads in prehistoric times, just as it was later. On the Ord Hill, overlooking the Kessock narrows on the north side, is a massive Iron Age hill-fort, suggesting a considerable population there and a chieftain of some importance and prestige. Matching it, on the south side, guarding the entrance to the Great Glen, and overlooking present day Inverness, is the hill-fort of Craig Phadrig.

Archaeological excavations on Craig Phadrig in the early 1970s under the direction of Alan Small, undertaken on behalf of the Inverness Field Club, provided evidence of occupation during the Iron Age, with a secondary Dark Age occupation. Craig Phadrig (Gaelic: 'Peter's Rock') lies just to the west of Inverness: in the last twenty years housing has crept up the hill almost to the base of the fort itself, no doubt destroying, even obliterating, an agricultural landscape of ancient field boundaries, hut circles and stock enclosures which had survived more or less intact, under later stone dykes and boundaries, for 2,300 years.

Aerial view of Inverness in the 1930s, before the completion of the Dalneigh housing estate, showing the River Ness winding down to the Beauly Firth.

The dating evidence for the rampart encircling the hilltop of Craig Phadrig came from within the rampart itself. A radiocarbon date for charcoal from the remains of timber used in the construction of the rampart provided a date of 350BC, placing the site well within a sequence of Iron Age forts in the Highlands, though distressingly few have, as yet, been excavated to modern standards. Craig Phadrig is a 'vitrified' fort; that is to say, the stones used in the rampart wall have been heated to such a high temperature (over 1,200 degrees Celsius) that the rock melted, turned into fluid, and cooled into a very distinctive glassy, sometimes bubbly surface. In the eighteenth century some thought the glassy rock indicated an extinct volcano; in the late twentieth century the fantasy of landing sites for flying saucers was raised. Both of these interpretations are clearly wrong! More rationally, there has been intense debate in archaeological circles as to whether the vitrification was part of the construction technique of the builders, or was the result of destruction, accidental or deliberate. The excavations at Craig Phadrig clearly showed, from the way the rampart had collapsed, that the vitrified rock, in the words of the excavator, 'could not have been a design feature of the builders.'

Our understanding of vitrified forts is much more complete now than it was even twenty years ago, though much remains to be done in the areas of both survey and excavation. It has become clear that 'vitrified forts' are not really a different class of Iron Age hill-forts. Many hill-forts suffered attack or destruction, in which the timber buildings and structures on the hill top, many leaning against the inner wall of the rampart, were set on fire. However, for the effect of vitrification to occur certain conditions must have been present: the rampart must have been of 'timber-laced' construction, the stones used to build it must have had a high silica content — and the attack must have taken place on a windy day, so that when the timber inside the rampart caught fire a furnace effect would have developed, providing the high temperatures needed for the rock to melt and vitrify.

Few finds from the Iron Age were discovered in the excavations at Craig Phadrig, but it is clear that the fort, in a strategic situation overlooking the mouth of the Ness, along with its partner on the Ord of Kessock (also vitrified), guards the entrance to the Beauly Firth.

The Picts

We know very little of the people who occupied the Iron Age fort on Craig Phadrig, but quite a lot about the folk who occupied the site towards the end of its life — the Picts. First mentioned in classical sources around 300 AD, the Picts were the most important people in this part of Scotland until at least the middle of the 9th-century, when, in the words of Isabel Henderson, 'under Viking pressure, Kenneth MacAlpin led the Scots from Argyll into the eastern Pictish districts of Scotland and set up the Scottish administrative centre there.' Her chapter entitled 'Inverness, a Pictish capital', in the Inverness Field Club centenary volume, *The Hub of the Highlands: the book of Inverness and District* (1975) summarises the evidence for Craig Phadrig as a Pictish administrative centre. That emblem of the Field Club, the Pictish Boar, comes from the Boarstone, a Pictish monolith located on the southern edge of Inverness, with the outline of a boar etched on the face of the stone.

Craig Phadrig features in the *Life of Saint Columba* written towards the end of the 7th century by Adomnan, the ninth abbot of Iona. To be sure, it is never mentioned by name by Adomnan, but Pictish and Dark Age scholars are generally happy with the idea that the fortress of King Brude of the Picts visited by Columba in the last half of the 6th century was at Craig Phadrig. Or to be fair, scholars are sure that Adomnan believed King Brude's fortress was at Inverness, and this site would fit in well with what we know of other Pictish forts and strategic sites in other parts of their kingdom.

A slight doubt remains. The archaeological excavations on Craig Phadrig *did* provide finds from a Pictish or Dark Age occupation, most notably part of a mould which would have been used in the manufacture of ornamental metalwork. The Craig Phadrig mould was used to cast an escutcheon for attaching a suspension ring to the side of a Pictish hanging-bowl; the plain, openwork pattern produced by the mould is thought by some scholars to be early in the chronology of hanging-bowls, perhaps fifth-century, while others go for a 6th-century date.

The mould is important, being the first evidence that major items of ornamental metalwork were actually made in Scotland, rather than arriving through trade. Evidence of trade with the continent *was* found, in the form of a class of pottery known as E-ware, typically found at Pictish royal centres and seen as evidence of an administrative or trading centre. However, little else from the Pictish period was found at Craig Phadrig suggesting a major Pictish stronghold, and the fort itself has none of the characteristics of Dark Age fortresses occupied by Pictish kings elsewhere. The 'nuclear' design, where the core fort on a craggy hilltop is surrounded by a series of defended terraces, is not found at Craig Phadrig. There *is* a site not far from Inverness where another mould was found, this time for an ornamental metal brooch, and where the site *does* have the requisite characteristic of a Pictish royal fortress. This is at Castle Urquhart, on Loch Ness.

So, the debate goes on. Sometimes in history what we *believe* to be the case becomes more significant than what really *was* the case, and perhaps we will never really know where Columba and Brude encountered each other.

An extract from the Ordnance Survey of Inverness, 1870.

St Columba and Nessie?

Adomnan's *Life of Columba* is also noted for containing the first documentary reference to Nessie, but not surprisingly, with plenty of ambiguity thrown in. According to the *Life*, Columba was travelling in Pictland when he saw somebody being buried on the banks of the river Ness, a victim of a water monster which inhabited the river. When he ordered one of his priestly followers to swim across the river to fetch a boat from the other side; the monster, 'whose hunger had not been satisfied earlier,' sensed the swimmer's presence:

> Feeling the water disturbed by his swimming, it suddenly swam to the surface, and with a mighty roar from its gaping mouth it sped towards the man as he swam in midstream.

Columba made the sign of the cross and commanded the monster to withdraw:

> 'You shall not advance further, nor touch the man. Go back with all speed.' Then the beast, hearing these words of the saint, fled back terrified at full speed, as if dragged away by ropes...

Both the 'heathen barbarians' and the 'brothers' were impressed by this miraculous demonstration of saintly power. The locals were impelled by the great power of this miracle, which they had seen with their own eyes, to magnify the God of the Christians.

This is the first eye-witness account of Nessie, and it has a vividness and immediacy which is impressive. Cynics might point out that river monsters are a well-known feature of the Pictish world, a fact of which Columba (and Adomnan) would have been well aware, so that it would have been in their interest to 'stage' an event where Columba counteracted the power of this heathen belief with a suitable miracle. It is worth emphasising that this episode took place not in Loch Ness, where Nessie now resides, but in the River Ness.

While Craig Phadrig has so far failed to produce suitably impressive evidence of a Pictish royal centre, an important find did turn up not very far away in 1807, during the construction of the Caledonian Canal. Reported in the *Inverness Journal* for January 1st 1808, with an accompanying illustration, a massive silver chain was found 'in the side of a large flat cairn, about two feet below the surface.' The find spot was 'in the eastern corner of Toreveon (Torvean).' The chain consisted of thirty-three circular links, in pairs, 18 inches in length and weighing 104oz. It would have been worn as a badge of office by high-ranking officials such as the *mormaers* who acted as regional governors on behalf of the king — or perhaps, who knows, even by King Brude himself?

One such *mormaer* — the title survived until supplanted by the arrival of feudalism with the Anglo-Norman invaders in the 11th century — was Macbeth, Thane of Cawdor and later King of Scotland. Shakespeare's version of the career of this man is entertaining, and great drama, but poor history. In Inverness we have Macbeth's Castle and King Duncan's well — or do we?

MacBeth (Gaelic: *mac-Bethad*, 'son of life') was, contrary to Shakespeare's calumnies, one of the best kings Scotland ever had. Born around 1005, he killed Duncan I in 1040 and succeeded to the throne — his queen was Gruoch, Shakespeare's Lady MacBeth, a granddaughter of Kenneth II. His father was the ruler of the province of Moray, and his mother also of royal descent. Gruoch's first husband was another ruler of Moray: the marriage produced a son, Lulach, nicknamed 'The Simpleton'. Powerful and prosperous, MacBeth travelled on pilgrimage to Rome in 1050, where he 'scattered alms like seed-corn'. So, he had firm connections with the north. In 1054 Siward, Earl of Northumbria, invaded Scotland

The Inverness Town Seal: the origins of the camel and elephant are unclear, but are thought to represent the town's trading contacts.

on behalf of Malcolm Canmore with an English army and defeated MacBeth in battle at Dunsinane, in Perthshire. Three years later, fleeing from a second invasion, and trying to reach the safety of his strongholds in Moray, MacBeth was cornered at Lumphanan, in Aberdeenshire, and killed there. His stepson Lulach succeeded him, but ruled for only a few months before he too was killed, and Malcolm III, Malcolm Big Head (or Great Chief) — Malcolm Canmore — took control.

So, where was MacBeth's Castle? It is very likely that there was a royal castle in Inverness in the eleventh century, and that when MacBeth became king, he took control of it. Despite local traditions that it lay to the east of the present castle, where Auldcastle Road now is, there are, and never have been, any traces on the ground of what should have been an artificial mound or motte, surmounted by a timber palisade and wooden castle buildings. Much more likely is that the eleventh-century castle was built on the Castle Hill, guarding the crossing point of the Ness, and that the present mound is, at least in part, artificial. The first stone castle was built, in all probability, in the 12th century, during the reign of David I, if experience in other parts of Scotland is anything to go by.

Between 800AD and 1150AD, much of the west coast of Scotland, the islands of the Hebrides, Orkney, Shetland, Caithness, Sutherland and Ross, were all occupied to a greater or lesser extent by the Vikings, or at least by the Norse settlers who followed on behind their warrior raiders. Although the frontier between Celtic Scotland and the Norse territories was the Dornoch Firth, and later the Cromarty Firth (Dingwall is a Norse name, suggesting an important administrative centre), there is no suggestion that Inverness was ever visited by Norse raiders. They very likely raided along the Moray Firth coast, where Sueno's Stone at Forres suggests a battle with a Norse Earl, but it seems they left Inverness alone.

Lords of the Isles

In the islands, Somerled led a revolt against Norse rule in the 1150s, and established the dynasty which later produced the MacDonald Lords of the Isles. The first to use the title *Dominus Insularum* was John of Islay, son of Angus Og who had fought for Bruce at Bannockburn. His son Donald of Harlaw, named after the battle of 1411 which was one of the great but inconclusive confrontations between Highland and Lowland Scotland, married Mary Leslie, heiress to the Earldom of Ross. Donald's son Alexander succeeded as Lord of the Isles in 1423, and after many adventures made peace with the Scottish monarchy and was appointed Royal Justiciar for Scotland north of the river Forth. He died at Dingwall in 1449 and was buried at the cathedral in Fortrose to reinforce his family's claim to the Earldom of Ross.

During this period Inverness found itself part of a culture and society which were unfamiliar to it, and which the leaders of the burgh did not understand. Even their nineteenth-century descendants did not always realise that the so-called Earls of Ross who controlled the area in the 15th century were in fact rulers even more alien than the Anglo-Norman intruders who were brought in to run mediaeval Scotland. Inverness under the MacDonalds was an uncomfortable experience, and when the Lords of the Isles lost the Earldom of Ross in 1476 and suffered their final forfeiture in 1493, a more familiar administrative and cultural environment returned.

CHAPTER 2
INVERNESS IN THE MIDDLE AGES

We really know far too little about the mediaeval period in the capital of the Highlands. We know that there was a town there, but we are not really sure of its extent. Archaeological excavations in the 1970s seemed to show that the mediaeval town, bounded by a fosse or ditch, was not as large as had been previously thought. In an article entitled *The archaeological investigation of medieval Inverness*, published in the Inverness Field Club publication *The Middle Ages in the Highlands* (1981), Jonathan Wordsworth reviewed the evidence as it existed then. Fifteen years later, there is not much to add to his summary conclusions.

Mediaeval Archaeology

The eastern line of the town ditch seems to have followed the line of what is now Academy Street, and Hamilton Street, at the western edge of the Eastgate shopping centre. Some think it ran along the edge of the Barnhill (Ardconnel Street), but excavations on Castle Street in the 1970s seemed to show that there was no development there until the middle of the 13th century, making a defensive ditch on the Barnhill unnecessary. On the west side of the river there is unlikely to have been any mediaeval occupation before the 13th century, when a bridge is first recorded. Thereafter, the boundary was marked by the line of what is now King Street, and Alexander Place. According to records from the reign of William the Lion (1143–1214), the state bore the responsibility of making the ditch, but the burgesses of Inverness were responsible for its upkeep, and for making and maintaining a palisade along its line.

Excavations by Wordsworth in Castle Street in 1979 produced evidence of a plank and clay-walled house constructed in the middle of the 13th century, covered by midden material dating to the late 13th and early 14th century, containing imported English pottery brought from Yorkshire. Typical pottery of the period, known as Scarborough-ware, was found in this midden. Then, in

Castle Street, the mediaeval Doomsdale, leading to the town gibbet.

the 14th century, substantial timber buildings were erected on the site, with property boundaries suggesting that Castle Street, or Doomsdale as it was then called, was expanded, perhaps to produce a larger market area than was available in Bridge Street.

Three properties were identified in the 1979 excavations, which stood for 50–80 years until destroyed by fire early in the 15th century, perhaps in 1411 when the town was sacked by Donald of Harlaw. Subsequently the sites were cleared and new buildings erected. To their rear, small hearths indicated small-scale industrial activity: one was used for smelting lead and others may have been small cooking ovens. As in other mediaeval burghs, it is likely that the buildings were multi-purpose, being used as workshops, shops and dwelling houses.

Robert Gourlay's contribution to the Scottish Burgh Survey, entitled *Historic Inverness: the archaeological implications of development* (1977), summarises the evidence for mediaeval Inverness. Both he, and Jonathan Wordsworth, stress the urgent need for further excavation in order to shed more light on the growth and extent of Inverness in the Middle Ages, but nothing more has been done since 1979. It is greatly to be hoped that the redevelopment of the town centre now planned, along Academy Street and in the Falcon Square area, will provide an opportunity for further archaeological work, without which the mysteries of mediaeval Inverness will be lost forever.

We saw at the end of Chapter One how the MacDonalds left their mark on Inverness, though on a day to day basis their rule was no better and no worse than anything else the burgh had experienced, and to the ordinary folk of Inverness it probably did not matter very much who their feudal superior was. The royal castle was destroyed by Donald of Harlaw in 1411, probably on his way back to his island realm after the battle. The castle was repaired and rebuilt the following year by Alexander Stewart, Earl of Mar, at a cost of nearly £640, according to the royal Exchequer Rolls. In 1491 Alexander of Lochalsh, acting on behalf of John, the last Lord of the Isles, occupied Inverness in a final futile gesture of defiance; his motives were mixed, and he was at least as interested in furthering his own claim to the Lordship as in confronting the Scottish state on behalf of the Lord of the Isles.

Mediaeval Burgh

While feudal superiors argued out their cases before King and Parliament, and ebbed and flowed across the political seascape, Inverness was becoming a political, military, administrative and religious centre, and through increasing trade, the economic hub of the Highlands.

It was during the Middle Ages, in the years between 1100 and 1600, that Inverness became an important centre of trade and settlement. Obviously the strategic position of the town was the determining factor in its growth, but without formal authorisation from central government, in the form of official Charters from the Kings (and Queens) of Scotland, the burgh of Inverness could not have flourished in the way it did.

Even so, it was not until the last quarter of the nineteenth century, with the arrival of the railway, that it became clear that Inverness, rather than, for example, Cromarty, or Dingwall, or Elgin, was going to become the main trading port and adminis-trative centre in the North of Scotland.

Charters

The earliest known mediaeval charter which applies to Inverness was issued during the reign of William the Lion, 1165–1214. It grants the right to the Burgesses of the Province of Moray to limit their financial liability to their own personal debts. Since at the time most of the burgesses in Moray were in fact in Inverness, this is sometimes regarded as the first Burgh Charter. Later charters during William's reign exempted the burgesses from the payment of tolls, gave them the right to hold a weekly market, and the exclusive right of trading within the shire, which at the time was a very valuable privilege. In one charter the King undertook to make a ditch or fosse around the town, which the burgesses were to protect and enclose with a palisade.

Because charters were in effect a personal contract between the King and certain of his subjects, they required to be renewed with each successive reign. Sometimes this procedure gives evidence of charters now lost, for example when in 1236 Alexander confirmed the right of the burgesses of Inverness to use the lands of Merkinch to support the burgh:

> Alexander, by the grace of God, King of Scots. To all good men of his whole land (clerical and laical) greeting; know all present and to come that we have given, granted, and by this our present charter confirmed to our burgesses of Inverness, the lands of Merkinch, for the support of our Burgh of Inverness, to be held by the said burgesses of us and our heirs for ever, freely and quietly, for sustaining the rent of our burgh of Inverness, so that they may cultivate the said lands of Merkinch if they choose, or deal with it in any other way that may be for their advantage; rendering therefor one pound of pepper at the feast of St Michael yearly...

A charter from David I, in 1344, extended the protection of the burgesses into the area of the law, ensuring that only the properly constituted royal official, the Chamberlain, could sit in judgement on them — and threatening any who disregarded this protection with the full power of the state:

> ...know that we command and order that no one presume to harrass or annoy our said Burgesses of Inverness in any way in face of this grant, under the pain of losing all that according to our royal laws he might lose...

Revenue for carrying out the obligations of the burgh came from grants of Royal bounty — grants of lands from which the burgh could use the rentals or produce to raise money. In 1180 the lands of the Burgh Haugh, and in 1236 the lands of Merkinch were granted to the burgh, and then in 1369, in a charter signed at Perth by David II, the lands of Drakies, along with the fishings, mills, tolls and petty customs of the burgh. In exchange for this privilege the burgh had to pay the King an annual assessment of 80 merks sterling.

The monies from these lands, along with the petty customs, became the foundation of the Inverness Common Good Fund. And it was the charter of 1369 which really made Inverness into a Royal Burgh; up until then the burgesses, first of the Province of Moray, and later, of Inverness, had paid rent to the King directly for their possessions, and were thus his direct tenants or vassals. From 1369 the Burgh itself, as a corporate community, became the King's vassal.

The Great Charter of 1591

This is the royal Charter most often referred to by modern Invernessians; sometimes also known as the 'Golden Charter', it confirmed all previous charters and defined the properties and privileges of the burgh. Most important, it confirmed the status of Inverness as the most important burgh in northern Scotland, and in particular, made it clear that Inverness had trading and market rights over other northern burghs, such as Dingwall, Cromarty and Tain:

> James, by the grace of God, King of Scots to all good men of his whole realm, Greeting; Know that we, considering the ancient erection of Inverness by our famous progenitors, into a free burgh of this kingdom, have ratified, and by this present Charter, do ratify, and perpetually confirm, all and sundry the Charters, confirmations, rights, liberties and privileges granted and confirmed by our progenitors, William, Alexander, David and James the first of that name, Kings of Scotland, to our said Burgh. Likewise the Charter and confirmation lately granted by our Grandfather James, fifth of that name; also the Charter granted in favour of Divine Service, and of the Ministers of God's Word, and of the Hospital, by our Mother Mary, Queen of Scots; and the lands, houses, churches, chapels, crofts, milns, fishings and all others mentioned in that Charter, of date 21st April 1567 years; moreover we of new grant and, in perpetual feu, set and confirm to the Provost, Bailies etc. of our said burgh, the lands, territories and commonty thereof, with all parts and privileges. As also all the lands of Drakies and the forest thereof; the lands of Merkinch with the pasturage thereof with the parks and woods; likewise the lands called Barnhills, Claypots, Miln and Milnfields, the Carse and the Carn Laws with the common muir of the said burgh; likewise the waters of the Ness on both sides from Clachnagaick to the sea, with all fishings, ports, havens, creeks, the stell fishing, the red pool, with power to

begin to fish in the said waters with boats and nets on the 10th of November yearly, and to use cruives and water kists; with the ferry of Kessock and the right of ferrying on both sides. Farther all the milns called Kingsmilns, the sucken and multures thereof, with the astricted and dry multures of the Castle Lands, and all corns which have, or shall receive fire or water, within the liberty, territory and parish of Inverness, as well out-sucken as in-sucken, to pay multure and knaveship of the said milns; with power and liberty of pasture, peats, foggage, turf etc. in all places used and wont; and particularly in Craig Phadric, Capulach Muir, Daveemont and Bogbayne with power of ferrying on Loch-Ness; with mercats weekly on Wednesday and Saturday, and eight free fairs in the year viz. on Palm Sunday; on July 7th St Andrew's Fair; on August 15th Marymas; in September Roodmas; on November 10th Martinmas; in December Saint Thomas Fair; on February 1st Peter Fair and April 25th Saint Mark's Fair; every fair to be held for eight days; with the Petty Customs of all cities, towns and villages within the Shire, and particularly of the Colleges of Tain in Ross, Merkinch, Chanonrie, Dornoch, Thurso and Wick in Caithness; that no ship break bulk between Tarbetness and Inverness; and our said burgh shall have Coroners and Sheriffs within themselves; and a Guildry with a Dean of Guild; that there be but one tavern; that no one in the Shire make cloth but the burgesses; with power to make statutes and rules for the burgh etc. etc.

The provisions of this 'Great Charter' are still of interest to the citizens of Inverness. The revival of the Marymas Fair in recent years has added an interesting festival to the civic calendar, and the provisions in the charter regarding fishing in the River Ness were of interest to anglers when Inverness District Council decided to regulate fishing on the river. Whether the anglers of Inverness, or anybody else for that matter, would be so keen to reintroduce the provisions of the Great Charter, if they realised it allowed for only one tavern in the town, is debatable!

John Major

One of the best sources for the turbulence of life in the Highlands in the Middle Ages is John Major: not the twentieth-century politician and prime minister, but his 15th-century namesake, whose *History of Greater Britain* gives a particularly unsympathetic view of Highlanders — people always referred to as 'Wild Scots'. Inverness figures in John Major's *History*, usually in terms of the running dispute between the Lords of the Isles (who were also Earls of Ross in the fifteenth century) and the Scottish state, which

John Major supported enthusiastically as a bastion of civilisation against the barbarisms of the Highlands.

He describes how in 1426 the castle of Inverness was restored by the king, and how in the following year a parliament was held there. All the local 'men of mark' were invited to attend, and all ended up in the restored tower, 'kept in close custody'. It was while he was showing off his captives to his friends that the king, James I, composed two lines of verse:

> Ad turrim fortem ducamus caute cohortem;
> Per Christi sortem meruerunt hi quia mortem.
> (Let us carry that gang to a fortress strong;
> For by Christ's own lot they did deadly wrong.)

John Major, trying his hand at literary criticism, was not impressed by this regal effort at versifying, but commented that 'some allowance may well be made for kings when they take to extempore verse-making'. As well as Alexander Macdonald, Lord of the Isles and Earl of Ross, and his mother, the Countess of Ross, daughter and heiress of Walter Lesley, Earl of Ross, various other 'Wild Scots' (the words are always capitalised as if to emphasise their exotic barbarity) are named: Angus Duff and his four sons, described as the chief of four thousand men in Strathnaver; Kenneth More and his son-in-law John Ross, chief of two thousand men. William Lesley, Angus of Moray — and a lot more besides:

> And many other Scots whose tempers were alike savage followed them, ever prone to do evil rather than good, and with no notion of a peaceful life. Many of these he put to death, and others he disposed in different castles, to be kept some here, some there. I have nothing but praise for this spirited conduct of the king, and the desire that he showed to deal justice upon all. Those men, all low-born as they were, held in utter subjection some seventy or eighty thousand others; and in their own particular tracts they were regarded as princes, and had all at their own arbitrary will, evincing not the smallest regard for the dictates of reason.

With this kind of attitude, and after the king's humiliation of all the Highland 'men of mark', it could hardly have come as a surprise when in 1429 the Lord of the Isles attacked Inverness and burned the town. The king collected an army and defeated the army of the Lord of the Isles in Lochaber, despite his undoubtedly notional numerical superiority — there were supposedly ten thousand men 'of Ross and the Isles' in revolt. In a hint of troubles to come, John Major was able to report that 'two of the wild tribes, clan Chattan, to wit, and clan Cameron, deserted Alexander of the isles and attached themselves like honest men to the king'. In a famous passage, John Major had another attempt at describing and interpreting the clan system for his lowland audience:

> There is kinship of blood among these tribes; their possessions are few, but they follow one chief as leader of the whole family, and bring with them all their relations and dependants. They lead a life of blissful ease; from the poor people they take what they want in victual; bows they have, and quivers, and they have halberts of great sharpness, for their iron ore is good. They carry a stout dirk in their belts; they are often naked from the knee down. In winter for an over-garment they wear a plaid.

In this passage there is almost a grudging acceptance that the 'Wild Scots' did, after all, have some of the trappings of mainstream society.

The Wardlaw Manuscript

The destruction of Inverness in 1411 by Donald of the Isles, father of Alexander, is described in some detail by Rev James Fraser (1634–1709), author of what has come to be known as 'the Wardlaw manuscript', by virtue of the fact that he was the minister of the parish of Wardlaw (now Kirkhill). Donald was on his way to the battle of Harlaw, in the hinterland of the city of Aberdeen, and was in no mood to be trifled with. He was attempting to consolidate his claim to the Earldom of Ross, and arrived on the east coast with an army of islanders to make it clear that his patience was exhausted and that he was no longer prepared to pursue his claim by legal means. Donald attempted to persuade Lord Lovat to join him, but was rebuffed, ironically because Lovat 'declined to be illegal' — advice which his Fraser descendants found it hard to follow. Worried that other clans, whom he hoped would march with him to Aberdeen, would be wooed by Lovat, Donald marched on Inverness, which was undefended, and burned the town. The Wardlaw manuscript gives the famous account of the valour of the only Invernessian who was prepared to stand up to this display of naked aggression, and describes the effects of Donald's attack on the town:

> M'kdonnel, fearing to be seased on by other clans, who would espouse Lovats quarrell, and also that he would loose his oportunity

by dallying, marches through, pillages and plunders all before him, attacks Inverness, burns the bridge, the famousest and finest off oak in Brittain, burns most of the town, becaus they would not rise and concurr with him. John Cuming, a gentleman burger in the town, putting on his armour and head piece and two handed sword, made such stout resistance at this nearest end of the bridge against the M'kdonels that Jo. Major the historian saith, Si essent decem tales in Invernesia nec pons nec urbs comburerentur, — and if there were ten more like him in Inverness neither bridg nor brugh had been burnt. But they prevailed, and proceeded through Murray over Spey with fire and sword against all that would not rise with them, came to Garrioch, and there fought the battle of Harlaw.

Forgiving Rev James Fraser of Wardlaw for his idiosyncratic spelling, we must admire his powers of description, and admit that he conjures up a scene of which Don Quixote would have been proud. One cannot but wonder why a painting of this scene was not produced long ago, to hang in the Town House of Inverness, to encourage local councillors in their contemporary combat with the forces of barbarism attempting to wield power over local affairs from the fortress of St Andrew's House in Edinburgh. We will encounter Rev Fraser once again for his eye-witness accounts of events in Inverness in the middle of the seventeenth century, during the religious wars and the Cromwellian occupation of the town.

And having again met John Major, we will leave the Middle Ages with the observation that as a young scholar by the name of John Mair from Glenhornie, near Haddington, East Lothian, one of his playground games, in the spirit of 'cowboys and Indians', or 'Tommies and Jerries', was to re-enact the battle of Harlaw, fought in 1411 between the 'Wild Scots' of the Highlands and Islands under the direction of Donald, Lord of the Isles and Earl of Ross, conqueror and destroyer of Inverness, and the lowland armies of the Earl of Mar.

Lords of the Isles and Earls of Ross

Local historians have failed to appreciate the impact of the Lords of the Isles on the area of Inverness and Easter Ross, largely because of unfamiliarity with the source materials, which until recently were largely inaccessible except to a very few ardent mediaevalists. However, the Scottish History Society volume, *Acts of the Lords of the Isles, 1336–1493*, edited by Jean Munro and R

W Munro, has allowed a wider readership to realise just how pervasive and important the influence of the 'Wild Scots' was, especially in the fifteenth century. The MacDonald Lords of the Isles, in their capacity as Earls of Ross, issued charters from Inverness, Tain, Dingwall, Fortrose, and other places well outside their traditional island territories, suggesting that they took their claim to the Earldom of Ross seriously and spent a considerable amount of time in this area. Indeed, the cathedral at Fortrose was the burial place of Alexander, son of Donald of Harlaw, who died at Dingwall in 1449. Alexander was powerful enough to issue a charter to Hugh Rose of Kilravock in 1440, granting him the lands of the barony of Kilravock in the sheriffdom of Nairn. This charter was issued at Kinmylies and witnessed by Lachlan Maclean of Duart, Macleod of Dunvegan, Torquil Macleod of Lewis, George Munro, and two members of the Macleans of Kingairloch family. Another charter, issued at Inverness a few days later, was witnessed by Fraser of Lovat, Donald of Calder (Cawdor), William Urquhart, George Munro, Robert Chisholm, John Grant, William Lesley, and others — all this suggesting that the two factions, the islanders and the locals, were absorbed into the details of administration under the lordship of Alexander, Lord of the Isles and Earl of Ross.

In what has been described as the earliest surviving bond of manrent, Thomas Fraser, Lord of Lovat, bonds himself to Alexander, Earl of Ross, Lord of the Isles and justiciar north of Forth in a document dated 18th January 1441. Its language seems strange, but the meaning is clear enough:

> Be it made kende till all men be thir present letteris me Thomas Frasar lorde of the Lovet to haf becummyn ande becummus lele man ande trew to a rycht he ande mychty lorde my lorde Sir Alexander of Ila erle of Ross ande lorde of the Ilis ande justice of the north half of the watter of Forth ande that I sall make to my saide lorde lele and trew service at all my gudely powar...

In 1458, John, Earl of Ross, Lord of the Isles and Sheriff of Inverness wrote a letter to John McCulloch, 'bailie of the girth of Sanct Duthowis' (Tain), saying that while he of course recognised the right of the king, James II to confirm the privileges granted by his predessors to the church and town of Tain, he was now making it clear to the Bailie of Tain, John McCulloch, that this did not mean that could ride roughshod over the accepted trading practices of the merchants of Inverness, who had been complaining bitterly to him about the effect of the king's interference on their own livelihood. Between the lines of this letter, couched in rather obscure and archaic Scots, there is clear evidence of an unholy row breaking out in Inverness:

> Forthi at is cumyn beto our heryng in maner of grewous complaynt be the aldirman, bailyeis and cumunite of Innernys our nychtbouris, that sinder of the inhabitandis the toun of Tayn and vtheris of the north partis of thar fredome of Innernys occupiis merchandis in buying, selling, cappyn and owthawyng of merchandice and gudis langand thar fredome fra thar burgh in grete hindering, scaithe, and lak to thaim, and in lessyng of ladding of thar schippis...

John warns Bailie McCulloch not to annoy the merchants of Inverness, not to put any impediment in the way of their trading, and not to get the idea into his head that somehow Tain could compete with Inverness for trade. However, the competition between the two burghs was to continue for many years to come.

In 1475–6 the MacDonalds came unstuck, and John, the last Lord of the Isles, was forced to give up large chunks of his lands, in Knapdale and Kintyre, and to renounce the earldom of Ross and the office of sheriff of Inverness and Nairn. By proclamation at Dingwall castle and at the crosses of Dingwall and Inverness John was summoned to appear before Parliament in Edinburgh on 1st December 1475. When he failed to appear, sentence of forfeiture was pronounced. Within four days commissions were granted to reliable and powerful nobles to execute the forfeiture. In contrite mood, John appeared before parliament in July 1476, and the forfeiture was rescinded. It was however, at some considerable cost. The note of renunciation signed by John in Edinburgh on 10th July 1476 has survived, and from that date he was no longer the Earl of Ross and took no further part in northern affairs, except to stir up trouble again. His son Angus, in Inverness in 1490 fomenting trouble, was murdered there by his Irish harper. As a result of the continuing and increasingly uncontrollable agitations by John and his supporters, in 1493 he was forfeited again by the Scots Parliament and forced to give up his remaining island lands and titles. The title of Lord of the Isles reverted to the Crown, where it still resides — it is one of the many titles bestowed on the heir to the throne, and the reason why the Prince of Wales wears the Lord of the Isles tartan on visits to the north.

Rev David Rag

The arrival of the Protestant Reformation in Inverness in 1560 must have been unsettling and exciting for the populace, but it is barely documented. The *Records of Inverness* give us the proceedings of the Burgh Court during this time of change, and in its records there is a little information about the first Protestant minister in the town, David Rag. It seems he was appointed by the end of 1560, and on 18th January 1561 the Burgh Court orders two local men to pay his salary, his 'fee'. Jasper Waus is ordered to pay ten merks immediately, and George Cuthbert has to pay eight merks 'betuix this Candillmes or Fastyrs Ewyn (Fasterns Eve, or Shrove Tuesday) nixt to cum, and the rest to be payit betuix that and Pasche (Easter)'.

Rag had a problem with women. He was evidently quite a ladies' man, greatly admired by the women of the town, and resented by their jealous husbands. More seriously, he was accused by Arthur Byrnaye of committing adultery with his wife. The case was tried before a jury on 13th December 1561 and Rag was acquitted, but his position in the community was fatally undermined. Byrnaye was found guilty of slander and assault, fined, and ordered to appear in church the next Sunday, there 'in tyme of prayaris confess opynlie his ofence and aske the foryvenes at our said minister for God's sake'.

Nothing is known about David Rag's origins, or about what happened to him after he left Inverness. In 1567 Andrew Rag was a reader in the parish of Cannisbay in Caithness, and it is tempting to think that he and David were brothers. The surname is unusual in Scotland, but Black's *Surnames of Scotland* identifies one or two other examples, in Edinburgh and Aberdeen, and dismisses the idea that it is a variant of Reoch or Riach. The name probably originates in Yorkshire, where there is a place called Wragby. *Wraghi* was a Danish or Norse personal name, so perhaps Andrew and David felt at home in the north of Scotland, where the Norse influence was so strong. David Rag was replaced by Thomas Hewison, by 1565.

Feasts and Fairs

Mention of the feast days and fairs in the Burgh Court records are still of some interest, in view of the successful attempt to revive the Marymas fair. These days were an important part of the social life of the town, a welcome relief from the daily struggle for survival. In the Burgh Court Records, these days are recorded as being celebrated: Lammas, Yule, Mary Day, Lettyr Mary Day, Roodmas, Ash Wednesday, Hallowmas, St Thomas's Eve, Fasterns Eve, Pasch (Easter), Corpus Christi Day, Michaelmas, Andrewmas, Beltane, Martinmas, Uphalye Day, St Boniface Day in Lent, St Duthus Day at midsummer, St Boniface Fair, Pardoun Fair, Bryde Day, Munroe's Fair, Feast of Midsummer, Feast of All Hallowmas, Rood Day, St Colme's Day (Columba), and Coan Fair. For many years after the Reformation, these days were used by town officials to delineate the civic calendar and to give people, often illiterate, a reference point in the calendar of their personal lives.

CHAPTER 3

INVERNESS IN THE SEVENTEENTH CENTURY

The history of the seventeenth century in the Highlands is dominated by the area's involvement in the religious wars which tore the nation apart from the 1640s to the 1660s, leading directly to the 'Revolution' of 1689 which saw the removal of James II from the British throne, sowing the seeds of the attempts in the next century to restore his son and then his grandson (Bonnie Prince Charlie) to his rightful place.

In the days before local newspapers, and when few ordinary folk could read or write, in English or in Gaelic, sources for the history of the seventeenth century in the burgh of Inverness are rather scanty. However, we are fortunate in having one eyewitness account of these years, from the pen of Rev James Fraser (1634–1709), minister of the parish of Wardlaw (now Kirkhill). His 'Wardlaw Manuscript' was published by the Scottish History Society in 1905, under the title *Chronicle of the Frasers*, and added immeasurably to our understanding of the period. Of course, Rev Fraser did not set out to write an objective history of the events he witnessed; his purpose was unashamedly to glorify his own family and clan, the Frasers of Lovat.

Montrose and the Religious Wars

Unfortunately, the chief of this family in 1646 was no more skilful in assessing the politics of his time than was his descendant one hundred years later: both took decisions which led directly to misery and suffering on a grand scale for their followers and adherents. When Montrose was sweeping all before him on behalf of king Charles I, winning battles at Tippermuir, Inverlochy and Auldearn, and winning the support of the Macdonalds, Macleods, Mackenzies and Mackays, the Frasers continued to support the Covenant, and indeed at Auldearn the Frasers fought against Colkitto, with disastrous results, as described in the Wardlaw manuscript:

The Frasers and McKenzies suffered most; in our country there were 87 widdowes about the Lord Lovates eares; this we got for our dissloyall, rebellious covenant which we fought for.

Montrose took his revenge: in April 1646, when he was unsuccessfully besieging Inverness, he allowed his army to overrun the Aird and Strathglass, the Fraser heartland, with devastating results:

> ...betuixt the bridge end of Inverness and Gusachan, 26 miles, there was not left in my countrie a sheep to bleet, or a cock to crow day, nor a house unruffled; so severe was the depredation, onely the garrishones were safe and preserved mens lives...these preserrved thousands of soules, men, women and children, who had recourse for safety to these forts to preserve their lives, otherwayes all had perished in the fury of this surprise and onesett.

Montrose started his siege of Inverness on the 29th of April, setting up his guns under a hawthorn tree on the top of the 'old castlehill'. The wooden bridge across the Ness was under the control of the town, but the water level in the river was low enough for horses to cross easily, and Montrose sent out patrols to harry the local population. The Rev James Fraser witnessed some of these depredations:

> I remember that Rory Mackenzie of Dochmiluag, with 6 horsemen, sallied out through the parish of Wardlaw, pillaging all along. He basely killed one John Makgeorge, tennant in Phoppachy, and Thomas Makthomas, an old man, miller to his own father in law, Hugh Fraser of Belladrum, at Rindowy.

The patrols did encounter some resistance, notably from Lieutenant William Fraser, known as William Geilach ('Highland William'), whose somewhat preposterous and quixotic stand ensured his immortality through the pages of the Wardlaw manuscript:

> [he] stopt the passe and common rode [road] above Rindowy in Blarnagale, having 4 men in arms with him, takes out a great barrell of strong ale out of the drinking house, and sets it on the high rode and rids stradling over it, broaches the vessell and calls to all going by to drink the King's good health. Not a man, horse or foot, came near him for two dayes; some road by below him, some above, and never any came neare him; all the while he appeared so formidable to Montross people. When he drunk a health it was accompanied with a shot; and there he continued like a centinell for some dayes untill the fury was over and all was setled and every man called back to his post at the seige of Invernes.

Running short of supplies, Montrose was forced to raise the siege on May 5th. The Inverness garrison acquitted itself well, 'securing the skirts of the city', and with the approach of General Middleton's army Montrose withdrew, moving his encampment to the Wood of Farly, two miles above Beauly. Rev Fraser himself handled two cannons which Montrose was forced to leave behind. They were taken into the town and

> lay uppon the street near the cross and Court of Guard for 6 yeares thereafter; which I have often seen and handled; never removed till the English came there 1651.

With the king now in the 'custody' of the Scots army, Montrose received a message from his monarch ordering him to disband his forces and to leave the kingdom: he was in Holland when he received news of the king's execution.

On February 2nd 1649 the Covenanters of Inverness mutinied and were subsequently overwhelmed by a force of Mackenzies and Mackays numbering around 700 men, both infantry and cavalry, and Rev Fraser was a closer witness of events than he would perhaps have wished. His description has an immediacy and excitement which stirs the blood, as he lapses into the present tense and relives the day's events. He gives a detailed account of the street fighting, and he himself was spattered with blood when Major Murray, the deputy governor of the castle, shot Sergeant John Mackenzie through the heart. As a fifteen year old schoolboy, out in the town for the day with one of his school chums, he observed things which stayed fresh in his mind all his life, and his eyewitness account, full of local colour and references to the streets and buildings of the town, and the people, deserves to be quoted in full, preserving the original spelling:

> Feb. 22, the Mackenzies and Mackyes and others got to a head, haveing mustered 700 horse and foot for the Kings service, in a compleit body crossed over the Ferry Kessok, and randivousing at Markinsh, in view of Inverness, about 9 in the morning Collonell Hugh Fraser, living then in Kinmilies, joined them with his retinue, and so they march forward towards Kill Baine, and crossed the foord above the Isle of Inverness, the river being extream litle (a good providence to their cause), then they drew up a battallian above the town at Aldniskiach, when they directed a trumpet and two single horsemen very martially with a message to the garrison to surrender. Major Murray, deput governour under Sir James Fraser of Bray, now at south (who was Collonell) goes about to secure the portes and put the fort

in a fensible postur. The whole town in a confusion, not knowing whom to owne.

The Major in the first place sets uppon secureing the castle street gate towards the south, where the besiegers lay, and, being bussied ordering the pillisads, a beame of wood fell uppon his brow and wounded him sore, which raised his passion and rankled him, a bad omen and introduction.

A muteny was made in the streets by his souldiers as he returned from the port. One Sarjant John McKenzie, a pretty man, having a sword in his hand, obviates the Major, who, drawing his pistoll, shot him dead through the heart, and fell instantly uppon a dunghill midding, and expired gasping. I can averr this for truth, being myselfe, with one John Cuthbert, my schoolfellow, closs by him, and got sparkles of his bloud uppon our cloathes, a mark of loyalty. The Major cryed out, Take thow that for heading a muteny.

One Lieutenann Eneas Makdonell was another of the muteiners who narrowly escaped the Majors fingers; haveing got one to appologiz for him, being the Cornols foster brother, bearing his liverey. The Major steping down the street met Lieutenant William Forbes, who told him that the magistrates had obscured themselves to shift him, and were not to be trusted, and therefore to look to himselfe and escape.

Uppon the east side of the Court of Guard stood Captain Cranstown ahorseback, with his troop drawn up in the street, who called with a loud voice, Major Murray, instantly horse and be gone, else yow are betrayed. In a trice they all road away in heast, and out at the east street, leaving the town as a prey to the invaders. The magistrates caused open the castle Port, making it patent to them whom they welcomed as loyall persones.

My father, Mr. William Fraser, one of the ministers, was called wast the country, and I with him. Bewest Bunchrive we meet Lieutenant High Fraser with a 100 men out uppon a party for deficiency in Urqhart, who instantly uppon the report returned to Lovat, and stayed in that garrison till his master the Collonell returnd. There was another Lieutenant with a 100 men in Strathspey quartering, which made the garrison weak. Thus the dissloyall fort and ramparts of Inverness are demolished and leveled to the ground.

Young Master Fraser was on the spot again on May 3rd 1649, when in response to the arrival of General Middleton in the north the Mackenzies mustered again:

and made a body of 1500; and comming over, some at Cessock, some at Beuly, crossed the bridge of Ness oppon the Lords day in time of Divin service and allarmed the people of Inverness, impeding Gods worship in that town; for, insted of bells to ring in to service, I saw and heard no other than the noise of pipes, drumms, pots, pans, ketles, and spits in the streets, to provid them victuals in every house and in their quarters. The rude rasacality would eat no meat at their tables untill the landlord laid down a shilling Scots upon his trencher that sat, terming this *argid cagging* [*airgiod cagainn*, chewing silver], cheawing mony, which every soldier got; so insolent they were. And here indeed they fealed of their conduct by a rupture among themselves...

Moonday, about 10 of the clock, they marcht from Inverness, well appointed and furnished with ammunition, mony, all maner of arms, provision in aboundance, nothing wanting that might incurrage men in a good cause.

After such an auspicious start, the force proceeded to Balveny, under the command of Lord Reay and Captain Thomas Mackenzie of Pluscarden, where they set up camp, celebrating in style with much eating and drinking. Early the next morning, Colonel Kerr and Colonel Strachan attacked with just two troops of horse, taking them completely by surprise. Four hundred were killed outright, and a thousand men captured, including Lord Reay and twenty officers. They were taken back to Inverness:

...where I saw them pass through, and these men, who in their former march would hardly eat their meat without monny, are now begging, and, like doggs, lapp the water which was brought them in tubs and other vessells in the open streetes. Thence conducted over the bridge of Ness, and dissmissed every man armless and harmless to his own home. This is mater of fact, which I saw and heard!

The officers were kept in captivity, and eventually ransomed, at the end of May. There was worse to come for supporters of the Royal cause. Montrose himself was defeated at the battle of Carbisdale, on April 29th 1650, and after being taken prisoner was conveyed to Inverness, where, on May 7th, James Fraser once again was an eyewitness:

But now I set down that which I was myselfe eyewitness off. The 7 of May at Lovat, he set uppon a little shelty horse without a sude, but a quilt of raggs and straw, and pieces of roaps for stirrops, his fett fastened under the horse belly, with a teather and a bit halter for a bridge, a ragged old dark reedish plaid, and a Montier cape called Magirky on his head, a muskatire on each side, and his fellow prisoners on foot after him. Thus conducted through the country, and near Inverness, uppon the rode under Moortoun, where he desired to alight, and calld for a draught of water, being then in the first crise of a high fever, and here the crowd from the town came forth to gase, the two ministers wait here uppon to comfort him, the latter of which the Marques was well acquaint with.

At the end of the bridge, stepping forward, an old woman, Margret Nin George, exclaimed and brauled, saying, Montross, looke above, view these ruinous houses of mine quhich yow occasioned to be burnt down quhen yow besieged Invernesse. Yet he never altered his countenance, but with a majesty and state beseeming him, keept a countenance high.

At the cross, a table covered, the magistrates treat him with wine, which he would not tast till allayed with water: the statly prisoners, his officers, stood under a forestare, and drunk heartely. I remarked Colonell Hurry, a robust, tall, statly fellow, with a long cut in his cheek. All the way through the streets he never lowed his aspect. The provost, Duncan Forbes, takeing leave of him at the towns end, said, My Lord, I am sorry for your circumstance. He replied, I am sory for being the object of your pitty. The Marques was convoyed that night to Castle Stuart, where he lodged.

At least it is clear where James Fraser's sympathies lay! His hero James Graham, Marquis of Montrose, was executed on 21st May, so at least did not have to endure his indignities long.

William Mackay, editor of the Wardlaw manuscript, thinks that 'it is the part taken by Inverness in Montrose's war that is probably referred to in the 'Phrophesie made before the situatioune of Invernes' preserved in the collection of Gaelic poetry made by Macrae of Inverinate in the seventeenth century'. This fragment of verse, published in *Reliquiae Celticae*, vol. 2, is as follows:

Invernish daill chlaisk
Dorire kaha tuirhghash,
i dig M'Pehaig i mach
Lea layn agas lea luhrich
Tuitti ni Ghayle ma saigh
Ma voirlumb toim nj hurich.

Inverness a-clashing!
A deadly battle will be fought,
In which MacBeth will come forth
With his blade and his mail;
The Gael shall fall over one another
About the Bordland of Tomnahurich.

Cromwell's Occupation

The Commonwealth now controlled the whole country, and in the spring of 1652 Major General Dean was asked, in the words of the Wardlaw manuscript, 'to spy out the most commodious situated places for forts within the kingdom'. In April he laid out the foundations of a fort, or 'cittadell', at Ayr, as being the port best placed for trade with France and Ireland. Other forts were laid out at Leith and Aberdeen, and in Inverness, where James Fraser was there again to record the event:

> in the end of May one Mr. Hanes, a German ingenire, came to Inverness and laid the line of that citadell, which was non of the least of them. I was present at the first draught cut in that ground.

This was 'Cromwell's Fort', of which now no trace remains, save the reconstructed clock tower. By 1655 it neared completion, and Rev Fraser's description of it is worth repeating:

> The Citadel of Inverness is now on a great length almost finished. They had first built a long row of building, made of bricks and planks, uppon the River side, of a great length, to accommodat the regiment, and ramparts and bulwarks of earth in every street in the town, and also fortified the Castell and the Bridge and the main Court of guard at the Cross. They bought a large plat of ground from the burgers called Carseland, where they built their cittadale, founded May 1652, and now finished, a most statly sconce. It was 5 cornered, with bastians, with a wide grast or trench, what an ordinary bark might sail in it at full tide. The breastwork 3 storys, built all of hews ston, lined within with a brick wall, Centinel houses of stone on each corner, a sally port to the south leading to the town, and on the north the great entry or gate called the port, with a strong drawbridge of oake called the blew bridge, and a statly structur over the gate, well cut with the Commonwealth arms and this motto TOGAM TVENTVR ARMA.
>
> The entry from the bridge into the Citadell was a statlie vault about 70 foot longs, with seates on each side, and a rod of iron hooks for picks and drums to hang on. In the center of the citadel stood a great foursquare building, all hewn stone, called the magazin and granary; in the 3 story was the Church, well furnished with a statly pulpit and seates; a wide bartasin at top, and a brave great cloak with 4 large guilded dyalls, and a curious bell. Southeast stood the great long English building 4 story high, so called being built by English masones; and Southwest the Scotch buuilding of the same dimensions, built by Scotch masones; Northwest and northeast lower stories for amunition, timber, lodgings for manufactories, stables for horses,

provision, brewing houses, a great long tavern quher all manner of wines, viands, beer, ale, cider, was sold by one Master Benson; so that the whole regiment was accommodat within these walls.

A cinquport or conduit run under ground from the on to the other side, with grates of iron at ends, which at flowing and ebbing carried away the filth and odor of all the citadel. All their oake planks and beames was carried out of England in ships to Cessock rode; all their firr, logg, spar rofe beames, sold ther out of Hugh Fraser of Struyes woods. I saw that gentleman receave 30 thousand marks at once for timber. Most of their best hews stone was taken from Chanory, the great Cathedrall and Steeple, the Bishops Castle, to the foundation, rased, the church and Abby of Kinloss and Beuly, the Gray Friars and St. Maries chappell at Inverness, and many mo; so that it was a sacrilegious structure and therefore could not stand.

At the digging of the trenches, every man got a shilling sterling wages a day, so that all the country people flockt in to that work, and hardly could yow get one to serve yow; and the soldiers made more money attending it than their dayly pay amounted to. This great work was finished in the 5 yeare; and commissary Coup, who advanced the mony to masones, carpenters, and others, told me that the whole expense of it amounted to about 80 thousand libs. sterling.

No doubt Rev Fraser would be gratified that so little now remains of Cromwell's Fort, still known by that name though of course Oliver Cromwell himself never set foot in the town. As he says, all of the buildings in the area containing dressed stone were raided, or quarried, for the Inverness fort: much of it was to end up in the stone bridge over the Ness built in 1685. Incidentally, its cost of £1,300 places the money expended on Cromwells's Fort in perspective — truly a major investment which underlines the importance with which the government viewed the strategic position of the town.

As a symbol of the Commonwealth, it was not allowed to stand after the Restoration. By an Act of Parliament in 1662 the citadels of Inverness and elsewhere were ordered to be demolished, and just as he had witnessed the laying of the foundations in 1652, now, ten years later, James Fraser was there again. And once again, it was an event which the whole community of Inverness participated in, and celebrated:

> The first part they cease uppon was the centinell houses, neat turrets off hewn stone, curiously wrought, and set up uppon every corner of the rampart wall. These were all broken down in pieces by the souldioures themselves. The next thing was the Commonwalths armes

pulled down and broken, and the Kings arms set up in their place, the blew bridge slighted, and sally port broken, the magazin house steeple broken, and great bell taken down.

All this done with demonstations of joy and gladnes, the souldiours shouting with God save the King, as men weare of the yock and slavery of usurpation which lay so long about their necks. I was eyewitness now of the first stone that was broken of this famous citadell, as I was also witness of the first foundation stone laid in the same, anno 1652, in May. This sconce and cittadell is the Kings gift to the Earle of Murray, to dispose of it at his pleasure.

On April 11th four hundred of the occupying English regiment of 1000 left for Leith, with their wives and children, and on the next day another four hundred marched out of Cromwell's Fort. Although he was glad to see them go, Rev Fraser recognised the human feelings involved:

Next morrow, other 400 marcht, with their arms, commanders, and colloures, to the great griefe of all the English souldery; never people left a place with such reluctancy. It was even sad to see and heare sighs and teares, pale faces and embraces, at their parting farewell from that town. And no wonder; they had peace and plenty for 10 yeares in it. They made that place happy, and it made them so. The cittadell was slighted, all the country in course called in to rase it. I saw it founded, I saw it flourish, I saw it in its glory, grandeur and renoun, and now in its ruins. *Sic transit gloria mundi.*

Inverness English

Incidentally, it is probably not the case that the enduring story about how well the people of Inverness speak the English language is anything to do with the English garrison stationed there for, after all, only ten years. The origin of this idea is probably Samuel Johnson, who remarks in his *Journey to the Western Islands* that

the soldiers seem to have incorporated afterwards with the inhabitants, and to have peopled the place with an English race; for the language of this town has been long considered as peculiarly elegant.

But while it is certain that there was 'incorporation', to use the learned Doctor's tasteful word, between the garrison and the locals, there is nothing to suppose that the soldiers themselves were capable of speaking anything but regional dialects. They were not educated men. Much more likely is the explanation for Inverness English offered by William Mackay, the editor of the

Wardlaw manuscript, who points out that in Thomas Kirk's *Tours in Scotland* of 1677 and 1681, it was noted that the people of Inverness were predominantly Gaelic-speaking: 'all in the town of Inverness do generally use that language, except some few of the better sort, that can speak Scottish. Mackay thinks that the origin of the 'good' English spoken in Inverness 'is to be found in the circumstance that the language was acquired by a Gaelic-speaking people whose native tongue was remarkably free from 'brogue' or accent, not from English or Lowland soldiers, but from educated schoolmasters and good English books'.

Signs and Wonders

In the preceding February the exodus from Cromwell's Fort had been presaged, according to the still superstitious Rev Fraser, by the arrival of an enormous whale, 116ft long, beached on the shore east of Inverness. There was an argument with Culloden about which jurisdiction it had landed in, but the town prevailed.

In August 1661 Rev Fraser tells us that a 12-foot long sturgeon was caught in the Beauly Firth, 'in the Yarr of Drumchardeny within our paroch of Wardlaw'. Nessie-watchers may wish to consider the possibility of occasional visitations by these enormous fish to the waters of Loch Ness. In 1932, a year before the famous sightings of Nessie which achieved so much national and international publicity, an Inverness lady spotted a 'crocodile' swimming up the river Ness — exactly how a sturgeon would look in such circumstances.

At any rate, the seventeenth-century sturgeon was sold for a great deal of money to some English merchants who were in Inverness, where it was pickled, barrelled, and sent to London. The superstition that the landing of such a monstrous fish presaged an important event, or the death of an important person seemed to come true again, when Alexander Campbell, a brother of the Laird of Calder (Cawdor) was killed just one month later, on 7th September 1661. On that day three large whales were found beached at Ardersier, and drew a crowd of spectators. Sea birds were swirling overhead, and Alexander Campbell drew his pistol and fired off some shots to disperse them. He sat down to reload, but:

> setting the pistoll to his boot toa fast, and the barrell mouth to his breast to draw out the rammer, the shot gat off, and two balls run

through his heart, killing himselfe stark dead, without ever speaking one word; a dreadfull dismall accident, sad blow to that famely: the prettiest man that ever came of it and the floure of all the Campbells in the North, a youth of wonderfull expectation, my trusty, true, and real friend, universally beloved, and universally bemoand.

But, the monarchy had been restored, and life could get back to normal:

The 29th of May, being the anniversary thanksgiveing for His Majestyes restautation, was solemnly kept here by preaching, singing of psalmes through streetes, ringing of bells, bonefires, small and great shot, and all other demonstations of you imaginable, and no difference observed tuixt presbiterian and Episcopalls. All are seemingly loyall, the lawes so strick and observant that non appeare to dissent.

Horse-Racing at Tomnahurich

Another sign of normality was the resumption, after many years interruption, of the annual horse races round Tomnahurich Hill, on 24–25th May. It was a great event, requiring a high level of planning and organisation: on March 1st the magistrates of Inverness had set up 'the port and pillars for the annuall horse race about the Hill of Tomnihurich, and advertisement sent abroad to that effect'. During the years of Parliamentary rule, the period of the Commonwealth, the prizes and paraphernalia associated with the races had been kept safely, and were now prepared for the great day: silver cups, saddles and a ceremonial sword.

There was a great response from all concerned. The Earl of Moray, the Earl of Seaforth, and Lord Lovat all attended, with their race horses, and the Lairds of Grant, Mackintosh, Foulis, Balnagowan, Lord Macdonald of Glengarry, the English officers from the Fort at Inverlochy, and many more:

The Provost and Magistrates of Inverness, with the citizens, came in procession over the bridge to their bounded march, and, with the usual ceremony, hung the silver cup with blew ribbons uppon the hookes off the painted port, the Sadle and the Sourd set uppon the top of it.

The race started at ten o'clock, and lasted for an hour. The riders were all in white, with distinctive ribbons of blue, red, yellow and green. The four main contestants were Lovat, Grant, Kilravock, and Captain Man, though everybody else with a horse joined the rear. Lovat tucked in at the rear of the main contenders, then, with half a mile to go, launched his attack, and won easily.

On the second day, May 25th, the main race was between the Master of Lovat, Kilravock, the Laird of Innes, and Bailie Finlay Fraser of Inverness. At the finish line Lovat and Bailie Fraser were so close together 'that it was scarce discernable; so that they cast lots, and Balife Fraser carried the cup and sword with approbation and applause'. The Laird of Grant paid Bailie Fraser £13 for his horse — and won the race on it in the next year!

Accidents and Disasters

Rev Fraser describes a few other incidents and episodes which would have been talking points at the time, and would have been remembered long after. In August 1661 the local schoolmaster, Mr Alexander Fraser, was drowned at the harbour in Inverness while trying to rescue one of his scholars. Two boys, Donald Bain of Tulloch and Hugh Fraser of Reelig, got into difficulties. Their schoolmaster took off his clothes and ran into the water to help them, saving young Donald, later Sir Donald Bain of Tulloch, but losing his life in the fruitless attempt to save Hugh Fraser: both he and the schoolmaster were drowned. They were both dragged from the water still warm, but 'though hung by the heeles till a great deal off water sprung out at their mouths' the attempts at resuscitation were unsuccessful.

On March 20th 1664 there was a great fire at the 'barnyards of Culcabock' in which eleven haystacks were destroyed — 'it made such a dreedful flame as put Inverness in a consternation, being so neare'. The local gossip was that the fire had been started by Glenmoriston men, in the settlement of some feud.

Peace Talks at Kilvean

In May 1664 there was a great gathering of the supporters of Mackintosh and Lochiel at Kilvean, then on the southern edge of Inverness, to sort out a boundary dispute. They put on quite a show. Mackintosh, with about 500 men, set up camp on the east side of the river, while Lochiel, with another 300 men, encamped at the base of Tomnahurich Hill. The Rev Fraser says that 'earth, water, aire, rebounded at the sound of bagpipes Martiall musick' — perhaps the equivalent of a modern pop concert or outdoor folk festival. It took three days to sort out the problems between the principals, with the Bishop of Moray acting as arbitrator, but they concluded the negotiations successfully, to the great disappointment of the lawyers: 'it prevented litigation and cost in law. This was a noble sight of gallant gentlemen, and the clergy in decent grave garbs'.

We even get some weather reports from Rev Fraser. On 22th June 1664 there was twenty-four hours of thunder and lightning, accompanied not by hailstones but with 'pieces of ice, inch thick and 3 inch broad'. In September 1664 there was an accident at the bridge in Inverness. While attempting to repair the bridge, which was leaning, a carpenter inadvertently cut through one of the main support beams, causing a portion of the bridge to collapse. For some reason, which is not mentioned by Rev Fraser, there were two hundred people on the bridge at the time, men, women and children. Perhaps it was just as irresistible in 1664 to watch other people working as it is today; perhaps they were aware of the risk he was running and could not restrain their curiosity. Four townsmen suffered broken legs, while another sixteen were badly bruised on their heads, arms and thighs; none of the children was hurt. A great flood followed, and for the rest of that winter the bridge could not be repaired, and a ferry boat had to be used.

Marymas Riot

We get a report of a riot in Inverness in 1666, at the Marymas Fair, on August 15th. On the hill south of the castle the horse market was in progress, and on the edge of the hill some women had set up stall selling bread and cheese to the crowds. Finlay Dubh, Black Finlay, a townsman, picked up a cheese and asked the price. Whether by accident or design, when he got the answer he dropped the cheese, which ran down the slope and into the river. The women quite reasonably demanded payment, while 'he (a crabbed fellow) gave her cross language of defyance'. A bystander could not resist interfering, and grabbed Finlay Dubh, giving the women his bonnet as surety, until he should settle his account. One of Finlay's relatives joined in, telling the bystander that it was all none of his business. But the bystander replied that he would see justice done, as a witness to what had happened. At which point, all hell broke loose, as the Wardlaw manuscript describes:

> To threatning words and as goods, they goe from words to blowes, till at length most of the hill markat is ingaged to a confusion. This allarms the whole town. The guards are called, who come in arms,

and John Reed, a pretty man, their captain, runs in betuixt the parties to seperat them. Severall other gentlemen present offer their mediation; no heareing, but swords drawn, guns presented, some vounds given. Provost Alexander Cuthbert is told that his guards are not regarded, puts on a steel cap, sword, and targe, caust ring the alarm bell, comes streight to the hill, and many pretty fellowes with him. The people cry for justice. The guard, being opposed and abused, let off some shot. Two are killed outright, and above ten wounded. The noise husted, maters examined, the guard blamd. If the Provost in a fury said he allowed and avowed quhat was done, for who durst disturb the kings free burgh at a market time?

Eventually tempers cooled, and a modicum of peace was restored. The two who were killed, and two more who died of their wounds, were buried at Kirkhill, witnessed, of course, by Rev James Fraser. The man who had precipitated the fracas was marked for life — not branded as a punishment, but by nature, for his beard was naturally white on one side and black on the other, so he was always easily identified.

The *Records of Inverness*

While the Wardlaw manuscript brings the immediacy of an eye-witness account, the official records of the burgh, though often dry and legalistic in their tone, do give us many insights into the way of life of the people. Two large printed volumes of extracts from these records, edited by William Mackay and published in Aberdeen by the Spalding Club in 1911 and 1924, provide much material of interest. Mackay drew on two sources: the Burgh Court Books, 1556–86 and 1602–37; and the Minutes of the Town Council, 1637–88. The records for 1586–1602 have not survived, and there is a gap in the Town Council minutes for 1655–1662, probably while the town was under the control of the military garrison in Cromwell's fort. It was intended to publish extracts down to the crucial period of 1745–6, but the projected third volume never appeared, and this remains a worthwhile project for some modern historian, though at least the minutes are safely in the custody of the Highland Archivist and available to researchers.

Many of the cases dealt with by the Burgh Court are to do with fairly minor squabbles among the citizenry, though occasionally there are more serious crimes and misdemeanours. Some cases deal with matters now under the control of Trading Standards officers: regulations on the quality of wheat bread and ale, on the control of trade within the burgh, and on the export of goods from the burgh.

Many of the personal crimes are for assault in varying degrees, from verbal abuse to serious physical assault. There are many cases involving non-payment of debts, or non-provision of services paid for. There are lots of examples of petty thefts. Sometimes the punishments handed out seem rather drastic by today's standards, though appropriate enough by the standards of the time. On 7th July 1618 Thomas McAndrew and John McVarraich were up before the Burgh Court for trying to break out of the town jail. Their sentence was that they were to be taken through 'the four streits of the toun' at eight o'clock on Saturday morning, scourged, and thereafter nailed by their ears ('luggis') to the Tron. There they were to stay until six o'clock at night, tied back to back, and then banished for ever, never to dwell in the burgh ever again. On June 18th 1613, Donald McAine, indicted as a vagabond and thief, was sentenced to have his ear nailed to the pillory at the cross for the period of one hour, and thereafter to be scourged through the four streets of the town, and banished; he would be put to death if ever found in the town again.

On December 2nd 1603 Donald John Mackferquhar, a miller, was found guilty of six charges of witchcraft by a jury of fifteen burgesses, in a trial which must have caused great interest in the town. His sentence was that for the using of charms, and for witchcraft, he was to be taken to the 'Haouche Heid' (the head of the Haugh) and burnt. 'Ordinary' criminals were beheaded on 'the heiding hil', and 'thair his heid to be stuckin of fra the bodie'. Magie Fischar, found guilty of murdering her newborn son, the result of an adulterous relationship with William Mcillichrist of Culloden, by drowning him in the Ness, was sentenced on December 5th 1610 to be hanged, while on October 29th 1611 John Ross was sentenced for a long series of thefts to be taken to the gallows of the burgh muir, there to be hanged until he was dead.

Occasionally the death sentence was more imaginative. On 2nd October 1615 Allister McConil was found guilty of stealing a 'littil browne horse' from Easter Drakies. He tried to sell it at a horse fair, but was caught. He also stole other property belonging to Alexander Cuthbert and sold it in Inverness, took some items 'under silence of nicht' from the house of Andrew Dow of Drakies, and some gardening equipment from Thomas Moir of Kinmaillies

(Kinmylies). He was indicted as 'ane commun notorius theif, ane maisterles vagabond, infang thief, outfang theif, ane ivil member for the common weil'; his sentence was 'to be tain to the brige, and cassin doun in the watter, and thair thow remain quhill thow die'.

Janet Brunto narrowly escaped a similar fate, by promising to exile herself from the town, at her appearance before the Burgh Court on 18th May 1612:

> That day Jonet Brunto, beinge accusit as ane commun harlot, nocht sparand na man, and fund as ane usand that form as ane craft, hes voluntarlie becum actit to exil hirselff presentlie, and that sche sal neuer be fund in this toun again, nycht or day, vnder the pain of puttinge of hir to deith and drouninge of hir, lyickas the Prouest and baillies hes inhibit ony persone to gif hir ludgeing vnder the pain of xl lib.

Obviously a real professional! Sometimes a bit of pettiness creeps in to the deliberations of the Burgh Court, as on 17th November when Alexander Merchand, exasperated by the deliberations of the Town Council, burst into one of their meetings and 'gave them money iniuriows wordis'. The Council took their collective revenge by depriving him of his privileges as a freeman of the burgh.

The Minute Books of the Town Council have more to do with the administration of local government in the town than with the administration of justice, but contain a great deal of interesting and important material which sheds much light on life in Inverness during the last half of the seventeenth century. Sometimes the entries are brief and to the point, as when on 27th November 1654 they appointed a new hangman, 'Allister Doun in Oberriachan' (Abriachan), allowing him all the 'casualities' (ie, casual perks) which his predecessors had enjoyed.

Sometimes the Town Council could be called upon to exercise a judicial function, as on 11th July 1681 when the Procurator Fiscal complained to them that Janet Leugach (*lugach*, having crooked legs), having been banished from the town, was back again in Inverness. She is described as 'ane vile & wicked person'. The particular cause of the fiscal's appeal to the Council was that

> not onlie for former miscariages, bot also for miscarrying herselfe & transgressing groslie yesterday, being the Lords day, in tyme of divyne service, in the Hie Kirk of this brugh, by being drunk & vomitting therin to the great dishonour of God and contempt of His Church.

She confessed to these misdeeds, and was sentenced by the Magistrates and Council to be taken to the Tron at twelve o'clock that very day,

> there to receive ten stripes on the bare back be the hands of the hangman, and therafter to be caryed throw the whole streetts and to receive sex stripes in each streett; and therafter to be banished this place for ever never to return therto under the payne of being lyable to punishment at the Magistrats discretion.

Anybody who helped her in any way would be liable to a fine of 'twentie pounds Scots money'.

A couple of weeks before Janet Leugach's outrage, on 27th June the Magistrates and Council decided to crack down on the language of the populace:

> the saids Magistrats & Counsell apoint, statut & ordain for the suppression of cursers & swearers that how oftensoever it sall happin any of the members of the Touns Consill to hear & notice any person or persons qtsomever to curse or swear on the streetts or elswhere within this Brugh & liberties thereof that they shall incontinent, as be ther presents they are authorised, to cause ane or mor of the burrow officers imprison any sua found cursing & swearing, there to remain ay & untill the Magistrats take ane course with the delinquents and inflict such punishment as their fault deserves; and also appoint the constables in their respective streetts to advert to the fulfilling of this act & obtemperance thereof in all points.

The Council could also crack down on filth in a more practical sense, as when on 9th July 1677 they attacked the problem of dunghills and middens in the town:

> ...finding that diverse of the inhabitants incroaches upon the Kings hie way & makes dunghills & middings therupon contrair to the Acts of Parliament and prejudicall to the leidges; they therfore have appointit intimation to be made be towk of drum at the mercat cross be tuo hours this afternoon requiring & commanding all the inhabitants that have any middings & dunghills on the Kings hie way betwixt this & the milne burn sall remove the samen within fourtie eight hours under the pain of confiscation of the middings & fyneing of the contraveiner at the Magistrats discretion.

It is interesting that the Council thought that threatening the populace with the confiscation of their middens was as much as a deterrent as the threat of a monetary fine. Another public nuisance that the Council decided on 9th July 1677 to try and do something about a problem that is still a matter of great concern today —

stray dogs:

> The Counsell considering the great prejudice the brugh sustaines throw the great number of curr dogs kept therein, especiallie their spoiling bigging in the thach thereof, their throwing down yaird dykes, their troubsomnes in the night, the inhabitants as they go under silence of night in the streets being bitten & hurt by the said dogis, with severall uther enormities by them comittit; the Counsell therfor for remeid have appointit statut & ordained that the owners of the saids cur dogs cause furthwith kill their saids cur dogs or pay tuo shillings Scots money to those will kill the samen for each dog.

In this way the burgh hoped to rid itself of this menace; there would be a further fine of forty shillings in Scots money for any transgressors.

The Old Stone Bridge

There is a great deal about the town bridge in the Town Council Minutes — the new stone bridge which was completed in 1685 and was swept away in the great flood of 1849. The Council took it upon itself to raise the necessary money — £1300 — by inviting contributions from leading citizens and important people in the area, in exchange for privileges, such as exemption from future tolls. Charges were computed on a proportionate scale: six pennies from each horseman or horse and load; four pennies for each horse or cow; two pennies for each foot passenger; 'and sua furth proportionallie for all sheep & uther bestiall passing alongs the said Bridge alse oft as they pass and repass the same'.

The Council passed toll exemptions for itself and Burgh officials and, doubtless at the behest of the church authorities, made it clear that inability to pay the toll would not be accepted as an excuse for missing church:

> the Counsell appoint that all poor people within Toun & Paroche... that are not weill able to pay toll at the bridge be exempt & frie on the Sabbath day in coming to and going from Sermon from paying of the said toll.

There were regulations about the opening and closing of the bridge. The gates were to be closed each night at ten o'clock, when the key would be handed in to the Captain of the Town Watch, who would keep watch during the night. The Town Guard had to make a round on the west side of the river during the night, and deliver the key to the toll master each morning at four o'clock so

A new cement structure on the site of the earliest mediaeval bridge over the Ness.

that he could open the bridge and start collecting tolls.

One of the final extracts from the Town Council Minutes printed in the *Records of Inverness* relates to the need for the town to protect itself in the unsettled political environment of the times:

> considering the countrey of the west highlands to be in a pnt. sturr and combustion by reason of the rebellion of McDonald of Keppoch and his adherents, and for secureing themselves and the whole inhabitants from the hazard incurssions of the saids rebels which may fall out through their slouth & negligence; Therefore the sds. Magistrats & Counsell for preveining therof have appointed & ordained that the present twelve Companies of this brugh be reducit to eight Companies considering the same to tend greatly to the safetie of the place...

They were not reducing the total numbers of citizens responsible for taking their turn in the nightly watch, but reorganising the number of companies, and commanding officers, involved — they had further contingency plans to reduce the number to four, under named commanders, in the event of an emergency. The same regulations mention the penalties for missing a turn at the watch — £5 Scots for each night missed, which was a massive penalty, showing how seriously the Council regarded the security situation. In passing, there is a reference to 'the knelling of the nyne hours bell nightly' — something which must have been part and parcel of the fabric of life in Inverness at the time.

The Magistrates also ordered all the Guild Brethren and Burgesses of Trades to arm themselves with

> ane fixt fyrelock and ane sufficient sword each of them, and such other tradesmen as are not able to have the forsds armes are hereby ordained to have ane deus ax or ane morneing starr with ane sufficient sword each person.

It appears that 'ane deus ax' is not, as the editors of the *Records of Inverness* thought, a 'Jew's axe', but a mis-reading of 'ane dens ax' — a Dane's axe, which would probably have been the large axehead with a curved edge, mounted on a long pole, familiar from West Highland grave sculpture. The 'morneing starr' is referred to in the records of other Scots burghs at the time, and was a long pole with an enlarged head of wood or iron studded with spikes (information from Dr David H Caldwell at the National Museums of Scotland). Also known as a 'Holy Water Sprinkle', it was a common peasant weapon throughout Europe for several centuries

The fine for not being adequately armed was £20 Scots.

CHAPTER 4
INVERNESS AND THE JACOBITES

The history of Inverness in the eighteenth century, and the effect of historical events on its people, is dominated by one date: 16th April 1746. On that day, in less than an hour, the last attempt to restore the Stuart dynasty to the thrones of Scotland and Ireland, and eventually, it was hoped, England too, came to a bloody and disastrous end on Drumossie Muir, at what we have come to remember as the Battle of Culloden.

Culloden Anniversary

In the Highlands of Scotland it is difficult to exaggerate the importance of this event. Its resonances linger on, and at the 250th anniversary of the battle in 1996 an estimated six thousand people, of whom only a handful were tourists, assembled on Culloden battlefield to pay their respects to the dead of both sides, in a simple commemorative service organised, as it is every year, by the Gaelic Society of Inverness. To their great credit they declined the temptation to invite the great and the good, and followed the same format as usual — a prayer and a simple commemorative address. It was all over in half an hour, and it is hard to imagine a gathering of greater dignity. Thankfully, those who had proposed to re-enact the battle for the entertainment of the assembled company were politely but firmly told, well in advance, to stay away. A simulated charge by a motley collection of surrogate clansmen armed with broadsword, pistol and targe sufficed to indulge their fantasies. On this occasion they managed to breach the Hanoverian line, and then returned the field of battle to those clan societies, families and individuals who had come to lay wreaths on the graves of their ancestors.

The 250th anniversary of Culloden produced a plethora of publications, of varying quality, including some notable contributions by Scottish historians. All are eager to nail the lie that Culloden was a battle fought between the Scots and the English. Nothing could be further from the truth. The Jacobite army was led by an Italianate prince (Bonnie Prince Charlie) at the head of an army of 4,000 Highlanders, Lowlanders, Irish and French troops — truly a cosmopolitan gathering — while on the Hanoverian side, it is estimated that up to 25% of the Government troops were Scots, serving in various regiments of the British Army, under the command of the Duke of Cumberland, the son of the usurping Hanoverian monarch.

The bitterness of the defeat at Culloden derives in large measure from events after the battle itself. The Jacobite wounded were shown no quarter, and two days after the battle parties of government soldiers were still hunting them down and bayonetting them without mercy. In the chaos of retreat, on the afternoon of 16th April, Government dragoons rode through the streets of Inverness, seeking out and killing anybody even suspected of Jacobite sympathies, including some civilians. All this has been well documented, in harrowing detail, including the famous account of how the Duke of Cumberland kicked Provost Hossack down the stairs, when he dared to ask for mercy for the defeated Jacobites.

Atrocities

Surprisingly, one of the most graphic descriptions of the atrocities committed by Cumberland's army was not published until 1841, when in the *New Statistical Account* of the parish of Croy and Dalcross the minister, the Rev Alexander Campbell, who from his surname would not be suspected of Jacobite sympathies, gives us his view of the events of 1746, and a first-hand account of one of the worst atrocities:

> The particulars have been so often and so minutely...narrated, that hardly anything farther can be said. It may, however, be proper to observe, that there was one deed of such atrocious and execrable foulness, as can hardly find a parallel in the annals of the most bloody and ruthless tyrants of ancient or modern times, and which, though denied by the sycophants of the court, is an incontrovertible fact: Early in the morning after the battle, orders were given by the Duke of Cumberland or General Hawley, par ignobile fratrum, to inspect the wounded and mangled, in whom there remained any symptoms of life, and collect them into two heaps, and apply a six pounder to each heap: yet, wonderful as it may appear, one Maciver, a private, though mutilated in several parts of his body, survived this massacre, a dismal memorial of Cumberland's tender mercies. The man died near Beauly, about the year 1796, where many are still living, who

may have known him; but to put the bloody deed beyond the shadow of doubt, the writer of this account knew for several years a John Reid, who fought that day in the second battalion of the Royal Scots, and heard from his lips, that he saw the cruel deed, and thanked God that he had nothing to do with the black wark. John fought at the battles of Dettingen and Fontenoy, and only died about the year 1807, in the 105th year of his age, and in the full enjoyment of all his mental faculties. He was a lively little man, and retained a correct and vivid recollection of what he had seen and heard.

The minister's account not only corroborates the atrocity by citing witnesses from both sides, but highlights very poignantly the internecine nature of the struggle, in which there were many examples of members of the same family confronting each other on opposite sides of the battle line.

Prince Charles Edward Stuart, born in 1720, had raised his standard at Glenfinnan, near Fort William, on 19th August 1745. Jacobite armies occupied Perth, Edinburgh, Carlisle, and reached Derby, less than one hundred miles from London, before the lack of Jacobite support in England convinced the commanders that to continue would be disastrous. Returning to Scotland, the Jacobites occupied Glasgow and Stirling, defeated Government forces at Falkirk, but on 1st February 1746, in the face of overwhelming odds, began their retreat into the Highlands. They entered Inverness on 18th February, and two days later blew up the government fortress there, Fort George, on the site of the mediaeval castle of Inverness. The town was occupied by Jacobite forces until the day of Culloden, 16th April 1746.

Jacobite Occupation

In the summer of 1996 Inverness Museum mounted an exhibition, *Calamitous Times*, based on contemporary accounts of life in the burgh during the Jacobite period. Some of the copy letterbooks of Bailie John Steuart (1676–1759) have survived, showing how an Inverness merchant, an Episcopalian and Jacobite sympathiser, came to terms with post-Culloden reality and supplied goods to the military garrisons which were the main bases for the Government occupation forces. *The Letter-Book of Bailie John Steuart*, edited by William Mackay, was published by the Scottish History Society in 1915. It is an excellent and amusing source of information on life in Inverness in the eighteenth century.

Writing to Robert Forbes, Bishop of Ross and Caithness, in 1748, John Steuart makes clear his apprehensions and devastating indictment of government policy in the Highlands:

> I should have wrot you long befor now annent what I could learn with certainty of the bloodie, barbarous transactions in this country for a long time after the memorable battle of Culloden...But by all I can learn I may say, without exagerting, that I doe not think there were ever greater, inhuman barbaritys and cruelties of all kinds perpetrat in anie countrie, either Cristian or Infidel, than was in this at that period; and all by order of the commander [Cumberland], as some of the officers then in that service have since told me. And those that comitted the greatest barbaritys, whither by murder, rape, rapin or fire, have since been most liberally rewarded and prefered. But God is the Lord to whom vengeance belongs.

By contrast, Duncan Grant's letterbooks, unpublished but surviving in the collections of Inverness Museum, show a prosperous Inverness merchant in happier mood. He was a long-time supporter of the Hanoverian cause, and had prospered by trading with government garrisons in the Highlands, set in place after the Jacobite rebellion of 1715. In May 1746 he wrote to an Edinburgh merchant:

> Now that our late calamitous times are happily near a period its time for me to look to some business haveing never seen my own house from the day the rebels took possession of this town till the day that our deliverer the Duke of Cumberland made them leave it.

Early Tourists

One of the most influential accounts of Inverness in the eighteenth century came from a three-volume work first published in 1724–7, but re-issued in many editions; that of 1753 includes some material on the 1745–6 rebellion, for example. In the style of eighteenth-century travel literature, the title was intended to be descriptive of the contents, rather than short and snappy: *A Tour thro' the Whole Island of Great Britain, divided into Circuits or Journeys, giving a Particular and Entertaining Account of whatever is Curious, and worth Observation; Interspersed with Useful Observations, Particularly fitted for the Perusal of such as desire to Travel over the Island*, by a Gentleman. And who was this anonymous Gentleman? None other than Daniel Defoe, English spy and author of *Robinson Crusoe*.

The comments in Defoe's *Tour* regarding the influence of Cromwell's soldiers in Inverness are often quoted, and were very influential with other writers, some of whom, unlike Defoe, had never set foot in the Highland capital. After describing the building of Cromwell's Fort, and how a garrison was posted there, 'to preserve the Peace of the Country and keep the *Highlanders* in awe', he says:

> It is observed, that at the End of those troublesome Days, when the Troops on all Sides came to be disbanded, and the Men dispersed, abundance of *English* Soldiers settled in this fruitful Part of the Country, from whence it received Two Advantages:
>
> 1. They learnt the Art of Husbandry in full Perfection, which they did not understand before; which, with the Help of a rich Soil, has rendered this Part of the Country more fruitful than the rest of *Scotland* to this Day. And to this it is in some measure owing, that the Harvest is so early, and the Corn so good, as is observed above.
>
> 2. As *Cromwell's* Soldiers initiated them thus into the Arts and Industry of the Husbandman, so they left them the *English* Accent upon their Tongues, which they likewise preserve to this Day; for they speak perfect *English*, even much better than in the most Southerly Provinces of *Scotland;* nay, some will say, as well as at *London* itself. And indeed their Way of Eating and Cookery, Dress and Behaviour, is pretty much according to the Southern Mode.

We will come back to Defoe's theories of language and accent, and confine ourselves for the present to a condemnation of his patronising remarks. However, in mitigation, he was not the last tourist to come to these parts and express surprise that the trappings of culture and civilisation were present in this savage outpost.

On a more positive note, Defoe gives an interesting description of the women of Inverness, which must have done the town no harm as a destination for tourists seeking an exotic location:

> To the Sides of the River *Ness* come the Women or Maid-Servants to wash their Family Linen, which they dry upon the Stones or Grass just by. Their Method of Washing is, by tradeing it in a Tub, naked up to their Knees, constantly turning round with an unusual Motion. Those who are not worth a Tub, tread it in the River, upon a large Stone, under Water; for they very seldom use Soap. We may see, in a warm Morning, the River Banks lined with these Women, and frequently as many Men admiring their Limbs.
>
> The Women here are remarkably handsome: many of them red-hair'd: they are generally taught to play on the Spinnet, to dance, *&c.*

This is racy writing! No wonder tourists flocked to Inverness throughout the eighteenth century, with the prospect of such attractions right in the centre of the town.

Some of the best accounts of eighteenth-century Inverness come from an English officer, Captain Edmund Burt, who was stationed in Inverness during the period of military road building in the 1730s. Writing to a friend in England, his letters, published in 1754, contain many interesting glimpses into town life, few of them flattering. These passages describe the condition of the ordinary people:

> ...here is a melancholy appearance of objects in the streets;- in one part the poor women, maid-servants, and children, in the coldest weather, in the dirt or in snow, either walking or standing to talk to one another, without stockings or shoes. In another place, you see a man dragging along a half-starved horse little bigger than an ass, in a cart, about the size of a wheel-barrow...Some of these carts are led by women, who are generally bare-foot, with a blanket for the covering of their bodies, and in cold or wet weather they bring it quite up over them...How miserable would be the children of the poor that one sees continually in the streets! Their wretched food makes them look pot-bellied; they are seldom washed...boys have nothing but a coarse kind of vest buttoned down the back...girls have a piece of blanket wrapped about their shoulders, and are bareheaded like the boys; and both without stockings and shoes in the hardest of the seasons.

Positioned in the street just outside the front door of the Town House in Inverness, in front of the Mercat Cross, is one of the most famous icons of the burgh of Inverness, the Clachnacuddin, 'the stone of the tubs', where the women of the town paused with their tubs of washing on their way to and from the river. Captain Burt has a good description of their exertions:

> Women with their coats tucked up, stamping, in tubs, upon linen by this way of washing; and not only in Summer, but in the hardest frosty weather, when their legs and feet are almost literally as red as blood with the cold; and often two of these wenches stamp in one tub, supporting themselves by their arms thrown over each other's shoulders.

So, it was a brave man, Mr Murdoch Macintosh, Sheriff Clerk, President of the Inverness Scientific Society and Field Club, who in November 1948 dared to question the Clachnacuddin story. In an address to the Club's annual meeting, he maintained that 'the

Inverness Castle around 1750, from Edmund Burt's Letters.

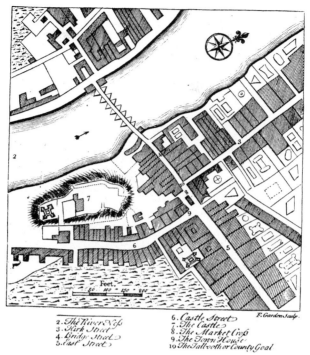

The earliest map of the town centre, published in 1754 in Edmund Burt's
Letters.

stone of the tubs' was a mistranslation. Quoting the traditional
explanation about resting their washing tubs while indulging in a
bit of gossip, Mr Macintosh said that he was not at all satisfied
with this explanation: 'The women of Inverness do not need a
tub to help them on with a bit of gossip'. His theory, sadly
unsubstantiated by any evidence, was that the stone marked the
place where baptisms took place at the time when Christianity was
introduced into the Highlands. Well, there was a tiny suggestion
of evidence: in 'an ancient history of Inverness' it was mentioned
that when the Clachnacuddin was moved to allow road-widening
operations, the people rioted — this proved, thought Mr
Macintosh, that sacrilege was involved: 'It must have had some
religious significance. The only washing it had anything to do with
was baptism'.

Invernessians at the Mercat Cross, around 1750, according to Edmund Burt.

More likely was his explanation for the canine population of Inverness. He pointed out that before the four main streets of the town were paved and levelled in 1672, householders threw their refuse and ashes out of their front doors, producing a surface more like a country road: 'The dogs were the scavengers in those days', he commented, 'which may account for the number of dogs which still wander around Inverness. It's probably hereditary'.

In contrast to Rev Alexander Campbell's 1841 account of how Cumberland's troops discharged a six-pound gun into a 'heap' of wounded, the Rev Hugh Calder, minister of the parish of Croy, writing in 1793, had an altogether more establishment view. In the first *Statistical Account*, edited by Sir John Sinclair, he wrote of

...the famous battle of Culloden, memorable for the complete defeat of the adherents of the house of STUART, in their last attempt to replace that deluded family on the British throne. The circumstances and consequences of that action are so well known, as to render it unnecessary to give any account of them here. Strangers still visit the field of battle, though there is little to be seen on it, excepting the graves of those that fell in the action, which are discerned by the green surface, while the rest of the ground is covered with black heath. Bullets, and fragments of armour, that are picked up by people in the neighbourhood, are anxiously sought after, and carefully preferred, by the virtuous, as curiosities and valuable relics.

Inverness in Pennant's *Tour*

Thomas Pennant's *A Tour in Scotland*, first published in 1769 and subsequently reprinted in many editions, was one of the most influential early accounts of life in the Highlands of Scotland. One of the many engravings in this book shows Inverness as seen from the east side of the river, opposite the Ness Islands. In the background the Ord Hill on the Black Isle looms dramatically over the Old High Church, while in the middle of the view the old stone bridge is prominent, its arches reflected in the river. The ruined keep of the castle blown up by the Jacobites in 1746 stands like a jagged tooth on the flat top of the castle mound, which is precipitous on its west side, overlooking the river. Other buildings, one with a slated roof, stand beside the castle. Between the castle and the church, obscured by the bridge and merging into the backdrop of the Black Isle, stand the buildings of the town of Inverness.

Pennant's account of the town is flattering, and inviting. He estimates the population at about 11,000, and describes the town as 'large and well built'. He notes that for many of the gentry in the surrounding countryside Inverness was 'the winter residence'. Ships of 200 tons can come up to the town's quay at high tide, while at low tide ships of 400 or 500 tons can approach within a mile of the town. Imports are listed as 'chiefly groceries, haberdasheries, hardware, and other necessaries from London'; in addition, 'six to eight hundred hogsheads of porter are annually brought in', to slake the thirst of the locals. Exports are listed as salmon from the Ness, herring, 'of an inferior kind' from the Firth, from August to March, 'cordage and sacking', and linen. In the aftermath of Culloden Pennant found the local economy somewhat depressed, noting that

> the commerce of this place was at its height a century or two ago, when it engrossed the exports of corn, salmon and herrings, and had besides a great trade in cured codfish now lost; and in those times very large fortunes were made here.

Pennant visited Cromwell's fort, but found it to be 'a pentagon, whose form remains to be traced only by the ditches and banks'. He mentions that 'there is a very considerable rope-walk near it'. He visited the castle — 'old Fort St. George' — noting that it used to be a royal castle; he talked to old people who 'still remember magnificent apartments embellished with stucco busts and paintings'. Many of today's tourists who congregate before Inverness 'castle' on summer evenings would agree with Pennant's assessment of the view:

> The view from hence is charming of the *Firth*, the passage of *Kessock*, the river *Ness*, the strange-shaped hill of *Tomman heurich*, and various groupes of distant mountains.

Sadly, the addition, in the foreground, of various concrete excrescences built on Bridge Street in the 1960s make the view somewhat less charming than it was in the eighteenth century, though the addition of the Kessock Bridge does add interest, compensating for the loss of the Kessock Ferry.

Pennant ascended the 'strange-shaped hill' that we call Tomnahurich. There was no cemetery there in his day, though the hill was wooded:

> The *Tomman* is of an oblong form, broad at the base, and sloping on all sides towards the top; so that it looks like a ship with its keep upwards. its sides, and part of the neighbouring plains, are planted, so it is both an agreeable walk and a fine object. It is perfectly detached from any other hill; and if it was not for its great size might pass for a work of art. The view from it is such, that no traveller will think his labor lost, after gaining the summit.

In a footnote, Pennant makes it clear that he had personally climbed the hill of Tomnahurich: he paced out the length of the top of the hill, which he reckoned at about three hundred yards, while the breadth was only twenty yards.

Back in the town, Pennant encountered the institution of the Dean of Guild, an early version of a planning officer:

> who, assisted by a council, superintends the markets, regulates the price of provisions; and if any house falls down, and the owner lets it lie in ruins for three years, the Dean can absolutely dispose of the ground to the best bidder.

Inverness in the 1770s, as engraved in a plate accompanying Thomas Pennant's Tour.

In another footnote, Pennant notes the prices of some basic commodities, which can be summarised as follows:

Beef	2d. to 4d. (22 ounces to the pound)
Mutton	2d. to 3d.
Veal	3d. to 5d.
Pork	2d. to 3d.
Chickens	3d. to 4d. a couple
Fowl	4d. to 6d. apiece
Goose	12d. to 14d.
Ducks	1s. a couple
Eggs	seven a penny
Salmon	1d. and 1d. halfpenny per pound

The hospital in Church Street is mentioned, noting that the interest from the capital of £3,000 is distributed 'among the indigent inhabitants of the town. Dunbar's Hospital was built in 1668, partly of stones from Cromwell's Fort, by Provost Alexander Dunbar, at his own expense, on land owned by him. It remains today as one of the oldest and most impressive buildings in the town. Its history is detailed in Captain Douglas Wimberley's book, *The hospital of Inverness and Dunbar's Hospital* (1893), summarised in Gerald Pollitt's *Historic Inverness* (1981).

Pennant found a library of 1,400 volumes in the hospital house — the Kirk Session Library now safely catalogued and housed in the Public Library in Inverness. It was, he says, founded by 'Mr. *Robert Baillie*, a minister in this town: but the principal benefactor was Doctor *James Fraser*, secretary to the *Chelsea* hospital'.

The discerning tourist would follow Pennant's instructions as he continued his journey into the wild heartland of the Highlands:

> Cross the *Ness* on a bridge of seven arches, above which the tide flows for about a mile. A small toll is collected here, which brings to the town about 60 l. [£60] a year.
>
> Proceed North; have a fine view of the Firth, which now widens again from *Kessock* into a large bay some miles in length. The hills slope down to the water-side, and are finely cultivated; but the distant prospect is of rugged mountains of a stupendous height; as if created as guards to the rest of the island from the fury of the boisterous North.

Well, he *was* writing this only 23 years after the battle of Culloden. Johnson and Boswell packed a copy of Pennant's *Tour* in their suitcases, and perhaps have more to answer for in the way of misrepresentation than Pennant, who, after all, was a Welshman, and a fellow Celt. Pennant did in fact visit Culloden Moor, which he describes as 'the place that North Britain owes its present prosperity to, by the victory of April 16, 1746'. There is, it has to be said, some truth in this assessment. That Pennant did recognise the excesses of the aftermath of Culloden, and felt more than a few qualms at what had happened there in 1746, is evident from this passage:

> On the side of the *Moor*, are the great plantations of *Culloden* House, the seat of the late *Duncan Forbes*, a warm and active friend to the house of *Hanover*, who spent great sums in its service, and by his influence, and by his persuasions, diverted numbers from joining in rebellion; at length he met with a cool return, for his attempt to sheath, after victory, the unsatiated sword. But let a veil be flung over a few excesses consequential of a day, productive of so much benefit to the united kingdoms.

Pennant notes that 'the young adventurer' stayed at Culloden House on the day before the battle, and evidently engaged in a little historical research during his short visit to Inverness, as he quotes, in a footnote, an 'account very recently communicated to me,…and that by an eye-witness':

> The *Scotch* army was drawn up in a single line; behind, at about 500 paces distance, was a *corps de reserve*, with which was the Adventurer, a place of seeming security, from whence he issued his orders. His usual dress was that of the Highlands, but this day he appeared in a

brown coat, with a loose great coat over it, and an ordinary hat, such as countrymen wear, on his head. Remote as this place was from the spot where the trifling action was, a servant of his was killed by an accidental shot. It is well known how short the conflict was: and the moment he saw his right wing give way, he fled with the utmost precipitation, and without a single attendant, till he was joined by a few other fugitives.

Pennant also notes that the battle was fought:

contrary to the advice of some of the most sensible men in the rebel army, who advised the retiring into the fastnesses beyond the *Ness*, the breaking down the bridge of *Inverness*, and defending themselves amidst the mountains.

Boswell and Johnson

The immediacy of Pennant's accounts of Inverness and its vicinity would have been greatly appreciated by his readers, who included Boswell and Dr Johnson. Indeed, during their visit to Ardersier and Fort George, Boswell writes that 'I looked into Pennant's *Tour in Scotland'*. However, despite the fact that these two famous travellers stayed in Inverness (at Mackenzie's inn) from Saturday 28th August 1773 until Monday 30th August, when they hired horses and proceeded on to Fort Augustus, there is no mention of Culloden, or the Prince, at this point in their account of their travels. Perhaps Boswell was a little touchy on the subject, as can be deduced from Boswell's entry for Sunday 29th August, describing breakfast with Mr Keith, the collector of customs at Inverness, and an old friend of Boswell's from Ayr:

Dr Johnson expatiated rather too strongly upon the benefits derived to Scotland from the Union, and the bad state of our people before it. I am entertained with his copious exaggeration upon that subject; but I am uneasy when people are by who do not know him as well as I do, and may be apt to think him narrow-minded. I therefore diverted the subject.

Dr Johnson bought himself a book in Inverness, but on the following Tuesday gave it away to the daughter of the landlord of the inn at Glenmoriston:

…a modest, civil girl, very neatly dressed…She told us, she had been a year at Inverness, and learnt reading and writing, sewing, knotting, working lace, and pastry.

The book, it transpired, featured frequently thereafter at dinner parties, as ladies expressed an interest in this book, and asked what it was. The answer always caused surprise, even laughter, for it was Cocker's *Arithmetic*. Dr Johnson was a little tetchy whenever it was mentioned, and on one occasion Boswell remonstrated with him:

> 'But, sir, is it not somewhat singular that you should happen to have Cocker's *Arithmetic* about you on your journey? What made you buy such a book at Inverness?' He gave me a very sufficient answer. 'Why, sir, if you are to have but one book with you upon a journey, let it be a book of science. When you have read through a book of entertainment, you know it, and it can do no more for you; but a book of science is inexhaustible'.

By chance, it turned out that the father of the recipient of this book, named McQueen, was a veteran of Culloden; he accompanied Boswell and Johnson for a few miles along the road, and regaled them with stories of the rebellion:

> He had, in 1745, joined the Highland army at Fort Augustus, and continued in it till after the battle of Culloden. As he narrated the particulars of that ill-advised but brave attempt, I could not refrain from tears. There is a certain association of ideas in my mind upon that subject, by which I am strongly affected. The very Highland names, or the sound of a bagpipe, will stir my blood, and fill me with a mixture of melancholy and respect for courage; with pity for an unfortunate and superstitious regard for antiquity, and thoughtless inclination for war; in short, with a crowd of sensations with which sober rationality has nothing to do.

In other words, Boswell was a true Scot, despite his years in the metropolis! At Kingsburgh, on the isle of Skye, they would later meet Flora Macdonald, and Dr Johnson would sleep in the same bed as the fugitive prince, twenty-seven years before. They heard the story of how Flora had aided her prince; Boswell took notes and published her account as an Appendix to his *Tour*.

The First *Statistical Account*

Writing in the *Statistical Account* in 1791, the Inverness ministers give a graphic account of the development of the town, and the effects of 1746 on the local economy. They describe how from mediaeval times right up until 1698,

> ...the inhabitants were an industrious, enterprising and thriving people. The principal source of their wealth was a commerce in corn and skins. The corn and malting trade was brought to a considerable height. The greater part of the town consisted of kilns and granaries...,

for the art of malt making in these days was understood in this country chiefly by the corn-merchants of Inverness.

But, says the *Statistical Account*, from the turn of the century up until 1746, the burgh suffered a gradual decline:

> So that at that time and several years after the town appeared little better than the ruins of what it formerly was. In the centre of the town were many ruinous houses, and in all the other parts of it, every second space, and that by far the larger, exhibited the ruin of a kiln, a granary or other building.

Attributing the decline of trade to the duty levied on corn for export, from 1688, and the transfer of the skin trade to the more lucrative markets of Glasgow, the *Statistical Account* is in no doubt of the cause of the revival of the town's fortunes:

> In the year 1746, the town began to revive, and from that period to the present [1791], particularly in the last thirty years, has been in a rapid progress of improvement. At this time it may be said to be wholly new built; its old limits are considerably extended, and yearly extending. The money circulated by the army after the suppression of the rebellion in the year 1746, the great influx of money from the East and West Indies, the establishment of manufactures, the consequent improvements in agriculture, the rise in the value of land, and the consumption of luxuries, are evidently the causes of the increasing prosperity of this burgh. The harbour is safe and commodious, and kept in excellent repair.

Amongst the industries mentioned in the *Statistical Account* are tanneries, a soap-boiler, a brick work, a hemp manufacture employing over one thousand men, women and children in spinning, dressing and weaving, a thread manufacturer employing, through its nineteen agents throughout the Highlands nearly 10,000 persons in 'heckling, spinning, twisting, bleaching and dyeing'; for this work 'they earn from 1s. 6d. to 2s. a-week'. The flax was imported from the Baltic, 'and when manufactured sent to London, from whence it is dispersed over the world'.

There were four whisky stills and twelve brewers of ale in the town and parish of Inverness in 1791, and about seventy 'retailers of ale and spiritous liquors':

> Of the lower class of people, there are some who love whisky rather much; but not so much, it is believed, as formerly, their inclination begins to change towards ale and beer, a good and wholesome beverage.

In 1754, the population of Inverness, according to Dr Webster's survey, was 9,730; by 1791, it had declined to only 5,107, according to an 'actual survey' conducted for the *Statistical Account*.

Amongst these were the prisoners in the Tolbooth, from 'the counties of Orkney, Caithness, Sutherland, Ross, Cromarty, Nairn, Moray and Inverness': the list of their crimes and misdemeanours is a gem of social history in itself:

Thirty for horse-stealing;
8 for petty thefts;
4 for threatening expressions;
1 for alleged wilful fire-raising, but liberated upon investigation;
1 for scandal and defamation;
3 for deserting their apprenticeships;
a boy for alleged murder, liberated on investigation;
3 for violent assaults;
3 for child murder;
1 for selling spiritous liquors without a license;
2 women of bad fame, for irregularities and misdemeanours;
5 men from Campbelltown [Ardersier] for breach of the peace;
1 for deserting his Majesty's service;
17 for civil debts.

Riots and Civil Unrest

In the last decade of the eighteenth century, and in the first decade of the nineteenth century, all over Scotland, and indeed throughout the length and breadth of the British Isles, there were periods of serious civil unrest which frightened the authorities in a totally serious way and brought down the full force of the state on the unfortunate perpetrators. It was a period of Revolution, in Europe and on the other side of the Atlantic; it was a period of total war against France and its military genius Napoleon; it was a time of economic uncertainty, caused by the political and social environment.

Especially in 1795 and 1796, meal prices soared and there were meal riots in most Scottish towns, but unrest had been building up for some years. The first serious unrest in Inverness occurred in April 1793, when there was a popular upsurge of unrest aimed at preventing the export of grain, leading to four days of disturbances. A vessel in Inverness harbour had, for some days, been loading corn destined for Grangemouth. Prices fluctuated in different parts of the country, and it is probable that the owner of the cargo knew that he would fetch a higher price if it was exported from Inverness. It was at a time when meal was in short supply locally, and when news spread of what was happening, a crowd gathered, burst open the hatches of the ship, and unloaded the cargo.

Demands were formulated and presented to the Magistrates: that the grain should be ground locally into meal and sold at 1s per peck, and that no more grain should be exported from Inverness that year. In court papers arising out of these events, and studied by Ken Logue in *Popular disturbances in Scotland, 1780–1815* (1979) it is made clear that the Magistrates considered that supposed food shortages were only a pretext for unrest. They claimed, rather dramatically, that the real reason was political, and derived from the population's awareness of the political and revolutionary theory of Thomas Paine, in his influential book, *The Rights of Man:*

> Paine's Book it is now known has been very industriously circulated among the Lower Class of our people and its damnable Doctrines eagerly embraced by them. Of Liberty and Equality they are constantly talking and of making laws and fixing prices on every necessary of Life.

Logue points out that 'it was said as early as November 1792 that the ordinary people in the Highlands were in possession of Paine's work 'translated into Erse' (Gaelic), probably in extract form.

The Magistrates in 1793 must have been close to panic. The day before the disturbances in Inverness there was unrest in Dingwall, a public meeting called by the 'Apprentices and Journeymen of the Trades Corporation', and an attempt to march to Castle Stuart, to prevent the loading of a grain ship there. Only direct action by the local militia, firing into the crowd and wounding several protesters, restored order. There were meal riots in March 1796 in Inverness, Dingwall, Nairn, Macduff, Portsoy, Peterhead, Aberdeen, Stonehaven, Montrose and Oban, as well as further afield. Small wonder that the Magistrates were in a state of extreme agitation and not in a mood to be tolerant.

One Invernessian who speaks to us across a gap of two hundred years is Grizell Chisholm, who in February 1796 had no meal to feed her family, and joined in the demonstrations at the grain ship. When she, along with many others, went along to unload grain from the ship, she found herself confronted by the Provost, Bailies and the local Volunteer Company. She joined with others in throwing stones at the authorities, and was arrested, and put in prison.

Incidentally, the 'Riot Act' which was read at such disturbances, and has passed into the English language as a pseudonym for a verbal roasting, was an Act of Parliament passed in 1714, in the reign of George I. In a tome of parliamentary acts it is three and a half pages long, so reading it in the teeth of an imminent riot does not sound very practical. However, one of the provisions of the *Act for preventing Tumults and riotous Assemblies, and for the more speedy and effectual punishing the Rioters*, to give it the full title, was that a proclamation should be made to the rioters, the form and content of which was laid down in the Act:

> Our sovereign lord the King chargeth and commandeth all persons, being assembled, immediately to disperse themselves, and peacable to depart to their habitations or to their lawful business, upon the pains contained in the Act made in the first year of King George, for preventing tumults and riotous assemblies. God save the King.

This proclamation, in the terms of the Act, had to be delivered by 'the justice of the peace or other person authorized by this Act'. This person, said the Act,

> shall, among the said rioters, or as near to them as he can safely come, with a loud voice command or cause to be commanded silence while proclamation is making.

Confrontations between mobs and officers of the law were thus a serious matter, especially because, if convicted of an offence under the Riot Act, the penalty was to 'suffer the pain of death and confiscation of moveables'. If the Riot Act was read, citizens were well advised to return to their homes.

Another glimpse of how the inhabitants of Inverness amused themselves at the end of the eighteenth century is to be found in the ministers' account of public entertainments:

> There are in the town subscription assemblies, and occasional balls and concerts of music. Companies of comedians find their way to Inverness, and it is believed they have no cause to discontinue their visits, nor is it improbable, that in a few years a theatre will be erected. In the town and country parish, we have several convivial clubs. Their meetings are frequent and stated; but they are strangers to the coarse excess of former times, and its unhappy consequences.

CHAPTER 5

INVERNESS BEFORE THE RAILWAYS

It was the Railway Age which created an Inverness which we would recognise, and which made it possible for the town to grow and flourish during the second half of the nineteenth century. The railway came to Inverness in 1855, and immediately there were local businessmen, merchants and people of importance who realised the opportunities this presented. This awareness came slowly to some; those who achieved it quickly made fortunes, but by the end of the century wealth and prosperity was within the reach of a wide range of local people.

Gunpowder Explosion

Early in the new century Inverness hit the headlines in the national press, when six barrels of gunpowder exploded in the town centre. *The Times* of London, on 20th March 1801 recorded the main facts of the disaster:

> Thursday last at 12 o'clock a dreadful fire broke out in a candlemaker's workshop in a bye lane in the town of Inverness near which six barrels of gunpowder had been lodged, and to which the fire communicated before it was discovered — the explosion was awful and its effects melancholy. Two young ladies, daughters of Captain Fraser of Finellan were passing at the time; the one was killed on the spot and the other so shockingly mangled that little hopes are entertained of her recovery.
>
> Three women and 2 children were buried in the ruins and many others lost their lives, but the numbers are not yet known. Most of the houses in the town are much damaged; few having escaped broken windows. The materials of the house having been blown to an immense height in every direction, fell with dreadful violence and wounded a great many people, but few dangerously. The roofs of houses at a considerable distance have also been greatly damaged. The Hunt House is so much shattered that it is about to be taken down. The shock was felt for many miles and afforded two persons an idea of an earthquake, with its direct effects.

So, several townspeople killed, widespread damage, and two young Fraser ladies killed — indeed a melancholy event. It took place seven years before the first local Inverness newspaper came on the scene — the *Inverness Courier* did not appear until 1808. A couple of paragraphs in the *Scots Magazine* for March 1801 add a few details: the explosion took place on Thursday 11th March, at 12 o'clock; the death toll was eight;

> and between 40 and 50 wounded or hurt by the timber, stones and slates which were thrown out in all directions. The Northern Meeting Rooms were dreadfully shattered, as were all the neighbouring houses, and scarcely a pane of glass in the town escaped.

The *Scots Magazine* went on to point out that there were municipal laws in all Scots burghs against keeping more that a couple of pounds of gunpowder in shops within the town. A similar accident had taken place not long before in the town of Haddington, when a house was blown up and several lives lost. The question had to be asked: 'Why do not magistrates make strict search and see the laws observed?'

An Ecclesiastical Tourist

A few years later, the Rev James Hall followed in the footsteps of the eighteenth-century 'excursionists' and published an account of his adventures in London in 1807. An engraving of Inverness taken just as the main road from the south (now Old Edinburgh Road) starts to descend into the town shows the remains of the castle prominently situated on a craggy mound much less land-scaped than it is today; the old stone bridge with its arches, Balnain House, the steeples of the Old High Church and the Tolbooth, and a dense concentration of two-storied houses, with chimneys and slate roofs. In the background of this interesting view of the town are the Beauly Firth and the hills of the Black Isle.

Hall's account of the town is brief, but sympathetic. Like many other visitors, he comments on the local dialect:

> At Inverness I found a strange medley of the Scotch and English language spoken in the streets...there are, as it were, two towns, and two different people, as the people that come from the country, and intend to speak Gaelic, live in one end of the town, and those that cannot, or do not intend to speak it, live in the other.
>
> It has been often and justly remarked, that the people of Inverness speak English with remarkable purity; partly because they are at great pains to learn it, not merely from vulgar conversation, but by book, as we do Greek and Latin; and partly because English garrisons from the times of Cromwell have, in a great measure, given the tone, in

respect of both diction and pronunciation, to the whole county, from Fort William to Fort George.

He comments that the salmon fishery on the River Ness is let to London fishmongers, and that Inverness is a town with thriving manufacturing industries, a busy and 'commodious' harbour capable of taking vessels of two hundred tons, and a busy 'inland trade'. He noted that ships of four or five hundred tons could anchor within a mile of the town, and commented that the town was 'admirably situated for both distant and domestic or inland commerce'. He estimated the population at about 6000. To the north, 'near the town', he saw the remains of Cromwell's fort, but 'of the castles of Macbeth, Malcolm Canmore, and the Cummins, nothing remains but rubbish'. A pity that he could not have been more specific as to the location of this 'rubbish', as later researchers and antiquarians have been unable to discover even that.

Hall's relatively enlightened and unpatronising attitude is summarised in his final remarks on Inverness, which are as relevant today as they were in 1807:

> Some of our Londoners, when they hear of Inverness, and that it is more than a hundred miles beyond Aberdeen, will perhaps think it the very skirts of the creation, and that to be condemned to live there would be worse than being sent to Botany Bay: but let me tell such cockneys, that there is scarcely an article, good, bad, or indifferent, to be found in London, but is to be found here also, excepting watchmen and patroles, of which, fortunately, there is no need.

Hall was very interested in the Caledonian Canal, which was under construction at the time of his visit to the Highlands. He quotes the official view that it would bring great benefits to the people of the Highlands, and stimulate the local economy, thus providing an alternative to emigration. However, his own natural scepticism and keen observation forced him to the conclusion that the vast expenditure on the new canal (£475,000 on construction alone) would not have 'the desired effect' of preventing emigration:

> Like a contagious fever, the spirit of emigration, when once it has become general, is not easily opposed; and the people of the Highlands, driven from their farms by the avarice of their landholders, will rather seek a scanty subsistence on a foreign shore than remain at home, to see their possessions, which they and their fathers occupied, in the hands of strangers, and turned into extensive sheep-walks. The high wages given for digging the Caledonian canal may detain some of these for a time; but, till they cease to hear of the

success of some of their acquaintance that have gone before them, or find themselves invited to improve the seats of their forefathers and the scenes of their younger years, they will never cease to wish to be gone, where hope induces them to think they will be happier.

Perceptive words indeed — and prophetic. Hall was particularly scathing — and for us informative — about the way in which 'American agents' were scouring the Highlands for prospective emigrants:

The truth is, the Americans, knowing the state of the Highlands, have agents in every part of it, who, by advertisements, hand-bills, promises, and flattering accounts, set the people agog, and render them unhappy till they are on shipboard, when their misery begins. From the promises and representations of the agents every young man thinks himself certain of a farm when he goes to America, and that whether he has money or not; and every young woman who has not found a husband in her own country hopes to find one there. If government cannot suppress the spirit of emigration, it should endeavour to give it a benignant and wise direction.

Hall seems to have visited Inverness in 1803, since he comments on the building of the canal basin at Clachnaharry. The number of workmen directly employed in construction he puts at 150 in 1803, rising to 300 in 1807. In addition there were tradesmen engaged to make and repair tools for the construction workers. At Clachnaharry he says there were workshops for blacksmiths and carpenters, storehouses for tools and utensils, and huts accommodating over one hundred men. The wages for labourers were 'on an average, about eighteen-pence a day'.

James Hall travelled the length of the Great Glen, and was particularly impressed by Urquhart Castle. He crossed Loch Ness — without referring to Nessie — and landed on the castle promontory:

The lake, with its woody borders, and the lofty mountains with which it is environed, render this a most romantic situation. Nor will it, after this, be so melancholy a place as it must have formerly been, as it will be approximated both in imagination and by the facility of communication to other places and countries, by means of the Caledonian Canal.

The Tourist Boom

Traveller's tales, such as those written up by Pennant, Burke and Hall — and numerous others of lesser quality — had a profound

The steeple of the Inverness Tolbooth, the only surviving part of the first Inverness prison; further down Bridge Street is the headquarters of the Highlands and Islands Development Board, now Highlands and Islands Enterprise.

affect on the Highlands in general and on Inverness in particular, as hundreds of tourists followed in the footsteps of these early travellers, while those who remained travellers of the armchair variety formed an impression of life in the Highlands which was sometimes true to life, but more often romanticised and misleading. While the tourist boom which followed the coming of the railway to the Highlands, with all its consequent infrastructure, from tartan shops and hotels to shooting lodges and improved roads, was to have a massive impact later in the nineteenth century, we should not ignore the effect of the first travellers who ventured into 'the very skirts of the creation'.

Caledonian Canal

The Caledonian Canal was formally opened in October 1822. On 23rd October 'the Lochness steam yacht' carrying the official party departed from the Muirtown locks at 10 am, arriving in Fort William at 5:30 pm on the following afternoon. Accompanied by two smacks, the flotilla sailed along the canal, reported the *Inverness Courier*

> ...amidst the loud and enthusiastic cheering of a great concourse of people. The morning was particularly favourable though rather calm. There was scarcely a breath of wind to disperse the smoke, which ascended unbroken after the firing of the guns. The banks of the canal were crowded with spectators, a great number of whom accompanied the party from the Muirtown Locks to the Bridge of Bught...We hear they will be met at Loch Oich by the Comet steamboat. Among the gentlemen on board we observed:- The Right Hon. Charles Grant, M.P., the Hon. Wm. Fraser, Mr Grant of Waternish, Mr Fraser of Inchcoul, Mr Mackenzie, Kilcoy; Mr Mackenzie, yr. of Gairloch; Mr Fraser of Culduthel; Mr Fraser of Lovat; Mr Inglis of Kingsmills; Mr Fraser of Torbreck; Bailies Simpson, Cumming, and Smith; Mr Edwards, solicitor; Mr Johnstone; Mr Cameron, yr. of Letterfinlay; Captain Edward Fraser; Mr Davidson and Mr Hughes, of the Canal. On the way they were joined by Redcastle, Foyers, Balnain, Glenmoriston, Glengarry, and many other proprietors.

Truly, a glittering array of the great and the good of Inverness and the surrounding country. Because accommodation was limited, only the gentlemen who lived along the route of the canal, or who were personally connected with the enterprise, were able to travel with the official party.

Public Hangings

Public executions were fortunately quite a rare occurrence in the nineteenth century, but when they did take place, they attracted massive audiences. At the beginning of the century the public hangman in Inverness was William Taylor. In 1810 there was a horrific crime committed at Speymouth, near Elgin: compared with trial reports later in the century the paragraph in the *Inverness Journal* of 4th September 1811 is indeed restrained:

Alexander Gillan, from the parish of Speymouth, in Elgin-shire, accused of murder and rape, committed on the body of Elspet Lamb, a girl under eleven years of age, was brought to the bar. The pannel pleaded *not guilty,* and after the examination of several witnesses the Jury were inclosed, and returned a verdict all in one voice, finding him *guilty.*

William Taylor was given the task of hanging Alexander Gillan, at the scene of his crime, on 14th November 1810. Gillan made the customary final address to 'an immense concourse of people, from every quarter, and of every age and sex'. However, the Inverness hangman did not perform his duties well. The victim was in a distressed state, though after prayers, Gillan:

> became more tranquil, ascended the ladder without hesitation, and awaited his fate with perfect resignation. He was detained in this state of awful suspence too long, by the unskilfulness of the executioner, whose concern seemed directed to the perquisites of the office more than the business in which he was engaged.

In other words, William Taylor had been drinking, with unfortunate consequences:

> When the drop gave way, so great was the fall, that he yielded his spirit without a struggle. Having hung an hour, he was cut down and put in irons, and he now remains suspended to his gibbet, a shocking example of the dreadful effects of vice, when permitted to usurp the empire of reason; an example which, it is hoped, will strike deep into the minds of the rising generation, and tend to prevent the recurrence of such terrifying spectacles.

The day ended badly for William Taylor too. On his way home he was set upon by some of the local youths, and badly roughed up. He died, either directly or indirectly as the result of this attack, and on February 1st 1812 the Town Council of Inverness caused the following advert to be placed in the *Inverness Journal:*

EXECUTIONER WANTED

There is an EXECUTIONER wanted for the Town of Inverness. Besides a comfortable house, and ample allowance for firing, there are many considerable perquisites annexed to the office, which would enable any sober man who holds it to live comfortably. Particulars will be learned by applying, at the Town Clerk's Office.

Inverness, 30th January, 1811.

And at the Circuit Court of Justiciary held at Inverness in April 1811, James McCurroch and John Dawson, both shoemakers' apprentices from Elgin, were found guilty 'of assaulting, stabbing, and otherwise maltreating William Taylor, late executioner at Inverness'. Their sentence was 'to be transported beyond the seas for seven years'.

The first of three public hangings in Inverness reported in the local press took place in November 1812. The *Inverness Journal* of 20th November reported that on the previous Friday, 13th November 1812, Robert Ferguson had been executed for the murder of Captain C Munro — the result of his intervention in a drunken brawl at Cromarty. The second and third public executions, in 1831 and 1835, attracted a vast amount of coverage in the newspapers, but in 1812 the *Inverness Journal* was content with a short account, despite the rarity of the event: 'So uncommon a spectacle in this part of the country attracted a great concourse of spectators'. He made a long speech, in Gaelic, to the assembled crowd, and

> mounted the drop without the least trepidation, and, after delivering a most impressive prayer, he was launched into eternity without a struggle. Throughout the whole of this awful scene the unfortunate man displayed the most heroic firmness and Christian resignation, and spoke with a clearness and consistency that astonished all who heard him. The body, having hung the usual time, was carried back to the prison, and given over for dissection, in terms of his sentence.

Vandalism

Throughout the century the columns of the local newspapers contain many instances of petty crimes and misdemeanours, but in the spring of 1827 an article in the *Inverness Courier* hints at a situation bordering on the breakdown of law and order, describing events which may seem all too familiar to residents of Inverness today:

> RIOTING AND THIEVING — these vices continue here from night to night without much abatement. Friday last a Butcher's stall at Waterloo place was broken into, and a quantity of fresh meat and hams taken away. The same night a Dyer's shop at the same place was entered, and a number of parcels stolen. The potato pits in the neighbourhood of the town have likewise come in for a part of the depredation, — and the thieves have hitherto too successfully eluded pursuit and detection. Other practices of a more wanton kind have been committed, — such as can only afford gratification to the most mischievous & malicious dispositions. Many of the young trees, both

in Abertaff's plantations, and in those of Mr Duff of Muirton, have been destroyed during the past week, — and such is the disorderly state of the town, that none but a brave man dare venture to be out after night-fall, liable as he is to be insulted, or to have his pocket picked.

This report moves from mischief to malice and ends with the town in a 'disorderly state', but an adjoining report on an apparent attempt on the life of the Postmaster, Mr Hay, tries to strike a balance between the necessity to tackle very real social problems of civic order, and not overreacting to an apparently exaggerated story. It was said that somebody had shot at the postmaster through his office window, but the Courier could not believe that such a thing was possible — 'we have reason to think that any thing done on this occasion was not done with a deadly purpose, and that the account of it has been greatly exaggerated'. However, the same story does reiterate that

> this town is at present in a state of immorality and disorder, scarcely ever remembered, and...the want of an efficient police has been the means of encouraging the riots and depredations which are so loudly complained of from day to day.

The Assynt Murder

From April to October 1831 the populace of Inverness were entertained, shocked and disgusted by the trial of Hugh Macleod for the murder of Murdoch Grant, a pedlar, in Assynt, on the 19th of March 1830. It was a brutal murder, but the ensuing circumstances of the investigation and trial only served to heighten public interest.

The case was given full coverage in the local papers. The *Inverness Journal* for the 29th of April reported Hugh Macleod's appearance at the Circuit Court in Inverness, and printed the charge in full, namely that Macleod did,

> on the south-side of a loch situated in the parish of Assynt and county of Sutherland, called Loch-na-eign, or near the road or footpath leading from Drumbaig and Lochindarroch, and at the distance of 100 yards of thereby from the said loch, violently, wickedly, and feloniously attack and assault Murdoch Grant, pedlar or travelling merchant, who travelled through the country, and whose ordinary residence was at Strathbeg, in the parish of Lochbroom, in the country of Ross; or in the county of Cromarty; and did with a hatchet, chisel, or some other sharp and lethal weapon to the prosecutor unknown,

inflict on him several severe blows on the head, face, breast, sides, and other parts of the body, by which the said Murdoch Grant was severely wounded and reduced to a state of insensibility, and died shortly thereafter in consequence of the wounds thus received, and was thereby murdered.

An additional charge was that Hugh Macleod had gone through his victim's pockets and taken £30 in bank notes, a leather purse containing £6 in silver, a red leather pocket book, several pairs of stockings, a pack or bundle of pedlar's soft goods, and more besides. Many of these items, as well as an iron hammer and a hatchet, were to be produced by the Crown in evidence, and ninety-one witnesses were cited. This was to be a major trial.

At first it looked very likely that the trial could not take place in Inverness. The fiscal, Mr Cunninghame, told the judge, Lord Medwyn, that new evidence had come to light in the last six days, with the discovery of the pedlar's pack, and he sought a post-ponement. More important, one of the most important Crown witnesses, George Mackenzie, a merchant in Lochinver, had failed to appear. The fiscal requested that he be arrested, and held in jail pending Macleod's trial. Lord Medwyn granted a warrant to arrest Mackenzie and hold him in Dornoch jail until the trial, which was likely now to take place in Edinburgh. Macleod was recommitted to jail in Inverness.

Worse was to come for the fiscal and his investigators. Mr Stewart, messenger in Dornoch, had been sent to Assynt to cite Crown witnesses, and while in that district he had heard that Kenneth Fraser, an apprentice tailor at Clachtoll, had some information about the murder, which had come to him in a 'vision' some nights previously. When tracked down and interrogated by Mr Stewart, Fraser had little to say for himself, and according to a report in the *Inverness Journal* from 'a respectable Correspondent in Sutherland', he

changed colour when pressed to speak out, but ultimately admitted that, during a dream, he had seen the murdered man's pack concealed in a certain quarter, where he could not say; but he added, that so forcible was the appearance of the place enforced on his memory that if he was brought to it he would recognise it. The officer persevered in the inquiry, and sent Fraser, with 3 other men, to search for the place where the pack was concealed, when, not a little extraordinary, Fraser in a short time pointed out the spot, and more singular still, the unfortunate pedlar's goods were found there.

It has since turned out that the prisoner (Macleod) and Fraser, were in a public house together, a few nights after the murder, when they drank nearly 20 half mutchkins of whisky. It is scarcely necessary to add, that Fraser is in custody; and it is expected, as he will have so much time to sleep and dream in jail, more important information will be obtained as to the commital of the horrible crime.

This was sensational stuff. In the middle of August it was announced that the trial would take place before the High Court of Justiciary at Edinburgh, on the 9th of September. The logistics of organising the safe transport of the prisoner, witnesses, and evidence to Edinburgh must have caused the Inverness fiscal more than a few sleepless nights.

In the end, though, the case was fitted in to the next Circuit Court of Justiciary, and took place in Inverness on 27–28th September, 1831. The Court began the hearing, under Lord Medwyn, at 9 o'clock on Tuesday morning and adjourned at 9 o'clock on Wednesday morning, sitting for twenty-four hours without rising: Lord Moncreiff and Lord Medwyn took turns in the Court. No fewer than 76 witnesses were called, of whom no more than half a dozen could speak any language other than Gaelic. Nobody had actually witnessed the crime, and Hugh Macleod denied any involvement, so the evidence against him was wholly circumstantial, and when he was found guilty, it came as a great shock. The jury took only ten minutes to reach a verdict, and were unanimous: guilty of both murder and robbery.

The death sentence was reprinted in its full horror in the *Inverness Journal* for 30th September 1831:

In respect of the foregoing verdict of assize, Lords Moncreiff and Medwyn decern and adjudge the said Hugh Macleod, pannel, to be carried from the bar back to the Tolbooth of Inverness, therein to be detained, and fed on bread and water only, until Monday, the twenty-fourth day of October next to come, and on that day, betwixt the hours of two and four o'clock in the afternoon, to be taken from the said Tolbooth to the common place of execution of said Burgh, or to such place as the Magistrates of Inverness shall appoint as a place of execution, and then and there, by the hands of the common executioner, to be hanged by the neck upon a gibbet until he be dead, and his body to be thereafter delivered over to the Professor of Anatomy in the University of Edinburgh, to be by him publicly dissected and anatomized, which is pronounced for doom; and ordain his whole moveable goods and gear to be escheat and inbrought to his Majesty's use; requiring hereby the Magistrates of Inverness, and keepers of their Tolbooth, to receive and detain the said Hugh Macleod, pannel, and to see the said sentence carried into execution, as they shall all severally be answerable at their highest peril.

After reading the sentence, his Lordship, in a most solemn and impressive manner, said, 'And may the Lord God Almighty have mercy on your poor soul'.

In the same issue as the lengthy trial report, the *Inverness Journal* reported that Macleod had confessed:

No language can convey an idea of the awful state of the unfortunate criminal on being removed to his cell. He tossed himself about in a manner which indicated the poignancy of his feelings and the secret workings of his heart. About an hour after he had been sentenced to die, the Reverend Mr Clark visited him, and the conversation which ensued effected a great change in the miserable man. He eagerly enquired whether it were yet possible to save his life, and on being answered in the negative, he made a full confession of his guilt to Mr Clark, in presence of Mr Lumsden, the Sheriff of Sutherland.

The *Inverness Journal* for 21st October 1831 announced the arrangements for the execution. Hugh Macleod was being kept in the 'condemned dungeon' in the Jail of Inverness. He was reportedly resigned to his fate, and wished

to address the multitude who will be collected around the gibbet, to witness this shocking example of the dreadful effects of vice, when permitted to usurp the empire of reason — an example which it is hoped will strike deep into the minds of the rising generation, and tend to prevent the recurrence of such terrific spectacles. The procession will leave the Jail exactly at two o'clock on Monday afternoon, the whole of the tenth Militia, now in Inverness, is to attend as an escort along with the Constables of the town, and before four o'clock the unfortunate man will be launched into eternity. It has been deemed prudent in the mean time to imprison Donald Ross, the executioner, to prevent his absconding.

We will meet Donald Ross again, when in one of its first acts under the local government reforms of 1832, the Council decided to dispense with his services.

The execution was carried out on Monday 24th October 1831. Both local papers, the *Inverness Journal* and the *Inverness Courier*, reported that day's happenings in full. For Hugh Macleod his last day on earth began shortly after seven o'clock in the morning, when the jailer, Mr Davidson, entered his cell. He was sitting up,

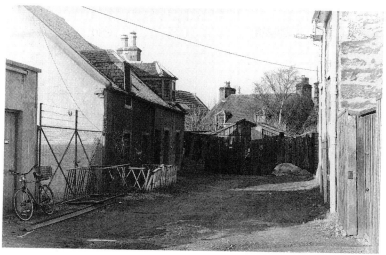

Early nineteenth-century houses in Queen Street, now demolished.

and said he had slept well. He breakfasted at nine o'clock, and an hour later the blacksmith came to strike off his leg irons. He behaved without emotion, but, reported the *Courier,* 'on the executioner pinioning his arms and taking off his handkerchief, he changed colour'. He was accompanied throughout his ordeal by two of the local clergy, Mr Clark and Mr Kennedy. One of the Magistrates arrived and asked him if he was able to walk to the place of execution — a cart was available if he needed it. He replied that he was well able to walk ten miles if necessary. The *Courier* account, printed two days later, describes his last walk, to the Longman:

> At half-past one, the party left the prison, and on gaining the street Macleod cast a wild astonished look on the assembled crowd. He then fixed his eyes on a Bible, which he carried open in his hand, and continued reading. He was habited in a long black cloak or gown, made for the occasion, and had on a white nightcap, with the halter round his neck — a part of the ceremony that might as well have been dispensed with.

The two ministers accompanied him, and also Mr E Davidson, schoolmaster, and Mr Mackenzie, shoemaker.

> The Magistrates also walked in procession, and the party, with a number of constables, and the Inverness-shire Militia, escorting the whole, then proceeded to that part of the sea-beach called the

Longman, where the gallows was erected. The day was wet and boisterous — exactly such a day the criminal said as that on which he committed the murder: but notwithstanding the unfavourableness of the weather not less than from 7000 to 8000 persons collected to witness the ceremony.

This is a truly astonishing crowd, quite possibly representing 80–90% of the population of the burgh — though presumably people came from far and wide to see Hugh Macleod's last walk. He ascended the gallows by himself, and there followed a short service, in Gaelic: a psalm, a reading from the Bible, prayers in Gaelic and English, and then it was Hugh Macleod's turn. It was customary for a condemned man to have the opportunity to address the crowd, and he took full advantage, speaking for more than fifteen minutes, in Gaelic. He was anxious to ensure that the younger generation would learn from his mistakes:

Young people, to you I address myself. — Whisky, whisky, women, Sabbath-breaking, and playing at cards brought me to this end. Though I would live 100 years, I would never put a glass of whisky again to my lips.

He admitted his crime, and insisted that he had acted alone, and especially, that Kenneth Fraser, 'the dreamer', had been completely innocent of any part in the dreadful deed. He absolved his parents from any responsibility for what he had done:

I was bred by honest and respectable parents; and if I had taken their advice, I would not be brought here. I hope none of you will come to this awful end; and I hope no person will cast up any thing to my parents and friends or to Kenneth Fraser, as they are all innocent. I beseech you take warning by my fate. My blessing and God's blessing be upon you all.

He handed his Bible and psalm book to one of the ministers, shook hands with all around him, kneeled and said a short prayer, and then mounted the 'drop'. The executioner adjusted the rope, pulled the cap over his face, and waited while Macleod sung another psalm, and then signalled by dropping his handkerchief that he was ready. He called out twice, 'the Lord receive my spirit', and was delivered into eternity:

The drop fell and he expired in a few minutes without the slightest struggle. After hanging nearly three quarters of an hour, the body was cut down, and being placed in a coffin was reconveyed to prison: it has since been transmitted, pursuant to sentence, to Edinburgh for dissection.

The *Inverness Journal* added some additional details. It describes how a company of the Inverness militia was drawn up in front of the Jail to escort the prisoner out to the Longman, where 'the rest of the regiment formed a square, with the gibbet at the centre, at the place of execution'. Still at the prison, one of the Magistrates asked if the proceedings could be conducted in English, as few of them understood Gaelic, but Macleod was having none of it: 'No, no', said the criminal, 'proceed in Gaelic, I have a greater Magistrate than these to look to to-day'.

At the gallows, the *Journal* adds the information that the psalm sung was the 51st, and the chapter read from the Bible was the 15th Chapter of Luke — about the Prodigal son. Macleod's last words are given as, in Gaelic, 'Lord Jesus receive my spirit', and one further detail about his coffin is given, which the *Courier* readers were spared:

> After hanging about three quarters of an hour, the body was cut down, placed in a plain black coffin, and conveyed to the Jail, where the corpse was put in a square box with a considerable quantity of salt.

The *Journal* concludes its report of the execution of Hugh Macleod by paying tribute to the militia:

> It is only justice to Colonel Gordon, the officers, and men, of the Inverness Militia, to say, that notwithstanding the immense crowd, supposed above 7000, and the very great pressure, they did not break their line; indeed, they could not have conducted themselves better had they been as many months as they have been days training and exercising.

That evening, three thousand people crammed into Rev Clark's church to hear a two-hour sermon, and it was reckoned that another three thousand turned out to hear him but had to go home disappointed. It was known that Macleod had made a full confession to Mr Clark, and in due course both it, and the two-hour sermon, were published. There is perhaps something slightly distasteful about the advert that appeared in the *Inverness Journal* alongside the account of the execution:

MACLEOD THE MURDERER.

> In the Press, and will be published on Wednesday first, a SERMON preached by the Rev. Mr. Clark of Inverness, on the evening of the day on which Macleod was executed, including a Sketch of his Life — Trial — Conviction — Conversion — and Execution.

PERTH AND INVERNESS ROYAL MAIL.

THE Earl of Lichfield, his Majesty's Postmaster-General, whose attention to the public accommodation is unwearied, having ordered the establishment of the above Mail Coach, through Dunkeld, Blair Athole, &c. &c., the public is respectfully informed that, on and after the 5th July next, it will leave the George and Star Hotels, Perth, every evening at nine o'clock, and reach Inverness at half-past ten o'clock A.M.; will also leave the Caledonian and Royal Hotels, Inverness, every morning at nine o'clock, and arrive at Perth at half-past ten o'clock P M., thus performing the journey in 13½ hours. The advantages, which a *daily* conveyance on this line of road hold out to the public, must be so apparent, that the contractors confidently expect that co-operation and support from them which can alone ensure its permanence.

☞ *Driven through by Two Coachmen.*

ROBERT WILSON,
ARCH. MACDONALD & Co., } Contractors

Royal Mail Coach Office,
   Caledonian Hotel,
Inverness, 1st July, 1836. }

The beginnings of public transport in the Highlands.

Both local newspapers had researched Hugh Macleod's life, and gave a full account of it. As he himself had said in his last speech, his downfall was drink.

Hugh Macleod was the youngest son of Roderick Macleod of Lynemeanach, (Gaelic: *Loinn Mheadhonach,* 'the middle field') in the parish of Assynt, where he was born in 1809, making him only twenty-two years of age at his execution. The family home was two miles from the coast, south of Loch Drumbeg, and only a few hundred yards from Loch Torr na h-Eigin, where the murder took place. His father was a crofter, or cottar, and known in the community as honest, hard-working and pious; he made many sacrifices to ensure an education for his children. Hugh was sent into service at the age of ten, and started to pick up some bad habits. When he was sixteen he heard that there was a vacancy for a schoolmaster at Coigash in Lochbroom; he applied successfully for the post, but left after only a year, already with a reputation for 'ardent spirits' — the dreaded whisky of which he spoke on the gallows. Soon he was in debt to every inn in the district, and having developed a taste for fine clothes, and young ladies, took to petty theft to defray his expenses. When he encountered the unfortunate pedlar, Murdoch Grant, in March 1830, he saw a chance to clear his debts, and succumbed to the temptation.

The case was incredibly well publicised, and as seen by the turnout for the hanging, it had captured the public's imagination, or perhaps more accurately, satiated their appetite for gruesome retribution for the crimes he had committed, which at that time were genuinely shocking to the public — it had, after all, been nineteen years since the last public execution in Inverness. This event, and the hanging of another murderer, John Adam, just two years later, were defining moments in the lifetime of anybody living in Inverness at the time.

Perhaps the experience at the Longman was all too much for one observer:

DEATH BY DROWNING.— AWFUL EFFECTS OF INTEMPERANCE.

On Wednesday evening a person enveloped in a camlet cloak was observed running down Fraser Street towards the Ness. A private of the Inverness Militia, who happened to be at the time on the banks of the river, states that on coming to the foot of Fraser Street the individual alluded to rushed into the river and instantly disappeared.

The alarm was promptly given, and the river dragged, but being much swollen, it is probable that the body was carried by the stream to near the mouth of the Ness ere a boat could be procured — the search for the body has consequently hitherto proved ineffectual.

The unfortunate victim turned out to be a tragic case: a Writer, that is, a lawyer, who had once been Town Clerk of the burgh of Nairn, and had held other public positions in that county, before his life was ruined by drink:

For several years past, however, the unfortunate man had acquired irregular and dissipated habits, which, in the debilitated state of his constitution, produced temporary fits of insanity. In this state he was observed strolling about the streets of Inverness on Wednesday afternoon, and it is most probable that he plunged into the river as described by the soldier, without being at all aware that he was rushing into eternity.

Cholera

Public health issues in nineteenth-century Inverness were never far removed from public concern: overcrowded housing conditions, inadequate sewerage facilities, poor drainage, worries about the public drinking supply, and the fear of disease and epidemic were continual topics of interest to the local press.

One of the worst epidemics was the cholera outbreak of 1832, which swept through the towns and villages of Caithness, Sutherland, Easter Ross, the Black Isle, Nairn and Inverness. It started early in September, and by the middle of the month it had taken hold in Inverness, and was causing fatalities — 117 deaths were reported by the 19th of September, out of a total of 363 cases. Extensive coverage in the local papers traced the course of the outbreak, and the *Inverness Courier* highlighted the fact that it was the most vulnerable people in the community who were most at risk, and noted with regret one particular death:

When medical aid is procured in time, there is little danger, but unfortunately a considerable number of those afflicted, from ignorance or prejudice, neglect this indispensable precaution...The deaths have been confined almost wholly to poor persons labouring under debility and ill health, and to the aged and indigent. The number of females attacked and who have fallen victims to the disease, are in the proportion of three to one male. Among the deaths reported this day is that of William Shaw, orderly or attendant at the Cholera Hospital, who died at 11 o'clock last night, after about eighteen hours' illness. Poor Shaw was a most valuable and indefatigable servant, and has literally died at his post. His interment this afternoon was attended by the medical gentlemen, as mourners. We understand that a subscription for his family is in contemplation.

Public subscriptions — fund-raising in the days before government compensation schemes, state pensions, life insurance and social security benefits — was a common feature of nineteenth-century life in Inverness, especially in response to disasters involving loss of life. The rigid class structure of Victorian society was jealously guarded by the middle classes, but in times of need they could react generously to the needs of the poor.

The cholera epidemic produced many cases of need:

Among the distressing incidents to which the progress of the disease has led, we learn that a labouring man and his wife were brought to the hospital yesterday from Merkinch, leaving three young children and a blind sister totally destitute and helpless at home; the latter has since been attacked by the malady, and is also now in the hospital. The medical gentlemen are unremitting in their exertions.

A week later, on 26th September, it was reported that William Shaw's replacement as attendant in the Cholera Hospital, Roderick Matheson, had also succumbed to the disease; so also did Dr George Forbes, one of the medical gentleman, the oldest medical practitioner in Inverness. Dr Forbes was aged sixty-six, and had come to Inverness to work at the new Inverness Royal Infirmary. By the end of October the epidemic had run its course: there had been 553 cases of cholera and 175 deaths as a result, which although tragic for the local community was not as bad as many similar communities in other parts of the country.

One of the unexpected results of the cholera outbreak was that it helped to launch the literary career of Hugh Miller of Cromarty, the stone mason who went on to write books on geology and fossils, and to become one of the best known literary figures of nineteenth-century Scotland. He had been contributing items of local news, and especially commentaries on the local fishing industry to the *Inverness Courier* for about five years, but his cholera story was something special. His report, published in the *Courier* of 10th October 1832, is too long to quote in full here, but a couple of extracts will suffice to illustrate the nature of his writing, which had a tremendous impact on Inverness readers and gave notice of the arrival of a new talent on the Scottish literary scene. This report was picked up by the Glasgow and Edinburgh papers, and Hugh Miller's success as a writer followed:

> The infection spread with frightful rapidity. At Inver, though the population did not much exceed a hundred persons, eleven bodies were committed to the earth, without shroud or coffin, in one day; in two days after, they had buried nineteen more. Many of the survivors fled from the village, leaving behind them the dead and dying, and took shelter, some in the woods, and some among the hollows of an extensive track of sand hills. But the pest followed them to their hiding places, and they expired in the open air. Whole families were found lying dead on their cottage floors. In one instance, an infant, the only survivor, lay grovelling on the body of its mother, wailing feebly among the dead, the sole mourner in the charnel house of the pestilence.

This represents the dark side of Hugh Miller, but he had a lyrical side as well, as can be seen in this passage describing how the news of the arrival of the cholera at Nigg was brought across the narrow strait to the town of Cromarty:

> It was one of those lively evenings which we so naturally associate with ideas of human enjoyment;- when from some sloping eminence we look over the sunlit woods, and fields, and cottages of a wide extent of country, and dream that the inhabitants are as happy as the scene is beautiful. The sky was without a cloud, and the sea without a wrinkle. The rocks and sandhills on the opposite shore lay glistening in the sun, each with its deep patch of shadow resting by its side; and the effect of the whole, compared with the aspect it had presented a few hours before, was as if it had been raised on its ground work of sea and sky, from the low to the high relief of the sculptor.
>
> There were boats drawn up on the beach, and a line of houses behind;- but where were the inhabitants? No smoke rose from the chimneys; the doors and windows were fast closed; not one solitary lounger sauntered about the harbour or the shore; the fearful inanity of death and desertion pervaded the whole scene. Suddenly, however, the eye caught a little dark speck moving hurriedly along the road which leads to the ferry. It was a man on horseback. He reached the cottages of the boatmen, and flung himself from his horse; but no one came at his call to row him across. He unloosed a skiff from her moorings, and set himself to tug at the oar. The skiff flew athwart the bay. The watchmen stationed on the shore of Cromarty moved down to prevent her landing. There was a loud cry passed from man to man; a medical gentleman came running to the beach; he leaped into the skiff, and laying hold of an oar, as if he were a common boatman, she again shot across the bay. A case of cholera had just occurred in

the parish of Nigg. I never before felt so strongly the force of contrast…

Since witnessing, however, the scene I have so feebly attempted to describe, I am led to think that the earth, if wholly divested of its inhabitants, would present a more melancholy aspect, should it still retain its fertility and beauty, than if wrapped up in a pall of darkness, surrounded by dead planets and extinguished suns.

Hearing of the problems in Cromarty, some of the local worthies of Inverness decided to pay a 'site visit' in order to see for themselves how the outbreak there was being dealt with. The *Inverness Courier* of 26th September 1832 reported, with some relish, on their experiences at the hands of the authorities in Cromarty:

SMOKING OUT THE CHOLERA! — Some professional gentlemen from this place having occasion to visit Cromarty last week, were seized at the entrance of the town, and told they must go to be smoked for the cholera, as they came from Inverness. They were accordingly conveyed to the sea-side, till they arrived at a wooden shed, where they were obliged to take off part of their clothes, wash themselves with a preparation of chloride of lime, and then enter a place strongly impregnated with sulphur and other ingredients, where they were locked up, until half suffocated. Having undergone this salutary and rational process, the Invernessians were allowed to dress and depart. This is really making the most of a misfortune.

The Hanging of John Adam

The last public execution in Inverness took place on Friday 16th October, 1835, at the Longman, before a crowd of over eight thousand persons. Along with religious gatherings, and electoral meetings, executions were amongst the most avidly supported public entertainments available to the general population. On this occasion, the victim was John Adam, aged 31, who had murdered his wife, in the words of the *Inverness Courier*, 'for the purpose of possessing himself of her little fortune'.

The *Courier* had reported his trial in great detail, and now, on the Wednesday following the execution, regaled its readers with a full account of the proceedings:

This ill-fated individual underwent the capital punishment of the law on Friday last, for the murder of his wife, pursuant to the sentence pronounced at the last Circuit Court of Justiciary, after trial and conviction, by Lord Moncrieff. The firmness and resolution which had all along characterised the criminal did not forsake him at the last. He slept soundly the night previous to his death, and in his waking moments conversed with the men appointed to look over him, on his adventures in the army, and other indifferent topics. He freely condemned his past life in relation to the two women whom he betrayed, as well as other cases of seduction he had committed, but he strenuously denied all knowledge of the murder.

There were few signs in Adam's early life of the troubles to come. Born in the county of Forfar on New Year's Day 1804, he came from a hard-working and respectable home. His father rented a small farm, Craigieloch, which John and his mother managed together after his father's death in 1821. He was educated locally, and attended church regularly. In his mid-twenties, the dark side of his character emerged. He seduced a deaf and dumb cousin, got her pregnant, and disowned the child. According to the *Courier*, 'the heartlessness and cruelty of his conduct roused the indignation of the people, and Adam was forced to fly from Forfarshire'. He worked for a time in Aberdeenshire as a farm servant, but committed a similar atrocity and was again forced to move on. After yet a third occurrence of this nature, he enlisted in the army at Glasgow, in 1831; his regiment was the Second Dragoon Guards. But his outrageous conduct towards women continued: as the *Courier* said, 'his engaging appearance and manners gave him easy access to unthinking females in the lower walks of life; and up to the day preceding his death, he used to recount with evident satisfaction the triumphs he had at tea parties, dances and promenades over his brother soldiers'.

He deserted from his regiment in Derbyshire, in March 1834, stealing some stores and money, and moved north to Dingwall, where he and 'a poor English girl', Dorothy Elliot, lived for nearly a year. As the *Courier* delicately put it, 'he promised marriage but never performed his engagement'. Later in 1834 he spent some weeks in Montrose, and in March 1835 returned there, married Jean Brechin, brought her to Inverness, and murdered her three weeks later on the road to Dingwall. He wrote a letter from prison to Dorothy Elliot two days before his execution, partly in his own blood, and on the night before she visited him, imploring him, without success, to admit his guilt.

The *Courier* gave what was clearly an eye-witness account of John Adam's final hours, on the day of his execution:

His fetters being struck off, the culprit washed and dressed himself in a long camlet black coat provided for the occasion. He partook of a hearty breakfast. About one o'clock he was brought into the Court House (which communicates with the jail), his arms and wrists being pinioned. The Rev. Messieurs Clark, Scott, and Kennedy, the Provost and Magistrates, and a few other persons were present. Adam seemed pale from his long confinement, but in good health. Mr Scott then delivered an appropriate and affecting prayer, after which Mr Clark gave out the two first verses of the 32d psalm, which were sung with much solemnity. Mr Kennedy delivered a prayer, and the party quitted the Court House for the place of execution.

To begin with Adam expressed a wish to walk to the gallows: 'he said he did not want to be driven to the gallows and hung up like a dog'. However, the authorities were worried that they would not be able to force their way through the dense crowds which thronged the streets, and when this was explained to him Adam readily agreed to ride in one of three carriages provided for the official party, sharing with Mr Clark, Mr Kennedy, and Mr Davidson, the schoolmaster. In the other two carriages were the Provost, Magistrates, Town Clerk and other officials. Adam thanked William Fraser, the jailer, and the turnkey, James Macdonald, who had been 'unceasing in their humane endeavours to soften the horrors of the prisoner's situation, which seemed to be felt by all but himself'. The procession set off; order was maintained by Special Constables who were sworn in for the occasion — 'their exertions preserved the utmost order throughout the day'. The *Courier* reporter followed the crowds — perhaps even rode in one of the carriages, and picked up the story at the site of the town gallows:

> The place of execution at the Longman, on the eastern shore of the Moray Frith, is fully a mile from the town, and the whole of the road and fields adjacent were filled with individuals hurrying to the spot where the gallows were erected. At the last execution here in 1831, it was calculated that about eight thousand persons were present. The number on this occasion was even greater, and the effect of the whole scene was indescribably striking and impressive. On alighting from the carriage Adam walked with a firm step up to the scaffold. He stole a glance at the vast crowd before him, but was calm and unmoved. His tall and handsome person, and respectable appearance, were the subject of universal remark.

After readings from the Bible and prayers from the clergy present, John Adam reaffirmed his innocence, saying that he was not afraid to meet his Maker; he also asked to be remembered to his mother and his friends. The executioner made his preparations, John Adam dropped a white handkerchief from his hand as a signal that he was ready, and 'the drop fell'. The *Courier* described the scene, for the benefit of the few townspeople unable to witness the event for themselves:

> He struggled for some minutes, but not violently. The crowd beheld this awful scene without any expression of sympathy or regret, as was manifested at the execution of Macleod. A feeling of astonishment at the firmness of the criminal, and at the hardihood of assertions of his innocence, seemed to be the prevailing sentiment among all present. It has since been interred, as enjoined by the statute, 'within the precincts of the prison', a part of the pavement being taken up and a grave dug in the passage leading from the private door of the Court house to the Jury-room and bench. It is perhaps to be wished that this part of the Act of Parliament were omitted, as in many of the jails, particularly in Scotland, there are no airing-grounds which can be used for the purpose, and there is something offensive as well as unwholesome in converting the interior of a prison or Court room into a charnel-house for dead malefactors.

Indeed! And when the Police office moved to Castle Wynd, John Adam's body was moved there too, to lie under the steps at the entrance. And again, in 1962, when the police moved to Farraline Park and the buildings at Castle Wynd were demolished to make way for the 'improvements' in Bridge Street, John Adam's bones were collected and eventually reinterred under the entrance of the new police headquarters at Culcabock, opened in 1975.

There is no doubt that Adam was guilty, even though the evidence against him was largely circumstantial. It seems he genuinely believed in his own innocence. The trial judge, and the gentlemen who visited him in prison, were astonished at his capacity for deception. In his defence, Adam had questioned medical evidence as to the time his victim's body had lain on the ground before it was discovered — the *Courier* noted that this was:

> ...a circumstance which none but the murderer could have known. No rational doubt could be entertained of his guilt, and when we consider that he travelled twice to Montrose, married the deceased, and brought her to Inverness for the purpose of possessing himself of her little fortune, and murdering her, it is probably as deliberate, cold-blooded, and atrocious a crime as ever was perpetrated in the kingdom.

Houses in Bisset's Close and Duff Street, all now gone.

To further the researches at the university in Edinburgh into the science of phrenology — the study of the bumps and confirmation of the head — a cast of John Adam's head was made, after his death, by Sir George Mackenzie, Dr Nicol, and Provost Cameron of Dingwall. The *Courier* reported that 'one or two gentlemen who were opposed to phrenology, have acknowledged that the case of Adam almost made them converts to the truth of this science'.

And who was the hangman? Two years before, Donald Ross, 'the common executioner of the town', lost his job in circumstances detailed in the columns of the *Inverness Courier* on Christmas Day, 1833. In these days of cut-backs in local government spending, it is interesting to note that attitudes towards the economics of local government, and towards the legal profession, remain unchanged, at least in some quarters:

> Retrenchment being the order of the day, the Council conceived they could dispense with the services of the executioner, which are seldom required here, and have hitherto been paid for, like the services of other high legal functionaries, at rather an extravagant rate.

Donald Ross had been appointed executioner in 1812, with a salary of £16 per annum. In twenty-one years he had performed just three executions, which the Council worked out must have cost the town nearly £400 for each execution! This figure was arrived at by combining his annual salary for twenty-one years (£336) with his £5 fee for each execution (£15) and an estimated annual income of an additional £50–£60 a year from various other sources. It was these additional amounts which irritated and concerned the Council most:

> It is very true, that many public servants are paid more for doing less; but we think the Council will effect a considerable saving, to say nothing of the cessation of a constant nuisance amoung our fish and meal, by dispensing with a regular executioner, and trusting to the services of a deputy from Edinburgh or Glasgow.

The 'constant nuisance amoung our fish and meal' refers to some of Donald Ross's financial activities, which the *Courier* listed as follows:

> As most public appointments of a rare and difficult nature are accompanied with fees and perquisites, independent of salary, Donald had various bites and nibbles at the public purse.
>
> *First,* he was provided with a house, bed, and bedding.
>
> *Second,* he was allowed thirty-six peats weekly from the tacksman of the petty customs.
>
> *Third,* he had a bushel of coals out of every cargo of English coals imported into the town.
>
> *Fourth,* he was allowed a piece of coal, as large as he could carry, out of every cargo of Scotch coals.
>
> *Fifth,* he had a peck of oatmeal out of every hundred bolls landed at the shore.
>
> *Sixth,* he had a fish from every creel or basket of fish brought to the market.
>
> *Seventh,* he had a penny for every sack of oatmeal sold at the market.
>
> *Eighth,* he had a pick of salt out of every cargo.
>
> *Ninth,* he was allowed every year a suit of clothes, two shirts, two pairs of stockings, a hat, and two pairs of shoes.
>
> Added to these fixed and regular sources of income, Donald levied *black mail* on the lieges in the shape of Christmas boxes, and had besides a sum of five pounds at every execution at which he presided.

These 'bites and nibbles' at the public purse gave Donald Ross a good living at the town's expense, so it must have been very disappointing for him to be dispossessed. The account in the *Courier* of the meeting of the Town Council at which his fate was sealed tells us that they decided to dispense with his services forthwith, but allowed him 'to remain in the possession of the house presently occupied by him until Whitsunday'. They went on to fill the vacant position of Jailor, for which there were thirteen applications; Mr William Fraser, messenger, was appointed at a salary of £40 a year, 'as formerly, exclusive of fees'. James Macdonald, lamplighter, was appointed turnkey, with a salary of

£20 a year. And just to show that the variety of business at Council meetings today is not a recent development in local government, we note in passing that at the same meeting it was decided to sell thirty old street lamps to the burgh of Nairn at four shillings each!

We presume that a hangman was imported to dispose of John Adam in 1835 — the records do not tell us if Donald Ross was recalled to perform his fourth execution. There is a brief reference to Donald Ross in Joseph Mitchell's *Reminiscences,* published in 1883–4. He remembered seeing an execution procession, and describes the site at the Longman where the gallows was erected:

> The penal laws were then very severe. Theft and sheep-stealing as well as murder were capital offences. To add to the misery of the unhappy criminals, the penalty was delayed for six weeks after sentence. The execution was conducted with great solemnity. The gallows was erected at the Longman, a green on the sea-shore about two miles from the town. Round the gallows, twelve feet from the ground, was a raised platform on which the clergy and magistrates stood, the culprit on the drop.

Joseph Mitchell also says that the hangman, Donald Ross, was 'a distinguished and awful functionary', and was himself condemned for sheep-stealing, and pardoned on condition that he agreed to act as hangman, 'an office very unpopular'.

We have already seen that William Taylor the previous town executioner, also came to a sticky end, in 1812. He had gone to Elgin on 'professional business', says the *Courier,*

> and was attacked on his return, about Forres, by a mob of mischievous boys and lads who maltreated him in so shameful a manner that he died on the spot. The most active of the mob were, however, very properly tried and transported.

Hogmanay Excesses

The issue of the *Inverness Courier* in which Donald Ross's dismissal was reported was published on 25th December, 1833, reminding us that the observance of Christmas Day as a public holiday is a comparatively recent development in the Highlands. Indeed, in the 1960s, it was still considered normal for offices to work normally on Christmas Day. New Year was always, until very recently, seen as the major mid-winter festival, though a Public Notice published in the same issue of the *Courier,* on 25th December, makes it clear that celebrations and jollifications among the population at large at both Christmas and New Year had been getting out of hand, and the town authorities took steps to reimpose control and good order:

PROCLAMATION
BY THE
PROVOST AND MAGISTRATES
OF
INVERNESS

WHEREAS it has been the unlawful practice of Boys and others, about the time of CHRISTMAS and NEW YEAR, to throw Squibs, Fireballs, Serpents, Garbage, &c., and to fire Guns, Pistols, or other Fire Arms, upon the Streets of this Town and Neighbourhood thereof, which has been often attended with very dangerous consequences to individuals as well as property, and much complained of by the inhabitants.

The Provost and Magistrates, being resolved to prevent a repetition of the same, do hereby strictly prohibit and discharge all persons whatever from throwing Squibs, Serpents, Fireballs, or any Garbage whatever, and from firing Guns, Pistols, or other Fire Arms, upon the Streets of this Burgh, or Neighbourhood, under the pain of being punished with the utmost rigour of Law. And they do most earnestly recommend to Parents, Schoolmasters, and Masters to take every proper measure to prevent those under their charge from transgressing these orders; and also recommend to all Shopkeepers and others to avoid selling Squibs, Fireworks, or Gun Powder, in any shape to children, or such as may be presumed to have it in view to use them in the manner above prohibited. Certifying to such Shopkeepers and others that they will be held responsible for any mischief which may follow in consequence of their disregarding this admonition; and to this Caution the Provost and Magistrates earnestly call their attention.

The Constables and Police Officers, are strictly enjoined to attend to the terms of this Proclamation.

Town Hall, Inverness   19th Dec. 1833.

Charles Grant, MP

One of the young men who left Inverness to make their fortune, and returned, was Charles Grant (1746–1823). Born the month before the battle of Culloden, in which his father fought on the Jacobite side, was wounded, and remained in hiding until the search for prisoners came to an end, he was a native of Cromarty. He left for India in 1767, returned to this country in 1771, married

Duff Street before redevelopment, 1960s.

Jane Fraser of Balnain in 1773, when he was twenty-seven and she was seventeen, and returned again in 1790, having made his fortune. He was a Director and Chairman of the East India Company, and MP for Inverness-shire from 1802 to 1818. The advances in parliamentary democracy since his day can be illustrated by the fact that he was elected in a three-cornered contest with Fraser of Lovat and Forbes of Culloden. The result of the election was as follows: Grant, 15; Lovat, 11; Culloden, 6. His election 'expenses' came to £600.

Joseph Mitchell says that the election of Charles Grant was fortunate for Inverness-shire,

> for through his influence civil or military appointments were obtained in India for almost every proprietor's son and suitable young man in town and county. A better class of men for India could not have been selected. They were of good family, well educated, brave, and hardy, accustomed to a rough climate and simple fare; and their Highland family pride qualified them to assume quite naturally the position of authority and command which necessarily devolves on our Indian officers.

When Charles Grant retired from parliament he was succeeded by his son, the Right Honourable Charles Grant, afterwards Lord Glenelg. A portrait of Charles Grant senior by Sir Henry Raeburn now hangs in Inverness Library.

Early Reminiscences

The title of this Chapter, 'Inverness before the railways', pays homage to the little book published in 1885, by Isabel Harriet Anderson. It seems to be a feature of many Inverness writers that they belong to a dynasty, and she was no exception. George and Peter Anderson published, from 1832, *Guides to the Highlands and Islands of Scotland*, printed in Edinburgh. In 1868, Peter Anderson produced the still excellent *Guide to Inverness:* he was Harriet's father. Her book, *Inverness before railways,* was the first of several informative and entertaining reminiscence works to reach a wider audience, of which the two most read today are *Reminiscences of Inverness: its people and places,* by John Fraser, published by the author in Inverness in 1905 (and reprinted in 1983); and Charles Bond's *Reminiscences of a Clachnacuddin Nonagenarian,* first published in 1842 but reprinted in Inverness in 1886. Every Invernessian should read these books. The 'Nonagenarian', John Maclean, was born three months before the battle of Culloden and lived, just, to become a Centenarian. His reminiscences, skilfully edited and presented by Charles Bond, editor of the *Inverness Herald* (1836–46), are compelling and fascinating, and an interesting early example of the technique of oral history recording.

John Fraser's *Reminiscences of Inverness,* described by its author as 'a walk through Inverness sixty years ago', that is, in 1845, is excellent for its descriptions of buildings, streets, factories, bridges, all now no longer to be seen, and also for early descriptions of many features of the town thankfully still with us. During his 'walk' around the town, John Fraser meets many old characters and local worthies, among whom the most interesting is perhaps the Nonagenarian himself, John Maclean, who is interviewed in the street while out for his evening stroll and tells his life story. The style is riveting, though just occasionally a little forced and artificial:

> 'Well, we'll be bidding you good evening, Mr. Maclean. You have seen many changes in your day?' 'Ay, many changes'. What do you think of that interesting old gentleman, now? Isn't he brimful of reminiscences, and altogether a source of great interest. We have lingered so long talking to him that we must now get away home, as it is getting on to tea time. Hark! there is Wells' Foundry bell just announcing the hour of six.

CHAPTER 6

LATE VICTORIAN GROWTH AND DEVELOPMENT

Harriet Anderson named her little book of 1885, *Inverness Before Railways,* and wrote about life in the town thirty-five years before. Inverness after railways was a different place altogether. If we think that Inverness has changed a lot in the last thirty-five years of the twentieth century, it is as nothing compared to the changes which took place a hundred years ago. Without the railway, Inverness would have withered and died; with it, it became a boom town, truly, in the phrase chosen by the Inverness Field Club for its centenary volume in 1975, *The Hub of the Highlands.*

The Highland Railway

The Inverness and Nairn Railway was authorised in 1854, and completed, and made operational, in 1855, bringing the Railway Age to the Highland capital. Once under way, the pace of change was rapid, and the railway network developed rapidly. In August 1858 the line from Nairn to Keith was opened, linking up with the Great North of Scotland Railway, and joining Inverness to the growing national rail network. To the north, the railway reached Dingwall in June 1862, and Invergordon in May 1863. Steps were taken to link Inverness more directly to Perth and the south, with the formation of various small companies, all of whom in June 1865 were amalgamated under the name of the Highland Railway. In July 1865 the Dingwall and Skye Railway was formed, itself amalgamated with the Highland Railway in 1880. In July 1871 the Sutherland and Caithness Railway was authorised, and opened in July 1874, with branches to Wick and Thurso; it amalgamated with the Highland Railway on 31 August 1884.

Once construction was authorised it proceeded rapidly: for example, when the link to Perth was authorised, to the line which had reached Dunkeld in 1856, the line from Dunkeld to Pitlochry was opened in June 1863, Forres was linked to Aviemore in August 1863, and the complete link was opened in September. The construction of the line linking Aviemore and Carrbridge to Inverness shortened the distance to Perth by twenty-six miles; it was completed in 1898. So, from the first Inverness and Nairn Railway in 1855 to the Highland Railway in 1863, with through trains from Inverness to London, took only eight years. It happened so quickly that it took a little longer for Invernessians to realise the full implications. Inverness was now a Railway Town, but without much of the infrastructure. Tourist hotels, guidebooks, tour operators, specialised shops and services, all had to be developed. Inverness had accommodated tourists since the eighteenth century, but never in the numbers now about to descend on the town. Apart from the spin-off of tourism, the Highland Railway in itself became one of the major industries in the town. Hundreds of men — and women — worked for the railway, and dozens of local families involved as Directors or shareholders followed its fortunes closely. They were not disappointed, and for some, it made their fortunes.

Joseph Mitchell

One name above all is associated with the Highland Railway, that of Joseph Mitchell (1803–1883), an extraordinary civil engineer who also chronicled the changes for which he was largely responsible in his two volumes of memoirs, *Reminiscences of my life in the Highlands* (1883–4). He was a little indiscreet about some leading figures in the Highlands, especially in the second volume, published 'privately' after his death. Both were fortunately reprinted in 1971, with the welcome addition of an index. What a pity that Mitchell did not live a little longer, but his *Reminiscences* are an excellent source for information about the people who brought the Railway Age to the Highlands.

Joseph Mitchell spent his boyhood in Inverness. His father was a superintendent of public works, in charge of overseeing the many improvements in roads, bridges and harbours throughout the Highlands (except for the Caledonian Canal). He was stationed at Fort Augustus, but then after another two or three years moved up to Inverness, to assume the office of General Inspector of Roads. The Mitchell family lived on the west side of the river, in a Canal house. Joseph Mitchell's description of Inverness, around the year 1810, is worthy of inclusion here:

The town on the west side of the river consisted then mainly of wretched little cottages or huts, occupied by peasantry and working people, many of them employed at the works of the Caledonian Canal. War was then raging in the Peninsula. A party of recruiting soldiers used to parade the street twice a week, with band and pipers, preceded by a dozen or twenty sergeants, gaily decorated with ribbons, and walking with drawn swords. There was therefore a great military taste throughout the population. The men who had returned from the wars, and who were engaged in recruiting, resided with their parents or friends in the cottages at Muirtown, and I used to make friends with them. I admired their beautiful dress, and had the privilege of putting on their belts and bonnets, and listened to their foreign adventures with great interest and delight.

Joseph Mitchell attended the Royal Academy, established in 1791, and obviously enjoyed his time there, in the company of the young sons of all the landed proprietors of the county. There was no trouble then with 'White Settlers':

At that time, besides the territorial chiefs, there were numerous small proprietors throughout the North, many of them related to the great houses. Selling a property except to a native was unknown; indeed, nobody would buy, for the North was separated by distance and difficulty of communication from the outer world. The small proprietors brought up their families with the feelings, tastes, and habits of gentle-folks, and when educated, the young men went forth into the world, and many became distinguished men.

The Inverness Academy was a training-school for many years for these young men. Still though much had been done for the town it was nevertheless a poor place. In 1810, it consisted of Bridge Street, High Street, and Church Street, with a beautiful and venerable old bridge, built in 1685 by subscription, and afterwards swept away by the great flood of 1849. The houses were almost all old, apparently built before 1745. Some of them were of considerable size, with turnpikes and pepper boxes outside, and narrow closes branching off. They were adorned with coats of arms and mottoes.

All beyond were rows of wretched huts. Petty Street, Maggot, and the west side of the river, consisted of a congregation of huts of the worst class, inhabited by the common people. Among them were a few good houses, but the outskirts of the town consisted chiefly of such wretched thatched hovels as I have described.

Joseph Mitchell went on to enjoy a distinguished career as the principal engineer with the Highland Railway Company. He served on the Town Council and was a Director of the Caledonian Bank.

He died in London in November 1883, but his body was brought back to Inverness, to his villa at Viewhill, and buried in Tomnahurich cemetery. He left £130,000 in his will; he gave generous donations to the Inverness Soup Kitchen and the Inverness Coal Fund, and in 1873 had given £500 towards the foundation of a Free Library in Inverness — it was opened on 16th June 1883. The first printed catalogue of Inverness Public Library, compiled by the Librarian, John Whyte, in 1883, is dedicated 'to Joseph Mitchell, Esq., C. E., of Viewhill, Inverness, whose munificent liberality has mainly contributed to the institution and equipment of the Library'.

One of Joseph Mitchell's other engineering achievements, apart from his Highland Railway, was the invention of a particular kind of concrete used in road-making, well suited for stretches subjected to very heavy usage. He used it in the approach to the goods yard of the Highland Railway in Inverness, on part of the George IV Bridge in Edinburgh, and even on a street in London. The *Inverness Courier* of June 8th 1882 praised the 'adamantine surface' of his concrete:

> There seems to be no doubt that it is tough, durable, clean, easy for horses' feet, and almost unimpressionable by fair even traffic.

Railway Excursions

The Railway Age brought a new range of possibilities for ways in which the working classes of Victorian Inverness could occupy their time. Railway excursions were a feature of the summer months, often arranged by the railway companies in conjunction with annual events such as agricultural shows, or on public holidays when special trains were run, for example, to the beach at Nairn.

The summer of 1876 produced a spell of sunny, settled weather in June, and on a Saturday at the end of the month the Highland Railway treated its workmen, together with their wives and friends, to their annual excursion to Aberdeen:

> The train, which conveyed upwards of 900 passengers, left Inverness at 5 a.m., and returned at a little after eleven at night. The excursionists were accompanied with the band of the Artillery Volunteers, who preceded them to the Aberdeen Drill Hall, where various games were engaged in to the satisfaction and enjoyment of old and young. On the whole, a very pleasant day was passed.

> (*Inverness Courier*, 29 June 1876)

Why 'on the whole'? Certainly one can imagine the journey home, at the end of such a very long day, might have detracted from the enjoyment of the experience, with tired, fractious children and just perhaps the odd railwayman slightly the worse for wear after a day out in the big city.

The process was reciprocal: the same newspaper report mentions that 'on Monday, a party of 435 excursionists from Dundee came over the Highland line' — at the remarkably cheap fare of 7 shillings for a third class return fare. Such an influx was no doubt greatly appreciated by the shopkeepers of Inverness, and is easily matched on practically any summer's day nowadays by ten bus parties, most of whom will have come from much further afield than Dundee. And, of course, today we call them 'tourists', not 'excursionists'.

Edmond's Menagerie

Tourist-watching was doubtless just as entertaining an occupation in the last century as it is today, but other forms of entertainment were also available to Invernessians. In July 1876 Edmond's 'Menagerie' came to Inverness, and encamped on the Maggot Green:

> The cavalcade entered the town by the eastern road, preceded by a splendid band carriage, which was drawn by two elephants — one of an immense size — and four Bactrian camels. It consisted of 15 large caravans, drawn by 50 draught horses. The collection, which is a superior one, embraced, it is said, about 600 living specimens, including an Indian rhinoceros, musical performing elephants, lions, and, indeed, animals and birds from every quarter. The opportunity of visiting such an extensive zoological collection should not be lost; and to-day is the last of the exhibition.

This was certainly an opportunity not to be missed. George Wombwell (1778–1850) was famous for his travelling circus; at his death his menagerie empire was divided between his widow and his daughter, his nephew, George Wombwell, junior, and his niece, Mrs Edmonds, whose travelling show came to Inverness. George Wombwell is buried in Highgate Cemetery in London; his tombstone is in the form of a lion.

Court Reports

The Burgh Police Court was a great source of entertainment for the avid readers of the Inverness newspapers. Whereas the High Court was the venue for trials involving serious crime, the Police Court was where minor infractions and misdemeanours were dealt with, by the Bailies of the Burgh, under the watchful eye of the Assessor.

Here, we can read of the real lives of ordinary citizens, as they occasionally overstepped the mark and fell foul of authority. A typical 'stairheid brawl', aggravated no doubt by the overcrowded housing conditions typical of the growing burgh in the last half of the nineteenth century, was reported in the pages of the *Inverness Courier* for 20th January 1876:

> THE BURGH POLICE COURT.— In this Court on Monday - Bailie Macdonald on the bench - there were some half-dozen uninteresting cases disposed of. John Sinclair and Mrs Sinclair, Wright Street, pleaded not guilty to a charge of assault, alleged to have been committed late on Saturday night upon their stairhead neighbours, the Camerons.

The substance of the dispute between the two families seems to have been 'a wordy dispute' — characteristic late-Victorian understatement — between Mrs Sinclair and Mrs Cameron 'as to who was to have the privilege of barring the outside door'. Numerous family members, including children were called as witnesses by both prosecution and defence:

> The Camerons swore they were half-murdered by the Sinclairs, while the latter swore to the very opposite; and all that could be gathered from the evidence was that there was a free exchange of wild epithets, and a general row, in which young and old took part, and out of which no one came unscathed.

The Sinclairs conducted their own defence, or rather, Mrs Sinclair did. When John Sinclair dared to speak,

> his wife gagged him by clapping her hand upon his mouth with 'Leave it to me, man; just ye show your bruised face to Mr Macdonald and Mr Dallas'.

Mr Dallas was the Burgh Police Court Assessor, there to see that the law was administered fairly and according to correct procedure. The Prosecutor, Mr Wyness, made the mistake of remarking that once Bailie Macdonald had disposed of the case against the Sinclairs, he intended to place the Camerons in the

Bell's Institution, Farraline Park, now the Public Library.

dock on similar charges. Mr Dallas was unimpressed: 'Not in this Court, so long as I am assessor of it. Such is not allowed in any court in the kingdom'. The problem being, of course, that the Camerons could not be charged on the same facts as in a previous case in which they had been called as witnesses.

Despite his procedural gaffe, Mr Wyness pressed on, demanding that the Sinclairs be convicted and bound over to keep the peace:

> The Bench, however, considering the nature of the evidence, found the charge not proven, and dismissed the prisoners from the bar.

Mr Wyness, knowing when he was beaten, decided not to proceed with the case against the Camerons. Three other 'uninteresting' cases heard before the same court that day resulted in fines 'for laying down ashes on the street before the doors of the houses in which they lived'.

In the *Inverness Advertiser* for September 3rd, 1878, there is a fairly typical report of proceedings in the Burgh Police Court, as disposed of by Bailie Black. The cases could, we would suggest, have been heard in an Inverness court only last week:

> *Drunk and Incapable.-* Charles Murray, a seaman belonging to Fort William, was placed at the bar charged with having been drunk and unable to take care of himself early on Sunday morning on High Street. Murray, a middle-aged man, appeared to feel his position, and

in an undertone pleaded guilty. The bailie, on ascertaining that this was the first time panel was charged with infringing on the rules and regulations of the Police Commissioners of Inverness, dismissed him with an admonition.

Disorderly Conduct.- Sophia Fraser, a young woman, was charged with having conducted herself in a disorderly and drunken manner on Grant Street on Sunday morning, by cursing and swearing, &c. It appears that Miss Fraser has been convicted of similar conduct half a dozen times during the last six months, and that she underwent imprisonment for periods varying from twenty to forty days. She pled guilty, and the bailie said that he thought he was doing an act of kindness by sentencing her to pay a fine of 40s, or go to jail for sixty days. Panel apparently thought otherwise, as she left the dock weeping bitterly.

A Cab Hire on the Cheap.- John Stewart forfeited a pledge of 5s for failing to appear to answer a charge accusing him of hiring a cab, and not paying for the same.

Queen Victoria in Inverness, 1873.

By the middle of the nineteenth century public observances and royal visits had replaced public hangings as community activities in Inverness. In September 1873 there was great excitement in the town when it became known that Queen Victoria would be passing through on her way from Fort William to Balmoral. Days of preparation ensured that the town looked its best, with banners, flags and decorations on many buildings. Thousands of people turned out in a carnival atmosphere to catch a glimpse of Her Majesty, who was greatly respected and greatly loved, it seems, by the entire population.

In the event, it was more of a Royal Transit than a Royal Visit. The Queen and her entourage had left Inverlochy Castle, Fort William at 8 o'clock on a Tuesday morning, and by 8.50 a.m. had arrived at Banavie, where they boarded the paddle steamer *Gondolier*. The party lunched on board the steamer as it passed through Fort Augustus; it reached Dochgarroch at 3.10 p.m., where they disembarked and, after all the luggage had been transferred, continued on their way in various carriages, accompanied by a detachment of the 2nd Royal Dragoon Guards.

The route through Inverness had been planned exactly in advance, and decorated accordingly. The *Inverness Courier* was disappointed that the Queen was not to pass along 'our fine modern thoroughfare, Union Street'. The procession approached the town along Glenurquhart Road, turning right into Ardross Street, crossing the river, and proceeding along Bridge Street and High Street to Inglis Street, where they turned left and followed Academy Street to Station Square.

In the event, because she was some nineteen minutes late, the Queen's visit lasted exactly nine minutes! The rather breathless report in the *Courier* certainly captures the atmosphere of what turned out to be a memorable day, although the centrepiece of the celebration was exceedingly brief:

> The first signal of the Queen's approach was the arrival of an attendant's carriage at five minutes to four, immediately followed by a second. Her Majesty approached at a rapid pace. The first of the dragoons came round Ardross Street at a sharp hard gallop, in advance of the open carriage, in which Her Majesty, the Princess Beatrice, and Lady Churchill were seated. The carriage was drawn by a couple of greys ridden by a postillion in a scarlet jacket. There was scarcely a pause as the royal cortege swept along the river side, amidst the scattered cheers of Her Majesty's loyal subjects. Crossing the bridge the bands struck up the National Anthem, the crowds cheered again, and Her Majesty bowed right and left most graciously. There was scarcely time for the continued swell of cheering which would certainly have greeted Her Majesty if she had driven through the streets at a slower pace. Every eye was bent forward to catch a glimpse of the sovereign lady, and the cortege had passed almost before popular interest was gratified. Still the demonstrations were very cordial, and Her Majesty acknowledged the reception with bows and smiles. In rear of the carriage the crowd closed in, dashing along the streets at a gallop, beyond the possibility of interference.

A hint of disappointment there, perhaps. Security was maintained by lining the streets with volunteers, militia and police, and at the station a detachment of 78th Highlanders from Fort George formed a guard of honour. The Provost, Magistrates and Town Council had marched from the Town House to the railway station at three o'clock, where they took up their position on the platform, along with a select two or three hundred spectators. A crimson carpet was laid from the station entrance to the platform. The *Courier* picks up the story:

> As the cortege entered the square at the station, the dragoons drawing up on either side, there was renewed cheering from the masses of spectators gathered all around. The gentlemen respectfully removed

their hats. Her Majesty bowed to the Master of Lovat and Provost Mackenzie, and John Brown having opened the carriage door, she at once alighted, followed by the Princess Beatrice and Lady Churchill, and attended by General Ponsonby. In walking down the platform, Her Majesty observed to Provost Mackenzie that she had enjoyed a very pleasant day and was delighted with the kind reception at Inverness. The spectators followed down the platform, cheering repeatedly. Her Majesty entered the royal saloon carriage. Everything was in readiness to start and there was not a moment's delay. As soon as the Queen was seated, the train moved away amidst renewed cheering, Her Majesty smiling and bowing her acknowledgements. The train had been timed to start at 3.45 pm, but Her Majesty having arrived nineteen minutes late, the engine steamed out of the station at four minutes past four.

The royal train arrived at Aberdeen at 7.11 pm, and left for Ballater at 7.23 pm. The Queen finally arrived at Balmoral after 10 pm — a journey of fourteen hours. Back in Inverness, the celebrations continued, as the populace made the most of the occasion. The Town Council and selected citizens met in the Town House to drink the Queen's health in wine from the cellars of Messrs Bell, Rannie and Co, and

the streets continued to be thronged during the evening, the crowd generally collecting in front of Messrs MacDougall and Co'.s shop, which was effectively illuminated. The letters V.R. with a star between, were formed by gas jets, which burned brilliantly. Messrs MacDougall also entertained their workmen to supper in honour of the occasion. The decorations generally had a new and pleasing appearance in the lighted streets. We cannot say less than that all the proceedings passed off with great credit to the town of Inverness.

(*Inverness Courier*, 18th September 1873)

MacDougall's Royal Tartan Warehouse was lavishly decorated with tartan and flags and a banner which declared: The Highlands welcome our beloved Queen — Mr MacDougall had exhibited at the Great Exhibition at the Crystal Palace in London in 1851, and his firm now pulled out all their patriotic and decorative stops to show their admiration of their beloved Sovereign.

One of the most impressive decorations in the town was at the west end of the suspension bridge, where a floral arch, resting on three ribs and surmounted by a floral crown, was constructed, with the permission of the magistrates. Mr Barnet, the gardener at Culloden House, supervised this production, and the decoration of the bridge itself.

Some citizens expressed surprise that it had been thought necessary for the Dragoons to defend the Queen's person — as if the people of Inverness could not be trusted — and the Provost made a reassuring speech, insisting that Her Majesty had wished to give the town 'a little more display than they would have had without the Dragoons'. However, even he felt compelled to refer to the fact that it had been 127 years since there had last been Dragoons in Inverness — in 1746, in the aftermath of the Battle of Culloden, when one of the Provost's predecessors had been abused by Cumberland and kicked down the stairs of his quarters, and when the Dragoons had hunted wounded Jacobites through the streets of Inverness, showing no quarter.

Religious Revivals

Religion was far more important to the average Invernessian a hundred years ago than it is today, though it has to be said that it is still more important in Inverness than in perhaps most other towns in Scotland. On Sunday mornings the streets on either side of the river are packed with cars, and Academy Street has its busiest 'rush hour' of the week. It will not be possible in this book to explore the church history of Inverness in any depth; the great, set-piece religious events of the nineteenth century were all recorded in detail in the local papers, and are there preserved for all to see. The Disruption, the religious and theological controversies which took the place in Victorian society for the common man and women now taken by politics, which for most of the nineteenth century was not open to ordinary folk, the opening of new churches, the arrival and departure of ministers, bishops and priests — all this is chronicled, though it has never yet been put together in a coherent and readable manner. Perhaps this is a project that some literate Invernessian with an interest in the minutiae of church history and the good eyesight required to scour the pages of newspapers on microfilm might care to undertake some day soon.

Outbreaks of revivalism enlivened the religious scene during the nineteenth century, even in Inverness, where there was already a wide choice available in the matter of religious observance. The activities of some of the nonconformist religions in the town should be studied more fully; they were important to a lot of

One of the prettiest Victorian buildings on High Street, originally the head office of the Caledonian Bank.

townspeople, and to varying degrees made significant contributions to the life of the town.

In the spring of 1865 an incident took place one Sunday which attracted an enormous audience. The *Inverness Courier,* in its issue of 23rd March, contained the following short report:

> PUBLIC ADULT BAPTISM.— On Sunday last two persons, young women, were baptised by immersion in the river Ness. The officiating minister was the Rev. Mr. Grant, the Baptist pastor of Grantown; and the ceremony took place in the middle of the day, between sermons, when there is usually a number of persons disengaged. A crowd consisting of from three to four thousand spectators assembled on this occasion. The day was cold and stormy, and the whole affair seemed a cruel as well as ostentatious display. It would surely be better to select some more private spot for adult baptisms, and some more suitable period of the year.

While it is true that baptism by immersion in the river Jordan would undoubtedly be a far more pleasant experience than in the river Ness on a bitterly cold March day, this somewhat snooty report surely misses the point of the exercise, which was to witness to the maximum effect. As a publicity stunt, staging a baptism in the Ness on a busy Sunday, at a time when a good audience could be assured, was surely an extremely worthwhile exercise.

The *Inverness Advertiser*, reporting the same event, includes much more detail and gives an altogether much more amusing

The Town House, a late-Victorian architectural extravaganza, replacing an earlier building; in front of it stand the Mercat Cross and the Clachnacuddin Stone.

and entertaining account — a useful lesson for historical researchers, who should not fall into the trap of relying solely on one source. Though sometimes tedious, it is often rewarding to see what different local newspapers have to say about the same events. The *Advertiser* estimated the crowd at about 2,000 — smaller than the *Courier* estimate but still impressive. In the days before public address systems, they were critical of the fact that Rev Grant's 'rather lengthy discourse' could only be heard in his immediate vicinity. The two young girls were baptised in the river:

> A general laugh from the spectators when the 'dip' was made, appeared to express their appreciation of the extreme ludicrousness of the spectacle. The same process being gone through with another girl, the ceremonial of the day was brought to a conclusion. Cabs were in waiting to receive the young women, who were driven off with the rev. gentleman and their friends amidst considerable noise and bustle, the crowd pressing forward to get a near look at the courageous damsels in their draggled garments.

This reporting is considerably more salacious than the more conservative *Courier!* On a more serious note, the *Advertiser* decried the need for the ceremony to be conducted quite so publicly, and highlighted a public safety danger which the Courier had ignored:

> we confess it was not without some trepidation that we saw some thousand persons hanging towards one side of the Suspension Bridge on the Sabbath. Very probably the bridge may be able safely to bear such a strain and much more, but in the interest of the public we beg to suggest that, in case there is any repetition of such observances in the same place - which the good sense of the parties should lead them to avoid - the magistrates should make it a point to see that the bridge is kept clear of crowding.

The *Advertiser* was willing to admit that the river baptism was carried out as a 'matter of conscience', but concluded that 'neither the time nor the place was very judiciously chosen'.

Moody and Sankey, the American evangelists, spent a week in Inverness in July 1874, as part of a wide-ranging tour. They were well received by the established churches, who often made their buildings and halls available for prayer meetings and assemblies. The *Inverness Advertiser* was impressed by their performance:

> Mr Moody speaks with decided earnestness, simplicity, and occasional pathos, throwing himself with the ardour of a strong, devoted temperament into the subject he handles. Mr Moody has a quaint way of telling the anecdotes which make up a great part of his preaching, which along with his earnest manner serves to impress his hearers. Mr Moody is generally accompanied by Mr Sankey, who sings hymns to the music of an American organ. Mr Sankey is in possession of a powerful voice, which he uses with much expressive earnestness.

They attracted large attendances in Inverness, at meetings in the Free High Church, the Music Hall, and outdoors, on the Castle Hill.

Much more popular, however, were the great open-air meetings which took place in Inverness in 1861, during the annual Wool Fair, from 11th to 13th July. The Inverness and Aberdeen Junction Railway Company ran special trains from Keith, Fochabers, Elgin, Nairn, and all stations along the line; for example, the return fare from Nairn was 1s 8d.

These meetings were part of a movement which was capturing the imagination, or ministering to the spiritual needs, of most of the population of Scotland. All over the country there were mass meetings, with outpourings of evangelical preaching, supported by the local clergy. In Inverness, the venue was Bell's Park, now Farraline Park — the area in front of Dr Bell's school, now the Public Library. Seats were laid out for an audience of six hundred in the area today occupied by the bus station, and collection boxes at the gates to Bell's Park were put in place to defray the expenses of the event. By 2.30 pm a crowd estimated at seven or eight hundred had assembled, and services began.

The star turn was Mr Robert Cunningham, from Glasgow, who the *Inverness Advertiser* on 12th July 1861 described as a person who:

> according to his own confession, has been a notoriously bad character in his day, engaging in all sorts of riotous misbehaviour - prize-fighting, drunkenness, &c. He delivered a powerful and impressive address, the more so that it was in the plainest and most homely language, and went to the hearts of all present. His hatred against publicans was expressed without disguise, as the principal cause of ruining poor people's prospects in this world and the next; and after that he directed his remarks against 'decent church-going folks', who sat listening to ministers whose 'religion was all doctrine stowed up the garrets of their heads'. Mr Cunningham's remarks produced a deep and evident impression on the assemblage.

Mr Cunningham was talking to the crowd in front of Bell's Institution from a temporary wooden platform which had been erected at the front entrance, in front of the pillars. While he was stirring up the 'decent church-going folks' in English, in the back playground, now occupied by Post Office buildings, a similar service was being conducted in Gaelic, with a large audience there too. The audiences reached a peak of 4000, distributed between the front and back of Bell's School.

They paused for an hour at five o'clock, then resumed for three more hours of uplifting evangelism — and resumed the following day at noon! This 'revival' lasted for several days.

Street-Preaching

The authorities had not been so sympathetic to religious expression in Inverness the previous year, when the infamous 'street-preaching' case occupied the minds of the religious establishment, ably supported by the police and the Sheriff. The *Inverness Advertiser* waged a campaign in defence of Mr Colin Young. It was a classic case of over-reaction by the police, leading to consequences far beyond what was justified. The initial press

Union Street, and the Station Hotel; part of the late-Victorian redevelopment of the town centre.

report, on 26th May, stated the facts, reporting on proceedings in the Police Court:

> The circumstances which gave rise to the case occurred on Thursday evening. Mr Colin Young, cabinetmaker, supported by some other gentlemen, were engaged in devotional exercises in the open air on the stone at the Exchange, commonly known by the name of the Clachnacuddin stone. A crowd had collected round the said gentleman; and on Mr Young preparing to address the people he was ordered by the Superintendent of Police to desist, on refusing to do which the gentleman was rudely dragged up to the Police Office, and acquitted on finding bail for his re-appearance before the magistrate next morning.

In the Police Court, Colin Young conducted his own defence, while Bailie Johnstone got himself into a muddle, and fined him half-a-crown. Worse was to come:

> Yesterday (Friday) evening, whilst Mr Colin Young was engaged in preaching at the same place, he was again laid hold on by the Superintendent of the Police, backed by some half-dozen policemen, his cap thrown off, and otherwise roughly handled, forcibly dragged from the stone, and taken up to the Police-Office, followed by a large crowd, who gave vent to their feelings in a manner anything but

Two of the earliest tourist hotels, the Palace Hotel and the Columba, on the west side of the Ness.

flattering to the conduct of the officers concerned. After some conversation in the Police-Office, Mr Young was liberated without being called on for bail, for some reason best known to the officials. In an editorial, the *Advertiser* gave vent to its own feelings, describing what had happened as 'a display of intense beadledom and stupidity', which seems about right. Mr Colin Young fought back by obtaining an interim interdict from Sheriff-Substitute W H Thomson preventing the magistrates and police from interfering with his right to speak freely in the Exchange of any other public place. The case dragged on into September; there was a full hearing before the Sheriff Substitute, and then an appeal before a full Sheriff, and by this time the whole case had become so enmeshed in legal argument and technicalities that almost nobody could say who had won, and who had lost. The town authorities insisted that although Mr Young had the right to use the streets, as did any other citizen, he should apply to them for permission to exercise that right, when it was at the Exchange, and when it was street-preaching.

The case provoked the citizenry into an outraged correspondence in the local papers, of which this example from the *Inverness Advertiser* of 1st September is among the most entertaining, and gives an interesting insight into the street life of Inverness, which, it appears, is not so very different today from what it was in 1860:

> SIR, — Can you inform me what dreadful crime is involved in street preaching, that Sheriff Young and Bailie Johnstone must combine their intellectual force and official authority to put it down? Fiddlers, ballad-singers, brass bands, volunteers, auctioneers, showmen, all are to be tolerated, but when a man stands up in the streets to tell his fellow-sinners of their lost condition, and show them the way to salvation, he must be hauled off to the police-office, and a learned Sheriff from the bench must frown him out of existence. The thing passes my comprehension.

Writing to the *Inverness Advertiser* on 14th May 1862, Colin Young reviewed the legal muddle, and summed up his situation in eloquent terms:

> If I have a right to preach what I believe to be the best news a man can hear, why hinder me? and why ask a Magistrate for liberty to use my own right? I would not have gone a hairbreadth against the Magistrate's wish, but from the conviction that, in complying with it, I was sacrificing a right dear to every true British heart. How is it that in the bazaars of India, in the streets of China, and in the squares of Italy, preaching is not interfered with? But in Inverness it must not be tolerated; but fines or imprisonment be the portion of every one who feels called by this means to try to save his fellow-men.
>
> Thanking you for your unflinching advocacy of our common rights against a miserable clique, — I remain, yours &c,
>
> COLIN YOUNG

Population Figures

Figures for the population of Inverness are inevitably estimates, before the decennial Census started in 1831. Pennant (1769) had reckoned the population at around 11,000, while the Rev James Hall (1803) thought it was around 6,000. Official Census returns produce the following statistics:

1831	9,633
1841	11,592
1851	12,793
1861	12,509
1871	14,469
1881	17,385
1891	20,855

In 1891, of the population of 20,855, 6,356 were Gaelic-speaking and 11,113 were females. There were 4,566 inhabited houses in the town. One hundred years later, the population of 'Inverness Settlement Zone' in the 1991 Census was 41,766, to which the new estates around Smithton, Culloden and Balloch added a further 8,728, making a total of 50,494. By the time of the next Census it is anticipated that this total will have risen to over 60,000.

CHAPTER 7

SOME VICTORIAN NOTABLES

Inverness has produced many important and influential men and women over the centuries, so it is regrettable that it is possible in the present work to discuss the contributions of only one or two of these. The first is closely connected with Inverness Public Library — his books form the core of the local history collections. Although we have had to ignore many candidates for inclusion, we hope that our readers will realise that, using local history indexes and local history sources available in Inverness Library, and elsewhere, it is possible in most cases to find out quite a lot of biographical material about people who were significant in the Inverness community. Unfortunately, the local newspaper indexes end in 1900, but it is usually possible to find out the date of death of somebody who has died in the twentieth century, then find their obituary, and so trace their career through the pages of the local newspapers.

Charles Fraser-Mackintosh (1828–1901)

Born on 5th June 1828 at Dochnalurg, Dochgarroch, near Inverness, this influential but modest man was the son of Alexander Fraser, tacksman of Dochnalurg, who belonged to a branch of the large and extensive Fraser clan descended from William Fraser, second son of Thomas, the fourth Lord Fraser of Lovat, who was killed at the battle of Blar-nan-leine in 1554. This was the famous 'battle of the shirts'.

Two of the three sons of his father's grandfather Alexander Fraser, who lived at Achnabodach (now Charlestown) on the estate of Kinmylies (from which Charleston Academy takes its name), joined the Jacobite Rising of 1715, were taken prisoner, and transported to the American plantations. Eventually they settled in South Carolina, where several of their descendants occupied prominent positions as merchants in another Charlestown.

Charles Fraser's mother was Marjory, daughter of Alexander Mackintosh, tacksman of Dochgarroch, whose father William was the eldest son of Duncan Mackintosh, a younger brother of the

Charles Fraser-Mackintosh, lawyer, MP, and antiquarian, 1880s.

famous Brigadier Mackintosh of Borlum who was a Captain in Mackintosh's Regiment in the 1715 Rising.

Thus, from both sides of his family Charles Fraser inherited honourable Jacobite traditions, which were to become a great influence in his own contributions to public life and private historical research in his later years. At first, he embarked on a legal career, entering the law office of John Mackay of Inverness in 1842, at the age of 14. In 1849 he went to Edinburgh University to continue his legal training and studies, studying Civil and Scots Law, Conveyancing and Rhetoric. In 1853, at the age of only 25, he started up in business in Inverness and soon had a large and lucrative practice. He became assistant to the Sheriff Clerk, and in 1853, Procurator.

In 1857 took his first dip into local politics when he supported the Liberal candidate, Alexander Campbell of Monzie in the Parliamentary election for the Inverness Burghs against the Whig sitting member, Alexander Matheson of Ardross. The Whigs retained the seat, as they also did in 1859. On balance, this result was probably beneficial for Inverness, in that Sir Alexander Matheson, as he later became, worked tirelessly for the prosperity of Inverness; while not a brilliant politician, he was honest and hard-working, and through his own considerable financial investment coupled with considerable business acumen he contributed much to the development and improvement of Inverness, through his redevelopment of the west side of the river and his involvement with the Highland Railway.

In the same year that the young Charles Fraser was dabbling in politics his maternal uncle, Aeneas Mackintosh, died, stipulating in his will that if his nephew were to change his surname by adding Mackintosh to it, he would become a major beneficiary of his estate. Thus Charles Fraser-Mackintosh came into existence at the age of 29, and in due time a Royal License was obtained to ratify his new nomenclature.

His appetite whetted by a skirmish in national politics, Charles Fraser-Mackintosh was elected as a Town Councillor in Inverness in November 1857. He was re-elected in 1859 and again in 1861, but on 10th May 1862 he suddenly resigned, citing the pressures of business and health difficulties caused by overwork, and he retired completely from public life.

We now know that he was about to embark on a scheme which was both going to transform the town centre of Inverness and make his fortune. Along with three associates (George Grant Mackay, Donald Davidson and Hugh Rose) he embarked on the redesign of the area between the Railway Station and Church Street, which was a confusing network of old houses, workshops, closes and narrow lanes. The old buildings were purchased by the consortium and cleared away, and the work of building Union Street began. By 1864 the new street was finished, and from the first every office, shop and set of apartments was fully let.

Charles Fraser-Mackintosh and his three friends were the first to realise that the arrival of the railway in Inverness would lead to the expansion of the town and the growth of commerce and industry. There was plenty of room for the town to expand. It was surrounded by open fields, but only a few citizens seemed to be aware of the opportunities available. In 1863 Charles Fraser-Mackintosh bought the Drummond Estate, once the property of his relative Provost Phineas Mackintosh, and laid it out for feuing — that is, subjected it to a process of subdivision and town planning which involved the creation of new streets and property boundaries, and the creation of property divisions which people were then invited to purchase and build on, while still paying an annual fee, or 'feu duty' to the owner of the land on which the houses were to be built. In 1866 he repeated the exercise on the estate of Ballifeary, on the west side of the river to the south of Matheson's holdings.

Then, in May 1867, Charles Fraser-Mackintosh withdrew again from public life, retired from the legal profession, enjoyed the adulation of his fellow-townsmen at a public dinner, and, still under the age of 40, left Inverness. For a year he travelled on the Continent, enjoying the fruits of his investments, until towards the end of 1868 his Chief, Alexander Aeneas Mackintosh of Mackintosh, wrote to him in the south of Spain asking him to take charge of running the Mackintosh Estates. He naturally acceded to his clan chief's request, and for the next four years he acted as Commissioner on the Mackintosh Estates, carrying through many improvements.

In 1868 Alexander Matheson had vacated his parliamentary seat as the member for Inverness Burghs and had moved to the seat of Ross and Cromarty, as successor to his uncle. Aeneas William Mackintosh of Raigmore was elected unopposed to the Inverness seat; the anti-Whig party were taken by surprise and had no candidate ready. In 1873 they resolved not to be caught unawares again, and in response to a petition signed by over six hundred electors Charles Fraser-Mackintosh allowed his name to go forward as the prospective candidate. When parliament was dissolved in January 1874 he was in Algiers, but quickly he made his way home and was duly elected as Member of Parliament for the Inverness Burghs (Inverness, Nairn, Forres and Fortrose).

He and Raigmore were both personal friends and relatives, being descended from Duncan and Joseph Mackintosh, younger brothers of Brigadier Mackintosh of Borlum, so the electoral contest took place without personal acrimony, though hard-fought. In an electoral address soon after his adoption as candidate,

THE CALEDONIAN HOTEL,

INVERNESS.

(Facing the Railway Station and within one minute's walk.)

(UNDER NEW MANAGEMENT.)

THIS well-known First-Class Family Hotel is patronised by the Royal Family and most of the nobility of Europe. Having recently added fifty Rooms, with numerous Suites of Apartments for Families, and all handsomely Refurnished throughout, it is now the largest and best appointed Hotel in Inverness, and universally acknowledged one of the most comfortable in Scotland.

Magnificent Ladies' Drawing-Room overlooking the River Ness.

Spacious Smoking and Billiard Rooms.

In point of situation this Hotel is the only First-Class Hotel overlooking the River Ness, the magnificent view from the windows being unsurpassed, and extending to upwards of fifty miles of the surrounding strath and mountain scenery of the great glen of "Caledonia."

TABLE D'HOTE DAILY AT 5.30 AND 7.30.

TARIFF.

	Per day.—S. D.			Per day.—S. D.
Parlour, Bedroom, and Dressing-room, *en suite* -	from 10 6	Dinners - - -from	3 6
		Do., Table d'Hote- - -	4 6
Private Sitting-rooms - -	from 5 6	Do., in private sitting-room from	5 0
Bedrooms, Single - 2s, 2s 6d, to	3 6	Tea, plain - - - -	1 6
Do., Double - 4s 6d, 5s, to	5 6	Do., with meat and fish - -	3 0
Table d'Hote Breakfast - -	3 0	Luncheons, hot - - -2s to	2 6
Breakfast, with Cold Meat -	2 6	Do., cold - - -	2 0
Do., with Eggs- - -	2 0	Cup of Tea or Coffee - -	0 6
Do., Plain, with Preserves -	2 0	Attendance, per day - -	1 6

An Omnibus attends all the Canal teamers. The Hotel Porters await the arrival of all Trains. Posting.

George Sinclair, *Proprietor.*

The Caledonian Hotel, from a guidebook of 1893.

Charles Fraser-Mackintosh was unequivocal about his politics and allegiances:

> Though not inattentive to political matters, yet I have to the best of my recollections never made a political speech in my life...If I had been a political-monger, a frequenter of platforms airing common-places, I should not, I think, have attained the pleasant position I occupy of being generally liked by my townsmen.
>
> If any one chooses to refer to the newspapers he will never find my name as supporting any narrow or retrograde measures. It is true that in my literary pursuits, which all lay in the examination into and elucidation of the history of the past, I may have imbibed Cavalier and Jacobite sympathies. It was impossible to resist them, nor do I wish to do so, because they are part of those things which held to keep a man's mind fresh and open, and in my own case there is a circumstance which of itself binds me to the Stuarts and to the King of the Highland hearts, Bonny Prince Charlie.
>
> I claim your suffrages as an independent man tied to no leader, but if elected free to follow my judgment with regard to all measures, but always to recollect in making up my mind and giving my vote that nine-tenths of my constituents are Liberals, and that if I do not act in unison with them I simply misrepresent them. I cannot go in on any other condition and be a Government or Opposition hack as the case may be, and my coming forward will be uncalled for, as you have a man of that kind already if that is what you want.

This was his way of politely pointing out that while Mackintosh of Raigmore, the sitting member, was an honest enough fellow, and a worthy opponent, he was of limited value in advocating the reforms and changes which Charles Fraser-Mackintosh and his anti-Whig alliance regarded as essential if the burgh was to progress. He went on to allude to the aspect of his candidacy for which he was to become most famous outside of his home town:

> I also claim your suffrages as a Highlander speaking and familiar with the Gaelic, and ready to advocate in the highest quarters all the legitimate requirements of the Highland people, many of which have hitherto been overlooked and ignored.

In his first electoral address Charles Fraser-Mackintosh put forward a list of legislative reforms which he supported, covering the Game Laws, the Law of Entail, the rights of tenancy in labourers' cottages and most especially what he called 'the assimilation of the County and Burgh franchise'. That is, the abolition of the separate seats for the Inverness Burghs and

Inverness County, and their amalgamation, with other reforms, into the one Inverness-shire seat.

Indeed, Fraser-Mackintosh's support of the cause of Highland tenantry led him to be referred to in parliament as 'the member for the Highlands', and it was in this area that he made his mark. He succeeded in getting the Scottish Education Code amended, to encourage Highland School Boards to employ Gaelic-speaking teachers in schools attended by children whose only language was Gaelic. He supported the Conservative Government in two measures of interest to Highlanders: the Church Patronage (Scotland) Act, 1874, which he saw as paving the way to an eventual re-unification of the Presbyterian churches in Scotland, and the Entail Amendment Act, 1875, which embodied one of the reforms in the Land Laws which he advocated so strenuously throughout his career.

His efforts were recognised at a 'great Celtic demonstration' in Inverness on 24th April 1878, which was attended by representatives from nearly all the Celtic Societies and interest groups throughout Britain. At a mid-day meeting in the Town Hall he was presented with an illuminated address from the Societies, and in the evening he was entertained to a public dinner.

By 1882 a Liberal government was in power, and Fraser-Mackintosh saw his chance to make further progress on land reform. Numerous petitions from all parts of the Highlands had been presented to parliament in the previous two years, asking for the appointment of a Royal Commission to enquire into the grievances of the crofters, but nothing came of them. Then, in February 1883 Charles Fraser-Mackintosh prepared a Memorial to the Home Secretary, urging that 'under existing circumstances it was most important that a Royal Commission of Enquiry into the condition of the crofter and rural population of the Highlands and Islands of Scotland should be granted'. This Memorial was signed by twenty-one Scottish members of parliament, with the result that a Royal Commission was appointed 'to enquire into the condition of the crofters and cottars in the Highlands and Islands of Scotland and all matters affecting the same or relating thereto'. Under these quite generous terms of reference the Royal Commission collected evidence from a total of 775 persons during the summer and autumn of 1883, at 71 meetings in 61 locations in the crofting counties of Argyll, Inverness, Ross, Cromarty, Sutherland and Caithness, including every part of the island of Skye, and the Outer

Hebrides from Lewis to Barra, as well as Orkney and Shetland, with extra sittings in Glasgow and Edinburgh.

The Commissioners were Lord Napier, the Chairman, Sir Kenneth Smith Mackenzie, Bart., Donald Cameron of Lochiel, Charles Fraser-Mackintosh, Sheriff Nicholson of Portree and Professor Donald Mackinnon. The Napier Commission, as it was called, reported early in 1884 in five bulky volumes of Evidence with an accompanying Report. It forms one of the best sources we have for the lives of ordinary people in the crofting counties in the nineteenth century, and resulted in the passage of the Crofters Act of 1886.

Land Reform was at the top of the political agenda in the election of November 1885, coupled with legislation extending the franchise to all households. When parliament was dissolved and the election announced, Cameron of Lochiel decided to retire from his seat representing Inverness County, and Charles Fraser-Mackintosh resolved to try his luck. In a three-cornered contest he emerged successful, defeating his erstwhile colleague on the Napier Commission, Sir Kenneth Mackenzie, the official Liberal candidate, and Reginald Macleod, the Conservative candidate. Now all the crofting counties had members pledged to land reform, and although the issue of Irish home rule dominated national politics in June 1886, the Crofters Act was guided through parliament by Fraser-Mackintosh and his colleagues and received the royal assent on the day before parliament was dissolved.

He could not agree with Gladstone's politics on the Irish question and at the general election in the summer of 1886 was returned, unopposed, as a Unionist, a position he maintained until he was defeated in 1892 . He declined the offer of a knighthood and retired from public life, passing his time at his residences in London, Bournemouth and Inverness in the pursuit of literary and historical studies. He died in Bournemouth on 25th January 1901 and was buried in Kensal Green Cemetery, in London.

In 1876 he married Eveline May, only daughter of Richard David Holland of Kilvean, Inverness; they had no children.

Apart from his work on the Napier Commission, Charles Fraser-Mackintosh is remembered best today for his historical researches:

1865 *Antiquarian Notes,* short essays on local history.
1866 *Dunachton Past and Present,* on Clan Chattan.
1875 *Invernessiana,* historical material on Inverness, 1160–1599.

1890 *Letters of Two Centuries,* a letter from every year, 1616–1815.
1895 *The Last Macdonalds of Islay,* on the Lords of the Isles.
1897 *Antiquarian Notes: Second Series,* a series of parish histories.
1898 *The Minor Septs of Clan Chattan.*
1913 *Antiquarian Notes,* second edition, with introductory biography.

In addition, he contributed to the *Celtic Magazine* and *Highland Monthly,* and a series of twelve papers on 'Minor Highland Families' in the *Transactions of the Gaelic Society of Inverness* is still often referred to by Highland family historians.

The *Inverness Courier*, which had opposed his election vigorously in both 1874 and 1885, gave him a glowing obituary:

...he left behind him a record that may well ornament the annals of political rectitude and public duty. One of the most respected members of the House of Commons, a man who was always listened to with attention by the leaders as well as by the rank and file, and whose advice was sought and generally accepted in all matters affecting the North, his absence could not fail to be felt in Parliament, but Mr Fraser-Mackintosh, though he accepted his defeat with that manliness which was one of his most admirable characteristics, could never again be induced to court the fickle smile of popular favour, and he settled down to the life that after all suited him best — the quiet career of the country gentleman, the student of his native history and antiquities.

His wife survived him until 1920, and on her death bequeathed his extensive library of books on the history and culture of the Highlands to the town library in Inverness. It is now housed in the Reference Room at Inverness Public Library, an invaluable collection for scholars and researchers interested in Scottish history in general and the history of the Highlands in particular. It is entirely fitting that Charles Fraser-Mackintosh's library is there, and used by the Inverness Public, for he was very much involved in the foundation of the Inverness Free Library, and in fact performed the opening ceremony at its new building in the Castle Wynd, on Saturday 16th June 1883. The arrangements were announced in the *Inverness Courier* of 12th June and the ceremony reported in the issue of 19th June. The ceremony was held in the Town Hall next door, as it was felt the Library rooms would be too small. The time of the opening was fixed at 3 pm —

in order that the working men, who, it is hoped, will interest themselves in the institution, may find it convenient to attend.

The printed catalogue, dedicated to Joseph Mitchell whose generous donation had been the catalyst for the new library, was on sale for one shilling. The library contained 5,400 volumes, arranged in nine classes:

- Theology, Moral Philosophy and Church History
- History, Biography, Voyages and Travels
- Art, Science, and Natural History
- Law, Politics, and Political Economy
- Poetry, Drama, and Ancient Classics
- Fiction
- Miscellaneous
- Magazines and Reviews
- Works of Reference.

According to the reports of Fraser-Mackintosh's speech, the Library Act was adopted in Inverness on July 4th 1877 at a public meeting of the inhabitants of Inverness. Previously the existing Subscription Library was bought by the Town Council to form the core of a public library. By 1883, forty-five towns in England but only eight in Scotland had adopted the Free Libraries Act. Provost Fraser, introducing Fraser-Mackintosh, expressed the Victorian sentiments which gave rise to Free Public Libraries in Great Britain:

> The great advantage of these libraries is their freedom. I do trust our industrial population will take advantage of these privileges. It is on their behalf these Acts were adopted, and if they do, as I hope they will, nothing will be more gratifying to the promoters and those in charge. The best books and periodicals will always be there, and it is for this purpose that the yearly assessment amounting to about £250 is levied.

There had been a subscription library in Inverness from 1820, and local booksellers had also operated libraries of their own, but the commitment to the provision of a Free Public Library by the Burgh of Inverness was an important milestone in the cultural life of the town. At the time of the official opening, Charles Fraser-Mackintosh was engaged in the work of the Royal Commission chaired by Lord Napier, on the future of crofting in the Highlands, and in his address gives an interesting summary of the work of the Commission up to that date and the significance of its deliberations for the Highlands. His own books are still used regularly, and in many cases his researches into some of the byeways of local history are all that has ever been published. Perhaps some day somebody will build on the foundations he prepared over a century ago and attempt an updated reinterpretation of his conclusions.

Alexander Strother

Not every Victorian worthy was lucky enough to have an Inverness street named after him, but one gentleman who is immortalised in the town centre is Bailie Strother, preserved for history in Strother's Lane. He died on 2nd October 1889, 'from congestion of the lungs', according to the obituary published the next day in the *Scottish Highlander*. Like many other local lads, he left Inverness to seek his fortune in London, and did well enough to return to his native town and set up in business as a grocer and wine merchant in the old Post Office buildings, on the High Street.

He moved to premises on Academy Street, on the corner of his Lane, and built up his wholesale business there with great success, eventually 'extending its ramifications into all parts of the Highlands'. The *Scottish Highlander* thought that he was amongst the first in the Highlands to start up a wholesale business of any size.

He was elected as a member of the Town Council in 1866 and served until defeated in the election of 1874. He stood again successfully in 1874, and retired in 1883, 'feeling the effects of advancing age stealing upon him'. He sold off his business and retired to the family farm at Balmachree, Culloden. His standing as a member of the business community was recognised by virtue of the fact that he was a Director of the Caledonian Bank, the Tweedmill Company, the Rose Street Foundry, the Heritable Investment Company, the Cemetery Company, and others.

He served as a Bailie (magistrate) until 1869, and in 1880 failed by just one vote to be elected Provost. He died in 1889 at the age of seventy-six, leaving a widow and a large family. His wife, Anne Tolmie, died on 20th October 1896. His son was Dr Strother, the resident surgeon in the Infirmary, while one of his daughters was married to a Free Church minister and another to an Inverness solicitor.

Many streets, lanes and closes in Inverness bear the names of individuals, though in some cases nothing at all is known of them, apart from their names. Baron Taylor's Lane, now promoted to a 'street', is named after John Taylor who owned property in this part of Inverness in the 1730s, and by virtue of being a feudal 'superior' claimed the title 'Baron'. Previously it was the Back Vennel (from the French word *venelle*, an alleyway), because it was a lane or passageway running at the back of the properties on High Street and Bridge Street. In the nineteenth century, because of its reputation as a venue for drunkenness and street-fighting its name changed slightly to the more aptly designated Black Vennel.

An anonymous Invernessian, writing from Queensland to the *Inverness Advertiser* in a letter published on 9th April 1874, remembered the back streets of Inverness and their reputation for wild behaviour:

> We have five Aborigines to do outside household work, and have taught two of their boys to count their fingers — but beyond that their education is too difficult for me. However, they are learning the habits of honest, steady application to work, which is more valuable to them than any book learning it is possible to give them. When you have solved the problem of how to clean and Christianise the Black Vennel and the Maggot, and other similar portions of the metropolis of the Highlands, we may be able to solve the problem of Christianising the blacks of Australia!

Sir Alexander Matheson

One man who rather immodestly ensured that most of the streets on the west side of the river were named after various members of his family was Alexander Matheson of Ardross. In 1868 he bought the Muirtown Estate, and set about developing it, laying out streets, raising the level of the ground to prevent flooding, and generally creating the streetscape we see today. His factor and architect, Alexander Ross, was responsible for carrying out the sometimes grandiose plans, which were a source of continuous controversy in the town for over ten years. Alexander Place (formerly Tanner's Lane), Kenneth Street, Ardross Street, May Court, Mary Ann Court, Duncraig Street, Attadale Road, Harrowden Road and Lochalsh Road all commemorate either members of the family or places connected with them. Perceval Road is named after Spencer Perceval, the Prime Minister who was shot by a madman in the lobby of the House of Commons in 1812; his daughter married Sir James Matheson, Alexander Matheson's uncle. However, when Sir Alexander Matheson of Lochalsh died in 1886 the *Ross-shire Journal* noted that the deceased was thrice married — first in 1841, to Mary (who died that year), daughter of the late Mr James Crawford Macleod of Geanies; secondly, in 1853, to the Hon. Lavinia Mary Stapleton (who died in 1855), sister of the eighth Baron Beaumont; thirdly, in 1860, Eleanor Irving (who died in 1879), daughter of the late Mr Spencer Perceval of Elm Grove, Ealing.

So, perhaps the naming of Perceval Road was of more immediate family interest than his third wife's assassinated ancestor.

The street names of Inverness make an interesting topic of research, and further information about them can be found in Edward Meldrum's little article in the Inverness Field Club's *Inverness Miscellany: No 1* (1982), much of what he has to say being based on Charles Fraser Mackintosh's *Antiquarian Notes*, in which there are several sections on 'Ancient names and places in and about Inverness'. Gerald Pollitt, in *Historic Inverness* (1981), discusses some Inverness streets, though ignores many more. A reworking and republication of this material, with further research, would make an interesting and worthwhile project for an Invernessian wishing to contribute something more substantial to the local history of the burgh, especially by bringing the story up to the present, by canvassing the sprawling housing estates around Inverness for current gems, many either of spurious origin, wholly inappropriate to both the terrain and the historical context of places, or mis-spelled due to modern ignorance of the past. Caulfield Road and its wrongly spelled off-shoots are named after the eighteenth road builder William 'Toby' Caulfeild, who built most of the roads in the Highlands usually ascribed to General Wade. The grandson of Viscount Charlemont, an Irish peer (which might explain the unusual spelling of his surname?), Major Caulfeild's mansion was at Cradlehall — the name supposedly deriving from a 'cradle' attached to a block and tackle which was used to hoist large house guests who had consumed too much claret to the safety of their upstairs bedrooms. Between 1740 and his death in 1767 Caulfeild planned and built over 800 miles of roads in Scotland, beating the 240 miles of military roads achieved by George Wade (another Irishman), but falling just a little short of the 900 miles of parliamentary roads constructed under Thomas Telford's supervision.

Redesigning the west side of the town was not Sir Alexander Matheson's only claim to fame. At his death on 27th July 1886 the columns of coverage in the pages of all the local papers of his funeral, and the extensive obituaries, testified to the esteem in which he was held in the Highlands generally and in Inverness in particular. Although obituaries tend to be overly glowing tributes, they do provide a useful starting point when researching local worthies as they usually contain the essential biographical and career information from which it is possible to reconstruct their lives in as much detail as the researcher's time and patience allows.

Sir Alexander Matheson was born at Attadale in Ross-shire in 1805, and spent the early part of his life there. He attended the University of Aberdeen, and the story of his first journey there was oft repeated. He stayed the night at the Luib Inn, three miles west of the hotel at Achnasheen, sharing the accommodation of two box beds with a party of drovers on their way to market. As the son of a landlord, even a small one, young Mr Matheson got a bed to himself; six drovers shared the other box bed and the rest sat out the night drinking.

The small estate of Attadale had been in the possession of his family from the beginning of the 1700s, but it was sold in 1825, forcing Alexander to make his way into the world of business. His uncle, Sir James Matheson, found him a place in the family firm of Jardine, Matheson and Company, and Alexander's business career was launched. He first sailed for China at the age of 22; the voyage to Canton took ten months. He was good at languages: French, Latin, Chinese and Gaelic. After a few years in the orient he founded the house of Matheson and Company on his own account, with numerous branches in India and China, and became fabulously wealthy. That his riches were not always based on strictly legal trade is attested to by the opium poppy motifs on the gates of his house at Ardross in Easter Ross.

Matheson returned from the orient and set about using his money for the greater good of the Highlands, in a series of canny business investments which enhanced his reputation and added to his massive fortune. He spent some money buying up the former family estates in Lochalsh, including the estates of Letterfearn and Inverinate, and having established himself as a Highland proprietor got himself elected to parliament in 1847 as member for the Inverness Burghs, a seat which he held until 1868. In that year his uncle retired from parliament and Sir Alexander took over from him as the member for Ross and Cromarty,

MacDougalls' 'Tartan Warehouse', 1893.

— THE —

Clan Tartan & Tweed Warehouse
INVERNESS.

VISITORS to the Highlands should inspect the Stock of this Establishment, which is one of the best in the North to select from.

CLAN TARTANS IN

RIBBONS.	**SASHES.**	**SERGES.**
TIES.	**HANDKERCHIEFS.**	**SAXONIES.**
BELTS.	**DOROTHY BAGS.**	**SILKS.**

Shawls, Plaids, Travelling Rugs, Tam o' Shanters, & Hose.

REAL SHETLAND HAND-KNIT SHAWLS, GLOVES, SPENCERS.
CLAN CREST HAT PINS and BROOCHES. Any Crest Supplied.

GRANT'S
Clan Tartan & Tweed Warehouse
HIGH STREET, INVERNESS.

Grant's emporium on the corner of High Street and Castle Street, as seen in Finlay's Official Guide to Inverness, 1905, surmounted by the Three Graces: now demolished and replaced by a hamburger establishment.

127

returned unopposed, as he was subsequently in the elections of 1874 and 1880. He retired, due to ill health, in 1884, and was replaced in the Ross and Cromarty constituency by Mr Munro Ferguson of Novar.

In 1882 he was created a baronet by Gladstone, but although widely known in the Highlands as 'Ardross' from his principal seat, chose Lochalsh as the title of his baronetcy. He was the first Chairman of the Highland Railway Company. In the later years of his life he continued to acquire land and estates: Strathbran and Ledgowan near Achnasheen, Attadale, New Kelso and Strathcarron, Dalmore, Culcairn, Delny and Balintraid.

We have already noted Sir Alexander's singularly unlucky marriages: he was survived by a son and daughter from his second marriage, and by three sons and three daughters by his third marriage. His eldest son and heir was Kenneth James Matheson, born in 1854, educated at Harrow and Christ Church, Oxford. Kenneth's 'coming of age' in May 1875 was a lavish occasion of celebration.

The personal tributes in the *Courier* obituary, while praising the great man, are revealing in their sentiments, and are typical of late Victorian newspaper prose:

> In personal appearance Sir Alexander Matheson was broad and firmly built, unobtrusive in manner, with an air of resolution and sagacity in his firm lip and quiet penetrating eye. He did not pretend to be a public speaker, but in making a business statement on paper, nothing could exceed the clearness of his style. His speeches at the meetings of the Highland Railway Company were models of concise and lucid exposition. To mere acquaintances his exterior seemed a little cold and reserved, but underneath his shy demeanour there beat a heart of the greatest warmth and kindliness. It was not his habit to make lavish promises, but every promise he made he kept, and often when he declined to promise, he found the means to grant the request which was presented to him. No man was ever more loyal and steady in his friendship. Those who were admitted to his intimacy found him a most interesting companion, full of information and anecdote, hospitable and pleasant. He was always happier with one or two friends in his own room of an evening, than as one of a dinner party. The extraordinary accuracy of his facts was as marked in his conversation as in his public statements. Whatever he knew, he knew perfectly and in detail. He had a remarkable memory for figures, retaining in his mind not only the round sums, but the shillings and

pence of accounts and transactions. The man who to outsiders seemed brusque or reserved, was, in reality, most sensitive and tender hearted. If he could help it, he never parted with an old servant, or changed an old tenant. It is not surprising that he was served with the utmost devotion, and that his death is deeply lamented.

Sir Alexander died in London, at the age of 81, and was buried in the castle grounds at Ardross. The Highland Railway ran a special train from Inverness for those wishing to attend the funeral. Although he was an old man, his death came suddenly, and was a great shock to the whole Highland community. His former tutor, Rev Donald Sage of Resolis, was quoted as having said that he was never known to tell a lie.

CHAPTER 8

THE TOWNSCAPE OF INVERNESS

Since Gerald Pollitt's book *Historic Inverness* (1981) was published, it has served as the best summary of the architectural history of Inverness, and as a study of the development of some of the town's streets. However, there are many gaps in Pollitt's research, and a real opportunity for somebody to organise all the available material into a guide to the public buildings and streets of Inverness.

In 1992, the publication of John Gifford's *Highlands and Islands* in the *Buildings of Scotland* series introduced carefully researched academic scholarship into this field for the first time. However, Gifford's book, although meticulously accurate, covers the whole of the Highlands and Islands of Scotland, and the section on the town of Inverness is necessarily brief, taking the form of short architectural descriptions and notes on all the most important buildings.

Inverness Place-Names

William J Watson was the Professor of Celtic Languages and Literature at Edinburgh University, and before that, Rector of Inverness Royal Academy. His main work was entitled *History of the Celtic Place Names of Scotland,* but a small volume, *Prints of the Past around Inverness* gives derivations and explanations for many of the town's place-names. As the section of his book on place-names amounts to only ten pages, of which Inverness names form only a portion, it is possible to reproduce most of his town names here; items marked with an asterisk (*) are from *Glossary of some Place Names,* by John Macpherson, a student of Watson's, published by Inverness Field Club in *The Hub of the Highlands: the book of Inverness and District* (1975):

Abban of Abban Street means a more or less disused river channel; also a backwater (*aban*). The river once went by this route to the sea.
Altnaskiach — the hawthorn burn.
Ballifeary — in 1244 Balnafare as 'town of the watching' (*Baile na Faire*); in the olden times sentinels would be posted here to give timely notice of any hostile visit by the unruly neighbours of the town.

Balloch Hill — the Balloch (*Bealach*) was the old Gaelic name for the 'gap' through which Castle Street now runs. The Balloch Hill is at the top of Castle Street. 'Le Ballocis Hill', 1376.

Balnafettack — (*Baile nam Feadag*) Homestead of the Plovers. In names of places Bal- usually means 'homestead', the Scottish 'toon'.

Barnhill — formerly also Cott Hill. In the 18th century there were no houses here, only three thatched cots.

Broadstone Park — so called from a stone, now buried under the footpath in Kingsmills Road, which was bored to serve perhaps as base for a flagstaff. It probably means 'the *bored* stone'. [Macpherson adds: 'the stone is now outside the Thistle Football ground.]

Bught — Old Scots *boucht, bought,* a bending, bay, sheep-pen; the same word really is English *bow,* to bend.

Cameron Barracks — the ridge was formerly called Knockintinnel (*Cnoc an Tionail*), the rallying hill.

Castlehill of Inshes — the Gaelic is *Caisteal Still* — Castle of the Stripe (of land), of which the English is a corruption.

Castle Heather — so written at least as early as 1758, but the older name was Castle-leather or Leffare, from Gaelic *Lethoir,* a hill side. 'The Lordship of Leffare' is mentioned in 1460.

Clachnaharry — usually taken as for *Clach na h-Aire,* Stone of the Watch; the Gaelic pronunciation, however, is in favour of *Clach na h-Aithrigh(e),* Stone of Penance, or, of Repentance...

Cradlehall — so called, it is said, from a sort of lift or elevator used in the house by Edward Caulfeild, who was in charge of the roads after General Wade, and lived there.

Craigphadrick — Patrick's Rock. The name is said not to be very old, and to have been given after a tenant who lived near it.

Culcabock — (*Cuil na Cabaig*), Nook of the Cheese; the reason of the name is unknown.

Culduthel — (*Cuil-daodhail*); *cuil* means 'nook' as above; *duthel* is the same as in the parish name Duthil, the meaning of which is difficult.

Culloden (*Cuil-lodair*); this name, so prominent in Highland history, means Nook of the Marsh. *Cuil,* a nook, is common in place-names round Inverness.

Dalneigh* (*Dal an eich*) horse field.

Diriebught, in 1376 Deyrbowchte, commonly said to mean 'The poors' Land'; but it may rather mean 'The poor or barren Land'.

Doomsdale Street — the old name for Castle Street. It led to the place of execution.

Drakies (*Dreigidh*) is in 1369 Drakeis; in 1376 Drekechys; a Pictish name; meaning unknown.

Drummond (*Druiminn*) means 'at', or, 'on the ridge'. In old writings it is called Drumdevan, 'idle ridge', ie, 'uncultivated ridge'; (*druim diomhain*).

Dunain* — (*Dun an eoin*) is fort of the bird.

Haugh — a very old English, or rather Scottish name, mentioned in William the Lyon's charter of 1180. In 1360 it is written Halc, old Scots *halche*, flat land by a waterside. Gaelic-speaking people still use the old form almost exactly — *an Talchan*.

Holm — from English *holm*, an island in a river. Here again the old form is used in Gaelic, *an Tuilm*. Holm here means 'river-meadow'.

Inshes — (*Na h-Innseagan*) means the meadows (*innis*).

Inverness (*Inbhirnis*) means the confluence of the Ness (with the sea), ie, the place at the mouth of the Ness. *Inver* is Gaelic, probably changed from an older *aber*. The River Ness appears in Adamnan's *Life of Columba* as Nesa. Rivers were worshipped as deities by the ancient Celts, and Nesa was most probably a water goddess.

Kessock Ferry takes its name from St Kessock, who was specially connected with Loch Lomond side. There were often small chapels or oratories near ferries, and there may have been one here dedicated to St Kessock.

Kilvean — the *Cill* or Church of St Bean (two syllables).

Kingmills — a very old English name. A charter of Alexander II (1232) mentions 'our mill at Inverness'. The mill was subsequently granted to the town.

Kinmylies — in the same charter the land of *Kinmyly* is granted by the King to the Bishop of Moray; it is *Cinn a' Mhilidh*, 'warrior's head', or 'headland'; compare Carmylie in Fife.

Leachkin — (*An Leacainn*), the Hillside — a very common name.

Leys (*An Leigheas*), meaning uncertain.

Loch Ardle — the name of an old barony near Inverness revived in recent times.

Loch Ashie (*Loch Athaisidh*), also Drum Ashie, which has become famous in the form of Drummossie. The name probably means 'bare or poor meadow', from *ath-innse*, locative case of *ath-innis*.

Longman — an interesting name, thought to mean Ship-flat, which is unlikely to be correct.

Maggot — so called from a chapel of St Margaret.

Merkinch — The Horse Meadow (or, in this case, island). When Abban Street was a river channel, the Merkinch was an island, and a common grazing ground for horses.

Midmills — between Kingsmills and the Diriebucht mill.

Millburn — takes its names from the water which worked those mills.

Porterfield — from the Porter of the Castle, who was an important official.

Raigmore — (*Rathaig Mhor*), Rath, of which rathaig is a derivative, means a fortified homestead. The original Raigmore is in Strathdearn.

Scategate, **Scathegate**, or **Scatisgat** — the old name for the road to the sea by Rose Street, probably so called because *scat* or tax was there levied on fish brought into the burgh for sale. *Gate* in old Scots means road.

Scorguie — (*Sgorr gaoithe*), windy point.

Tomnahurich —(*Tom na h-Iubhraich*)— Hillock of the Yew-wood. The oldest form of the word *iubhrach,* a yew wood, is Eboracon, whence also the name York.

Torbreck — (*an Torr Breac*) — the dappled hill.

Torvean — (*Torr Bheathain*) — St Bean's hill; cf Kilvean.

To this discussion of place-names in Inverness should be added Edward Meldrum's article on *Inverness Street Names*, published by Inverness Field Club in their *Inverness Miscellany: No 1* (1982). He is especially good on the mediaeval streets of Inverness, when the town consisted of four main streets, or 'gaits', from the Scots word meaning 'way' or 'street', all converging on the Mercat Cross and Clachnacuddin Stone. Kirkgait, now Church Street, was originally the main thoroughfare of the town, leading from the Castle to the Parish Church; Briggait, or Bridge Gait, is now Bridge Street; Overgait (that is, 'Upper Way'), now Castle Street, was also sometimes called Dymisdale or Doomsdale, because it led to the town gallows; and Eastgait, later Hie Gait, now High Street.

In *The Place-Names of Roman Britain,* A L F Rivet and Colin Smith have some interesting things to say about the origins of the name 'Ness' for the river at the mouth of which Inverness is to be found. Possibly similar meanings are noted for the Nassogne river in Belgium, recorded in AD 690 as *Nassania fons;* and for two rivers with the name *Nestos,* one in Dalmatia and one in Thrace. The suggested Indo-European root is *ned-*, as in the Sanskrit *nadi,* 'river', German *nass,* 'wet', and Greek *noteo* 'am wet'. Clearly it is a very ancient name, far earlier than any of the thousands of Gaelic names in the landscape, or even than any of the dozens of Pictish place-names.

The Cameron Monument

A monument is not exactly a building, perhaps, but since there amazingly only two public monuments in Inverness, outside of the cemeteries, it seems fitting to describe them here. The more famous, and certainly the more photographed, is the monument to Flora MacDonald in front of the Castle, looking down the Great Glen for her Prince to appear, her faithful sheepdog at her side.

The other monument, which for most tourists will be the first one they see as they arrive by train from the south, is the Cameron Monument in Station Square, a Cameron Highlander 'in full regimentals' with a sphinx at his foot. The regiment served in Egypt in 1808, during the Napoleonic war, and again from 1882 to 1887, in Egypt and the Sudan. The base of the monument bears the names of the campaigns in capital letters: KHARTOUM, GINNISS, ATBARA, KOSHEH, and the famous TEL-EL-KEBIR, in which 15,000 British army troops attacked 38,000 Egyptian rebels, and carried the day, spearheaded by the Highland Brigade's attack on the 'enemy' trenches.

The Cameron Monument lists the names of seventy-seven men killed in battle or who died of their wounds, and of a further thirty who died of disease, in the Egyptian campaigns. The monument was unveiled on Friday 14th July 1893, by Lochiel, the Chief of the clan Cameron, in front of a large crowd of onlookers. It was erected by the 79th Queen's Own Cameron Highlanders in memory of their comrades who had died in the campaigns in Egypt and the Sudan, in 1882 and 1885. The ceremony coincided with the annual Wool Market, so the town was full of farmers from all corners of the Highlands, who, according to *The Northern Chronicle,*

swelled the numbers of the vast crowd of citizens who assembled to witness the unveiling of what has the additional distinction of being the first statue erected within the precincts of the burgh.

There had been some debate about where to site the statue: the site on the Castle Hill now occupied by Flora MacDonald was deemed appropriate by some, in view of the fact that it would have faced Lochaber, the ancestral home of the Camerons. Mr Wade, the sculptor, who could not be present at the ceremony, had favoured the location in station square, and in this opinion he was supported by Lochiel.

Lochiel's long speech was reported in full in the newspapers: in it he gives an interesting summary of the history of the regiment. Their entitlement to display the sphinx and the word 'Egypt' on their regimental colours derived from an earlier visit to that land during the Napoleonic campaigns. As he finished his speech

Lochiel then pulled the cord, and, after a slight hitch, which was soon rectified, the statue stood revealed. While this was being done, the soldiers presented arms, the band played the National Anthem, and a general cheer rose from the crowd.

Major Hunt, the officer commanding the company of Camerons in Station Square, moved a vote of thanks to Lochiel — 'which Lochiel acknowledged by lifting his bonnet, and the proceedings

The 'Auld Reekie' of the Highlands, 1930s.

terminated — not, however, before the scene had been photographed'.

Newspaper reports of the time often include references to photography at public events, and some of these photographs have survived. There are two archives of old photographs in Inverness. One, representing the efforts of Joseph Cook, is in the custody of the *Inverness Courier,* and for some years an example from the archive has been selected every week and discussed by a knowledgable local historian. The other, in the custody of the Highland Council, is the Whyte Collection, housed at the Old School at Clachnaharry. These two sources, though often irritatingly incomplete, provide an excellent window into the life of the past. Pictures from both collections have been published in book form over the years, most notably in Joseph Cook's *Inverness* (1992) and in the Inverness Field Club's *Old Inverness in Pictures* (1981), which also includes photographs from many other sources.

Flora MacDonald Statue

The other Inverness statue, that of Flora Macdonald, was unveiled six years after the Cameron Highlander, on Wednesday 26th July 1899. It was donated to the town by Captain J M Henderson Macdonald of the 28th Highlanders, who bequeathed the sum of £1,000 for the purpose. Mrs Fraser, his daughter, performed the ceremony on behalf of her late father. Captain Henderson had died in 1894; his wife survived him by only six months.

Several thousands of people witnessed the unveiling procedure.

The Provost, Town Council, Magistrates, Town Clerk and other officials, along with Mr and Mrs Fraser and their son Frank, marched in procession from the Town House to the Castle-hill. Provost Macbean made a speech, extolling the virtues of Flora Macdonald, and detailing her encounter with Bonnie Prince Charlie. The sculptor was Andrew Davidson of Inverness, whom the Provost described as:

> a sculptor born and brought up amongst us, whose genius is pronounced and undoubted — a work of art in bronze, of heroic size, of a typical Highland lassie looking anxiously and expectantly across the sea for the long-delayed boat that contained the fortunes of a Prince, whose future for weal or woe lay in her hand. (Cheers). And now, ladies and gentlemen, it remains for me to perform the pleasing duty of requesting Mrs Fraser, in your name and in the name of Celts scattered throughout the world, to unveil the statue of Flora Macdonald — a statue which is the result of the admiration of her late father, Captain Macdonald, for the Highland heroine. (Cheers.) I am sure that my request meets with your approval, and the approval of Highlanders at home and abroad. (Cheers.)
>
> After ascending the dais, Mrs Fraser pulled a cord, which released the cords that bound the white cloth in which the statue was enveloped. On seeing the statue for the first time the gathering raised loud cheers.

Thus the *Inverness Courier* reported another outstanding public ceremony. Flora stands there on the Castle-hill yet, photographed by hundreds of tourists every season, larger than life — she is nine feet in height, on a pedestal sixteen feet tall. But, behind the ceremonial was a certain amount of disagreement and petty manoeuvring which had preceded the unveiling. Two months before, a lath model of Flora was erected on the Castle-hill site, so that the Magistrates and Town Council could see how she would look. The model was positioned on the west corner of the Castle, and they did not like what they saw. It was moved down into the middle of the carriageway, but that did not look right either. It was put on the plot of grass at the head of the carriageway, but the worthies could not make up their minds. They moved across the river to Ardross Street, to look at a possible site there, and to see how the model in front of the Castle looked from the other side of the river.

In June the Town Council met, and decided, after some debate, to persist with the Castle-hill site. The Town Clerk informed them that they did not own the ground on which the statue was to stand,

Aerial view of the town in the 1930s, centred on the Chapel Yard; the Gasometer and the 'Destructor', which incinerated waste to produce electricity, are both now gone.

and that they would have to negotiate a deal with the County Council, who did. Final arrangements were worked out at a special meeting of the Town Council held on the Friday before the public ceremony. There was more bickering about whether the Council should provide a cake and wine banquet afterwards; it was decided that it was a waste of public money, and should be dispensed with, at least on this occasion. On the Monday the bronze statue was placed on its pedestal, and covered with a white sheet, which on Wednesday Mrs Fraser removed, no doubt unaware of the dissent behind the scenes.

The *Highland News* added in its report the additional information that:

> A cinematograph film of the procession moving to the esplanade and of the crowd after the unveiling of the statue was taken by Mr John Mackenzie, Inglis Street, and general photographs of the crowd were taken by nearly all our photographic artists.

The *Highland News* also added a short paragraph about other attempts to commemorate Flora Macdonald, ending with the hope that the present attempt would fare better than previous efforts. Apparently her son, over fifty years after her death, provided a

Looking across the Waterloo Bridge to the Merkinch and the Canal Basin, in an aerial photograph taken just before World War II.

thin marble slab for her grave at Kilmuir, Skye, but it was cracked while being unloaded on the beach. Despite being broken, it was placed on the grave, 'but in a few months every fragment of it was carried off by tourist vandals'. More recently, 'a costly granite monument in the form of an Iona cross was erected over her grave, but it also came to grief' — it blew over in a gale.

Inverness Bridges

Having dealt with the public statues of Inverness, it is perhaps worth discussing briefly the problem of the bridges of Inverness. At the time of the opening of the latest bridge across the Ness, the Friar's Bridge, in 1987, there was some talk in the local press about one of the prophecies of the Brahan Seer, to the effect that when the ninth bridge over the Ness was completed, something drastic would happen in the town.

Alexander Mackenzie first published *The prophecies of the Brahan Seer* in 1899, with more than a hint of millennialist foreboding. He drew on oral traditions, which he collected together from various sources, and on the small amount of printed material which others had produced over the years. Mackenzie quoted the 'prophecies' as best he could, and gave his own commentary and

Inverness town centre in the 1930s, showing the Suspension Bridge.

interpretations: his book was reprinted in 1970 and is easily available to the modern reader.

Unfortunately, his work does not bear very close scrutiny. Elizabeth Sutherland, in *Ravens and Black Rain*, showed that either Coinneach Odhar lived to be a very, very old man indeed, or else the 'prophecies' attributed to him were in fact either folk traditions from various sources, or actual prophecies and sayings by more than one person.

The prophecy concerning the bridges of Inverness is given (by Mackenzie) as follows:

> When two false teachers shall come across the seas who will revolutionise the religion of the land, and nine bridges shall span the river Ness, the Highlands will be overrun by ministers without grace and women without shame.

Alexander Mackenzie thought, in 1899, that this was 'a prediction which some maintain has all the appearance of being rapidly fulfilled at this moment'. Certainly there are plenty in Inverness today, one hundred years on, who would argue that there are far more 'ministers without grace' and 'women without shame' in the Highland fleshpots now than there ever were before! In Mackenzie's time it was suggested that the 'two false teachers' from overseas were none other but Moody and Sankey, the American evangelists; it is difficult to know who today's equivalents might be. Mackenzie calculated that the eighth bridge across the Ness had been completed the previous year, and that the ninth was nearing completion. He could not resist adding a few comments of his own:

> If we are to accept the opinions of certain of the clergy themselves, 'ministers without grace' are becoming the rule, and as for a plenitude of 'women without shame', ask any ancient matron, and she will at once tell you that Kenneth's prophecy may be held to have been fulfilled in that particular any time within the last half century. Gleidh sinne!!

Save us, indeed! Mackenzie's two exclamation marks do hint at a little ambiguity as to whether or not he really feared 'women without shame!!'

However, when we start to compile a list of all the known bridges over the river Ness, it appears that the prophecy may have been fulfilled some time ago, if at all:

1411 wooden bridge, 'the famousest and finest off oak in Brittain', destroyed by Donald of Harlaw

1620 replacement wooden bridge destroyed in flood.

1624 timber bridge built: it fell down in 1664 and was not replaced for twenty-one years.

1685 stone bridge of seven arches built, using stone from Cromwell's Fort.

1808 Black Bridge built, of timber (replaced 1896).

1829 bridge from Ness Bank to Ness Islands.

1834 bridge from Ness Islands to Bught. The stone bridge, and the two Ness Islands bridges, were all washed away in the great flood of 25th January 1849 (6.15 am).

1849 temporary wooden bridge constructed.

1853 one Ness Island bridge replaced.

1853 second Ness Island bridge replaced.

1855 main Suspension Bridge opened on 23rd August.

1863 Railway Bridge built: it collapsed in 1989.

1877 Infirmary Bridge built.

1882 Greig Street Bridge built.

1896 Waterloo Bridge opened, 26th February.

1939 contract for a new granite bridge: temporary wooden bridge built a few yards upstream.

1959 Suspension Bridge of 1855 closed; temporary bridge built.
1961 New concrete bridge opened on 28th September.
1982 Kessock Bridge opened in August — not over the river Ness, but included for completeness.
1987 Friar's Bridge opened.
1990 replacement railway bridge.

A total of twenty bridges, not counting the Kessock Bridge! Perhaps we are now safe from Coinneach Odhar's prophecies? Not counting replacement and temporary bridges, we have, with the dates of the current bridges in brackets: the Infirmary Bridge (1877), the Greig Street Bridge (1882), the Waterloo Bridge (1896), the main Ness Bridge (1961), Friar's Bridge (1987), the Railway Viaduct (1990)

Celebrating the Millennium

As the nineteenth century drew to a close the town took the opportunity to welcome the advent of the twentieth century. Its arrival was celebrated in some style, and there was no nonsense about when the new millennium began — January 1st 1900 passed unnoticed, and the new century was welcomed on January 1st 1901. The weather was mild, with no frost or snow, and hundreds of people, mostly young, many of them children, filled the streets around the steeple of the old tolbooth on Bridge Street. The *Courier* disapproved of some aspects of the celebrations, but was prepared to make allowances, in view of the exceptional circumstances. They complained about the 'immense number of boys and girls who swelled the throng', and went on to note that:

> Another unpleasant feature of the lively scene was the too palpable proof of over-indulgence in intoxicating drink. Civil and military police paraded the streets, but we dare say took a more lenient view of their duty than they usually do. Fireworks were thrown into the air on all hands, and it seemed surprising that no injury was inflicted by the falling lights on persons in the crowd. All were in good humour, and although the noise and din prevented many from hearing the strokes of the steeple clock, the drum clock in Bridge Street showed that the year and the century had gone, and hands were shaken and greetings for the new year cordially exchanged. The bustle and the fireworks were both kept agoing for some time after midnight, and there were displays of lime-lights at different point, the one at the west end of the Suspension Bridge beautifully illuminating the Castle and the river. Rockets were sent up here and elsewhere.

Elsewhere in the town many of the churches held religious services on the stroke of midnight. There was a large attendance at the Methodist Church, and in St John's Episcopal Church. St Mary's Roman Catholic Church was full, and the Salvation Army held a service in the Music Hall. Afterwards, they organised a torchlight procession through the streets of the town centre, singing hymns as they went. The *Courier* noted regretfully that 'their reception by the crowd was not wholly sympathetic'. In their issue published on Tuesday 1st January 1901, the first day of the new century, they reported on the midnight festivities and announced the public arrangements for the day to come:

> To-day being the first day of a new century, the Provost, Magistrates, and Town Council have arranged that a united religious service will be held in the Town Hall, beginning at 11 a.m...The usual charitable entertainments will be given in the different institutions, and a football match between the Partick Thistle and Clachnacuddin teams will be played in the afternoon. There will be performances of the pantomime in the afternoon and at night.

An editorial on the 4th of January took time to reflect on the excesses witnessed three days before:

> There are those who think that the nation is hurrying to ruin along the slippery path of drink. It is unfortunately true that the noisy witnesses of much hard drinking were to be met in our own streets in large numbers. Men of all ages and some women were unmistakeably under the influence of liquor...The public opinion of the present day emphatically is that there is no credit in being, or having been, intoxicated. A staggering man is a painful sight...There is much to deplore in the spectacles too often to be seen on the streets of all our towns, but the growth of opinion is adverse to its existence. This is something to be thankful for, and cannot be without effect.

The Editor hoped that a measure of optimism for the prospects of Britain in the new century would not be misplaced:

> The spirit by which our Empire has been built up is the spirit by which it must be maintained. Whatever the new century may have in store, we trust we shall not depart from the principles which have yielded such results in the past, and which have thereby proved themselves to be the true foundation of Empire.

Meanwhile, in the Poorhouse, the inmates were entertained to dinner by the Parish Council. Bailie Sinclair sent a large bun for the inmates, whose numbers suddenly swelled for the day to over one hundred, while Messrs Macdonald and Mackintosh donated a supply of oranges, and Mr George Gallon sent apples. On the previous Saturday night, inmates and visitors at the Cottage Home, Charles Street were treated to an evening's entertainment, with Mr Mackenzie's cinematograph, musical accompaniments, and with 'the gramophone making a pleasant variety in the evening's enjoyment'. The football match at noon on New Year's Day was scrappy, with Clachnacuddin prevailing over their Glasgow opponents by four goals to three. And Donald McCuish, a cattle-man, a native of North Uist, was found drowned in the Caledonian Canal. He was about sixty years of age, a widower, without any family, and 'travelled about a good deal'.

Death of Queen Victoria

Then, only three weeks later, the nation's mood of celebration for the new century changed to one of mourning for the death of the monarch who had, since 1837, been the symbolic cornerstone of the British Empire. Queen Victoria died at her home at Osborne, on the Isle of Wight, on 22nd January 1901, and for days and weeks thereafter the country's entire energies seemed to be absorbed with the consequences. Kenneth Macdonald, the Town Clerk of Inverness, inserted a public notice in the *Courier* of Friday 25th January announcing the civic arrangements for the Proclamation of King Edward VII at the Cross at noon:

> Deputy Lieutenants of the County, Justices of the Peace, Officers of the Regular and Auxiliary Forces (in uniform), and Persons holding Official Positions under the Crown or under the Burgh or County, are invited to meet in the Town Hall, at 11.30 forenoon.

Underneath this official announcement on the front page of the Courier a local entrepreneur inserted a notice of his own:

THE QUEEN'S DEATH
THE DRAPING OF PULPITS,
PUBLIC BUILDINGS, &c.
MESSRS A. FRASER & COY.,
HOUSE FURNISHERS,
UNION STREET, INVERNESS,
Having a LARGE STOCK of MATERIAL on hand
will undertake Town and Country Orders.
TELEGRAMS - FRASER, UPHOLSTERERS, INVERNESS.

THE LIFE AND TIMES OF INVERNESS

The flag over the Town Hall flew at half-mast, the Longman Battery fired a royal salute, a guard of honour of one hundred men paraded at the Cross, the Proclamation was read by Sheriff Grant, standing on the Clachnacuddin stone, and Provost Macbean called for 'three hearty Highland cheers for the King'. The printed Proclamation was then duly posted on the Town Cross. The Editor of the *Courier* struggled to find the right words to express the feelings of the community:

> The long and gracious reign of Queen Victoria has come to an end. The Sovereign lady whose character shone with growing lustre throughout so many eventful years has passed from earth to her eternal home. The world moves so rapidly that already, two days after her departure, the sad event seems remote. The Proclamation of the new Sovereign has awakened fresh feelings and interests, and the thoughts of men are gradually turning to the future. But the past cannot be forgotten, and the light of such a life as the Queen lived, placed on a pinnacle of greatness before mankind, will not soon lose its splendour. It will never indeed fade from the memory of the nation, but will remain as one of its most fondly cherished possessions…The character of the Queen has done much to unite the peoples that form the British Empire. She has made the link of the Crown a real and effective bond, not only among English-speaking races, but among all the races that owned her sway. In Scotland we cannot forget how she understood the people, how she loved them and trusted herself among them, and how she touched their hearts. The Highlands and Highlanders had a peculiarly warm place in her affections…She stood forth as an example of enlightened Christian faith, as one who ruled her own home with love and firmness, who kept her Court pure, who realised the responsibilities of her lofty station, and walked in the fear of God. The manifold blessings of Queen Victoria's reign can hardly yet be computed, but she was loved and honoured in her lifetime, and her name will be remembered with reverence.

One hundred years later, it is difficult to relate to these sentiments, given the difficulties encountered by the Royal House of Windsor in the meantime. The pages of the *Courier* were filled for days with accounts of the Queen's life, of events in London and other towns and cities throughout Britain, and detailed descriptions of the public observances in Inverness. Unusually the newspaper even included illustrations: of the Queen as a young widow, of the Queen's apartments at Osborne, and of Her Majesty in later life. During the period of mourning, the columns of the paper were separated by thick black lines.

144

In Inverness, public life came to a standstill. The news had arrived in the town by telegraph, and immediately the Town Clerk sent word to the bell-ringers of all the churches:

> The news was quickly spread in the dark night by the solemn strokes of the bells of the Old Steeple. The notes of the United Free High Church bell were soon joined by those of the High Church, the West Church, and the Cathedral, and, in little time, all knew that the end of a great and glorious reign had come.

Provost Macbean send a telegram of condolence to the Secretary of State for Scotland in Whitehall, and preparations were made for commemorative services. The funeral took place in London on 2nd February: Mr T A Wilson, General Manager of the Highland Railway, inserted a notice in the local papers to intimate that 'all Trains on the Highland Railway will be Stopped from 2.30 pm for Ten Minutes'. All the churches held memorial services to coincide with the Queen's funeral, with the Provost, Town Council and civic dignitaries attending the one in the High Church.

The day of the funeral was observed as a fast day in Inverness, and all places of business were closed, including all licensed houses and restaurants, except for the refreshment rooms at the railway station. The *Courier* was pleased to note that 'although there were many people perambulating the streets, good order prevailed'. Many people wore black clothes, and many buildings and businesses in the town were draped in black or purple cloth. In private houses the blinds were drawn. The church services were well-attended, with people standing in the aisles. The 'official' service in the High Church was filled to overflowing; there was a prevailing sense of national unity. All of this was fully reported, with thick black columnar lines, in the local press.

The Highlands in Mourning

And then, within days, the Highlands buried two of its own leading figures: the Rev Dr Stewart — who wrote extensively on Highland history under the pseudonym 'Nether-Lochaber', and Charles Fraser-Mackintosh, perhaps the finest local historian Inverness ever produced. 'Nether-Lochaber' had been writing for the *Courier* since 1859, and was well-known throughout the Highlands, while Charles Fraser-Mackintosh, member of the Napier Commission on crofting, and MP for both the County of Inverness and for the Inverness Burghs, had been a leading figure in local affairs all his working life.

Two years later, in July 1903, the community had recovered its enthusiasm and was preparing for two important events: the opening of the Highland and Jacobite Exhibition in the Free Library Buildings; and on the same day, a ceremony in the Town House conferring the Freedom of the Burgh on two of the most important men in the Highlands, with Jacobite pedigrees of varying success— Lochiel and Lovat.

Highland and Jacobite Exhibition, 1903

The speeches by Provost Ross, Lochiel and Lovat were reported in full detail in the *Inverness Courier* for July 17th 1903, and still make for interesting reading. The Exhibition was opened by Lochiel, and his speech on 'Jacobite Sentiment' in the Highlands was well received. Timed to coincide with the tourist season, the Highland and Jacobite Exhibition was a tremendous success. In the first nine days, 2,500 visitors had passed through the doors and £120 had been made from ticket sales and from the sale of catalogues — one of which still survives in Inverness Library. The atmosphere was enhanced by the efforts of the String Band, a group of Glasgow instrumentalists who presented a different programme every day.

It was a busy summer in Inverness. Late in July the Invergarry and Fort Augustus Railway finally opened, bringing yet more tourists into the town. By the end of the month 3,300 had seen the Exhibition, to which more Jacobite memorabilia was being added almost daily. Evening sessions for townspeople were popular: the admission price was 6d after seven o'clock, compared to the daytime price of one shilling. In August, Lord Roberts, Commander-in-Chief of the British Army, visited Fort George and Culloden Battlefield, where he was photographed on top of the Cumberland Stone. He dined in Inverness that evening, but the *Courier* does not tell us that he visited the Jacobite Exhibition.

By the beginning of September 12,000 visitors to the Exhibition were estimated, and earnings amounted to £501. It closed at the end of the month, just as the 12th Annual Mod was opening; the final accounting showed a total of 17,060 paying visitors. To this were added sundry extras: Orphanage children, inmates of the Blind Institution, Opening Day invited guests, Mod competitors, and season ticket holders, making a total attendance, according to the organisers, of 20,551, producing a total income of £777 —

'and a few more pounds are still to come in'. It had been an outstanding success: it was suggested that the anticipated surplus should be used to establish a permanent exhibition of Jacobite memorabilia in Inverness.

At the closing ceremony, Mr Leslie Fraser, convener of the Musical Committee, raised a laugh at the expense of the band by suggesting that perhaps they might have appeared in Highland Dress. When he had mentioned this to Mr Turner, the double-bass player, he had replied 'that he would have to play from the inside of the double bass instead of the outside if he donned the kilt'.

Inverness Maps

One of the best ways of seeing how the townscape of Inverness has changed over the years is by studying old maps of the town. The very earliest maps are not of a large enough scale to show very much detail of the town centre, though Timothy Pont's manuscript map of the 1580s does show, in miniature, the castle, bridge, church, monastery and streets. The Blaeu map of 1654 can be used to illustrate the fact that areas now considered part of Inverness are depicted as villages well outside the core of the town, and the map of the area compiled by the Board of Ordnance around 1750 can be used in a similar way. More useful is William Roy's *Military Survey of Scotland,* 1747–54, at the scale of one inch to one thousand yards.

Roy's map was intended as a military document, to be used in the event of further disturbances in the Highlands, in the aftermath of Culloden. It covers the whole of the mainland of Scotland. The army engineers who made this map are said to have been quartered in Balnain House during their stay in Inverness. The depiction of the Inverness area is sufficiently detailed to show the streets and built-up areas of the town, though in the town centre, not individual buildings. Roy's map exists only in manuscript form, and the original is held in the British Library Map Room, in London, from where photographic reproductions can be obtained. Highland Archives have this invaluable local history source in the form of 35mm colour slides, which can be consulted on the premises at Farraline Park, though reproductions are not possible.

The first large-scale map of any real use is John Hume's plan of Inverness, published in 1774. It shows streets, houses and property boundaries, with a note of property owners. It is the only large-scale map of Inverness before the Caledonian Canal transformed the landscape. John Wood's 1821 plan of Inverness is also extremely interesting and useful in historical research, though it covers a smaller area than Hume's map; showing only the area from Cromwell's Fort in the north to the recently opened Northern Infirmary in the south, with a smaller scale insert showing Clachnaharry, Muirtown and Merkinch.

After that, the map published with a volume on the boundaries of burghs prepared in connection with the creation of parliamentary electoral divisions in 1832 is of interest. From then until the advent of the Ordnance Survey in the 1860s, there are no large-scale printed maps of Inverness. However, when the Ordnance Survey arrived, they produced maps of such accuracy and quality that they can answer almost any question about streets and buildings in the last half of the nineteenth century. The first edition of the 6 inches to one mile map was published in the 1860s, and then in the early years of the twentieth century a second edition was published. A version of this survey at the scale of 25 inches to one mile was also prepared, for the town of Inverness and adjacent populated areas only.

Census Records

From the last years of the nineteenth century onwards we can consult valuation rolls for Inverness, showing property values, proprietors and tenants, and for many buildings the house plans prepared for the Dean of Guild Court have survived in the Highland archives. Using the records of the Enumerated Census it is possible to find out who was actually occupying a property, on the night of the decennial census. Every ten years, from 1841 to 1891, these records are available — there is a complete set on microfilm in Inverness Library. The Census records for 1901 will become available to researchers in the year 2001 — there is a hundred year ban on access, for reasons of confidentiality.

Using all these sources, and what can be gleaned from newspapers and printed books, it is possible to built up a very detailed picture of what life was like in Inverness. The Census records reveal overcrowding and high mobility of the population, while the valuation rolls and Dean of Guild plans can give the detailed history of a building. Unfortunately, and inevitably, there are gaps in these records.

The episcopal cathedral, with the hill of Tomnahurich behind.

In the last years of the nineteenth century Inverness began to expand, and new housing estates developed on the edges of the town. The first of these was on the Barnhill — what is now known as The Hill, and Crown districts of the town. Empty fields were subdivided, or feued, and sold off to property developers and builders, in a process which has continued, interrupted only by wartime, to the present day. The study of the streets and buildings of Inverness is a fascinating topic, made more interesting when one can find out information about the house one is currently living in. There is an abundance of material: all that is needed to turn it into fascinating history is time, and patience.

CHAPTER 9

INVERNESS IN THE 20TH CENTURY, 1900–1950

The men and women of Inverness fought for their country or served their country in two world wars in this century at great cost, as can be seen from the hundreds of names on the town's War Memorial in Cavell Gardens — named after the nurse who was shot as a spy by the Germans while serving in Belgium. Public life was affected during the war years, and public entertainments curtailed.

Votes for Women?

A topic which interested at least half the population of Inverness in the first years of the twentieth century was women's suffrage— votes for women. We think today of the militant wing of this struggle — the suffragettes — as a group of proto-feminist, radical, usually privileged females, who chained themselves to railings and threw themselves in front of racehorses. This is a gross over-simplification, and ignores a long tradition of campaigning for women's suffrage, even in places thought by the metropolitan leaders of this movement to be remote and marginal.

For example, in 1871, fully thirty-five years before the issue hit the national headlines, Miss Jane Taylour of Belmont, near Stranraer, addressed a meeting in the Inverness Music Hall, on a wet, Thursday evening, advocating the right of women ratepayers to be included in the electoral franchise. It should be remembered that at this time, the franchise for the male population was limited to ratepayers — the 'universal' franchise for either men or women was considered too revolutionary and destabilising a concept to risk, in the prevailing social and political climate of late-Victorian Britain.

The meeting was well attended, despite the inclement weather. Bailie Simpson, taking the chair in the absence of the Provost, made it clear that while he did not agree with the proposition that women should be admitted to the franchise, even in a limited way, he was prepared to accept that Miss Taylour had substantial support. The *Inverness Courier* reported, in September 1871, that

The War Memorial, Cavell Gardens.

Bailie Simpson 'had listened to her address with pleasure as a fine exhibition of womanly spirit'. Before we cringe too much at this patronising comment, we have also to consider that Miss Taylour's argument for the extension of the franchise to women seems equally suspect, seen from the perspective of our politically correct age:

> Miss Taylour maintained that elections should be so conducted as to prevent annoyance and persecution; that the position of woman was to be a helpmeet for men, and that society was best and purest when men and women mingled on terms of equality.

The Rev Mr Robson of Ardross Street argued that 'he could not see the justice of a law which would refuse to give a vote to a woman like the Baroness Burdett Coutts, and would give that vote to her coachman if he only possessed a house of a certain value'.

In September 1909, the suffrage superstar, Mrs Emmeline Pankhurst, visited Inverness. The Inverness organiser for the women's suffrage movement was Helen Fraser, and the local President of the Inverness Women's Suffrage Society was Mrs Hunter; their branch was affiliated to the Scottish Women's Suffrage Society. There was a North of Scotland Federation, with societies in Inverness, Elgin, Lossiemouth, Nairn, Forres, Beauly and Fortrose.

Mrs Pankhurst addressed a large audience in the Music Hall, speaking for more than an hour. The *Inverness Courier,* reporting the meeting in its issue of 10th September 1909, was impressed:

> her easy command of language and effective diction, in a speech that covered the whole question as it now stands, held the appreciative attention of the meeting, and many of her strokes against the feckless male legislature were warmly applauded.

Mrs Pankhurst returned to Inverness in the following year, in pursuit of the cause of women's suffrage. Her activities, both on the national stage and on her Scottish tours, were reported in detail by the *Inverness Courier.* The editor, James Barron, was an active Liberal Unionist; that is, he supported the Tory oppostion to the government of the day, and was anti-suffragist. However, both his wife and daughter were active in the Inverness Women's Suffrage Society, and perhaps this is why the subject is treated so fully in the pages of his newspaper. After Mrs Barron died, aged 62, in November 1912, the editor ceased to report on suffrage activities for a while. The Burgh MP, J Annan Bryce, like James Barron, was opposed to the Conciliation Bill — an extremely weak and excessively moderate attempt by the Liberal government to defuse militant suffrage campaigning — and had his moment of glory in the House of Commons when he seconded an opposition amendment effectively killing the bill for that session. Like Barron, his wife and daughter were pro-suffrage.

So, this issue divided households in Inverness, as elsewhere. On the outbreak of war in August 1914, the suffrage campaign ceased, though the issue continued to be debated. In March 1910 the Inverness Women's Suffrage Society held its first annual meeting; by then it had attracted 188 members. Some research on the activities of suffragists in Inverness is held on file in Inverness Library, though much remains to be done: it would make an interesting project for a modern woman interested in the radical roots of feminism before the First World War.

Nessie-Watching

In the 1930s Inverness and Loch Ness hit the headlines nationally because of a spate of newspaper stories about the Loch Ness Monster. Although it is often said that the first recorded sighting of Nessie was the one referred to in Chapter One, by St Columba and his entourage in the sixth century, it was not until the tourist boom of the 1930s, and the sterling work of the *Inverness Courier*, that the putative monster of Loch Ness impinged upon the national consciousness.

Perhaps the article which appeared in the *Courier* of 2nd May 1933 — 'Strange Spectacle on Loch Ness: What was it?' — might have passed unnoticed as a quirky little story in a provincial newspaper, had it not been for the interest of the national press, and perhaps most of all, the espousal of the cause by the local Member of Parliament, Sir Murdoch Macdonald. Indeed, the original story in the *Courier* referred to the fact that 'a few years ago' a party of Inverness anglers had encountered something in the loch — 'either a very large seal, a porpoise, or, indeed, the monster itself!' The story, apparently, had received 'scant attention and less credence' at the time, although reported in the press.

This time, however, Nessie received better publicity. Alarmed by the prospect of national papers offering rewards for her capture, dead or alive, Sir Murdoch wrote in December 1933 to the Secretary of State for Scotland, and received assurances that he had been in touch with the Chief Constable, who had stationed constables at five points around the loch — though none of them had, as yet, seen the monster.

Then, in the summer of 1934, a stroke of luck for Nessie — a sighting by none other than Sir Murdoch Macdonald, MP himself. His letter in the *Courier* of 14th August is bursting with his excitement:

> Sir: I informed you by 'phone on Thursday last that I had had an unusual experience while passing along Loch Ness on the previous morning, Wednesday 8th August...At 6.45 a.m. my son and I were within four miles of Glenmoriston. He was driving and I was naturally keeping an eye on the loch in case I should have the privilege of seeing the famous Monster.

And see it he did! Two hundred and fifty yards from the shore he noticed an object floating in the water, in unusually calm conditions — the hills of the opposite shore were reflected in the water. And what did he see?:

> What we saw was two hummocks, each about equal length and separated by a space equal to about each of them, the whole being, I should estimate, about fifteen feet long.

His son noticed that it seemed to be moving slowly in the direction of Fort Augustus. They wakened a caravaner and borrowed his

Station Square, guarded by a Cameron Highlander.

binoculars, but in the end had to continue on their way without absolute proof of what they had seen. Their destination had been Portree, where they were to meet the Secretary of State for Scotland for a discussion on harbours, piers and ferries, so no doubt when they arrived at their meeting they would have taken the opportunity to reinforce the necessity to ensure that Nessie was fully protected.

In November 1950 the national *Daily Herald* ran a story about Nessie, claiming that the sightings could be explained as Admiralty mines laid in 1918. The *Inverness Courier* was unimpressed, reporting the gist of the story but adding that it was 'patently absurd' and that it 'certainly failed to take-in any readers in the Highlands, where it has instead aroused great mirth'. It appears that the *Daily Herald* was 'spoofed' by naval 'experts', as it was claimed that soundings had been taken in Loch Ness to a depth of seven miles. The true depth, said the *Courier*, was more like 754 feet.

Over the years there have been many more sightings, and many more stories in the newspapers. They do tend to coincide with the onset of the tourist season, and at least the local tourist authority is honest enough to feature Nessie as part of its logo. One or two local 'sightings' have seemed to be fortuitously linked to fairly blatant attempts to cash in on the interest of the national

The north side of Station Square, once the head office of the Highland Railway Company.

press, at times when little else was happening in the newsrooms.

However, Columba and Sir Murdoch Macdonald are not the only two Highlanders to be sure that they have had a genuine sighting of something not easily explained, and the search goes on, conducted both scientifically and otherwise. It is now even possible to find Nessie on the Internet, lurking in the depths of cyberspace!

Second World War

Inverness during the years of the Second World War, 1939–45, was an extremely busy place. North and west of the Great Glen was a Prohibited Area, used for training of commandos and army units, while the sea-lochs and island anchorages were used for assembling convoys. Life was restricted, and difficult. It was difficult to get information about what was happening in the war, in Britain or overseas, because of censorship. Nevertheless, a reading of the local newspapers for the war years reveals much of interest and gives many insights into the way of life, and the many changes that were taking place.

The main contribution of Inverness to the war effort was the involvement of AI Welders in the PLUTO project, without which the D-Day landings on the coast of Normandy in June 1944 would not have been possible. PLUTO, standing for Pipe Line Under The Ocean, was the means by which fuel was carried across the Channel to supply the armed forces fighting to liberate Europe.

The story of AI Welders is soon to be published, and wartime Inverness has been comprehensively chronicled by Mr Harry Benyon, in an outstanding piece of work combining personal interviews and newspaper research, as yet shamefully unpublished, but available in typescript. An excellent production from the School Library Resource Centre on *Inverness During the Second World War* combines newspaper extracts, advertisements, photographs and personal memories.

'Bomb Explosion in Inverness'

In May 1946 the legacy of war was brought home forcefully and explosively to Invernessians when one boy was killed and seven seriously injured when they discovered a bomb in Kingsmills Park, home of Inverness Thistle Football Club. The park had been occupied by the army during the war, and had been vacated a week or two before by a Polish Army Pioneer unit. But as a non-combative unit there was no reason why they should have been in possession of an unexploded mortar bomb. Some speculated that it had been found on a rubbish heap, perhaps abandoned there by one of the army units who had occupied the huts in Kingsmills Park earlier in the war.

The incident took place on the evening of Sunday 19th May, 1946. It had been a hot, sunny day, and one local householder, when interviewed by the *Inverness Courier,* knew from the sound effects that a bomb had exploded, but he thought it had been set off by the heat of the sun. As ambulances arrived and crowds gathered, it became clear that a tragedy had occured.

The ensuing public enquiry got under way at the Sheriff Court in Inverness on June 27th, ironically reported in the *Courier* on the same day as an account of an atom bomb test at Bikini Atoll. In the course of the evidence presented by twenty-five witnesses it became clear that the bomb had been found some weeks before the accident by an eight-year-old boy. It had been in a ditch in the Thistle park, possibly a trench dug by one of the units which had been stationed at the ground. All of the children questioned, including those seriously injured, knew that it was a bomb, and that it was dangerous. The child who had found the bomb had

Flora Macdonald, looking down the Great Glen from the Castle Hill, watching out for her Prince.

taken it home to his mother, but she had told him to get rid of it, and he had taken it back to the park, and he and a friend had given it to a Polish soldier, who put it in a waste basket, and forgot about it. Various other adults knew of its existence, but nobody thought to report it, and when the Polish unit left, the bomb was left behind, still in the waste basket. The boy who was killed, who was thirteen years old, had known it might be dangerous, but, thinking it was a dummy, had dismantled it, with fatal results.

In giving his findings, Sheriff Grant congratulated those who had administered first aid to the casualties, but bemoaned 'the widespread lack of any proper feeling of responsibility to take active steps to prevent accidents'. He found that the only persons who had acted correctly were the two boys who had handed the mortar bomb to the nearest available soldier, a Polish sergeant, and that the Polish unit were primarily to blame for what had happened, with secondary responsibility attributed to the military and civil representatives of the Deputy Commander, Royal Engineers, for failing to dispose of the bomb in a proper manner and for permitting access by the children to the park.

In the course of the evidence to the public enquiry a list of the units which had occupied Kingsmills Park was given, which is of some interest now:

Feb 11 1941–Oct 9 1942:   6th Battalion, Cameron Highlanders
Oct 9 1942–12 June 1943: R.E.M.E.

The statue of Flora Macdonald, in front of the castellated courthouse on the Castle Hill.

12 June 1943–4 Dec 1943:   637 Coy, R.A.S.C.
4 Dec 1943–17 Aug 1945:   42nd Fire Fighting Unit
17 Aug 1945–Nov 1945:   Camp Commandant, Highland District
3 Jan 1946–1 Feb 1946:   172 Corps Military Police
2 Feb 1946–7 May 1946:   17th Polish Construction Coy

From 7th May until the day of the accident (19th May) the park was unoccupied. Army representatives testified that only the Cameron Highlanders would have had live ammunition.

American Influence?

A more frivolous effect of the war was highlighted in a letter published in the *Inverness Courier* on 27th September 1946. The writer, signing himself as an anonymous 'Highlander', complained bitterly about the dancing of reels and country dances at public dances in the Inverness area. Or to be quite accurate, he was complaining about the way in which the dances were being performed:

> They are nothing less than shambles, and the noise defies description. It seems that the striking up of the music is the signal for everyone on the floor, male or female, to open their mouths wide and yell at the tops of their voices.

He had been standing next to the band at one dance, and they had been almost completely drowned out by the noise. All enjoyment had gone, and dances had become a 'free for all and devil take the hindmost'. And who was to blame for this decline of standards, this 'extraordinary behaviour?' There seemed an obvious source:

> Can it be a legacy from our friends across the Atlantic, who, ever eager to attempt a reel, have made up in noise for their lack of skill with their feet? If so, it is high time that we rid ourselves of their pernicious influence and ceased to give such a noisy display of bad manners when engaged in our own national dances.

While accepting that the occasional 'hooch' was an essential part of proceedings, our 'Highlander' complained that

> 'hooching' is an art in itself, and the strange animal noises which issue from the throats of the present-day exponents of the reel cannot be identified with such a term. Apart from destroying all pleasure which some of us take in dancing reels, these performances must make our visitors wonder if they have not come into a strange zoo or madhouse...

He suspected that the dancers were using the power of their lungs to disguise their own ignorance of how a reel should be properly danced, and noted that the pernicious influences complained of were not confined to Inverness:

> a recent broadcast of country dances from a Masonic Ball at Crieff was marred by exactly the same type of 'noises off'. Cannot we in Inverness give a lead to the rest of Scotland by ceasing from employing these jitterbug tactics, and giving back to our own national dances the dignity and expertness which is their due?

It is humbling to observe that essentially the same letter could re-emerge into the columns of our local newspapers next week, or indeed, that it expresses sentiments which have been expounded in exactly the same terms by the 'older generation' at any time in the last fifty years!

Could it have been displays of public disorder of this kind which the Town Council had in mind when they agreed to the purchase of a 'Black Maria' van for the police. the Burgh Treasurer objected, arguing that 'Inverness had not fallen so low that a van was needed to pull in the drunks. However, the Dean of Guild thought that 'it was a bad advertisement for the town when arrested people were dragged 400 yards through the streets by the police'. It gave visitors a bad impression of the town, and it was far better that they should be taken in a covered van. So, the Council decided, by 12 votes to 7, to acquire a suitable police van.

Food Rationing

Another way in which traditional Highland culture was being challenged in post-war Inverness was in the government's decision to include oatmeal in its rationing programme. Britain was desperately short of cereal crops, and rationing, which had been introduced during the war in the face of desperate shortages, was to continue as a pervasive fact of life well into the 1950s.

When the decision to ration oatmeal was announced, in mid-July 1946, the War Time Emergency Committee of the Inverness Grocers' Association sent an urgent telegram to the Minister of Food, Mr John Strachey:

> Inverness Grocers' Association extremely disturbed at threat to put Oatmeal under points scheme. This is staple food of hundreds living in remote glens who derive no benefit from restaurants, fish and fruit or vegetable allocations. Sausages and cooked meats available to town dwellers. Please consider excluding North from this restriction.

But the government did not relent, at least, not regarding oatmeal. Mealy puddings also suffered the same fate. Haggis, however, remained unrationed, and Dr Edith Summerskill, Parliamentary Secretary at the Ministry of Food, felt compelled to explain the distinction:

> I must point out that this decision was not to prevent an uprising in Scotland but because haggis contains the heart, lungs and liver of a sheep, chopped up with suet, onion and oatmeal, while mealy puddings contain oatmeal and fat, and so rate as flour confectionery.

The Inverness MP, Sir Murdoch Macdonald, did manage to wring some concessions for farm workers out of the Ministry of Food. It was permitted for farmers to continue to give their employees oatmeal as a supplement to their wages. People living in remote areas would be allowed to buy oatmeal in bulk, and they would be allowed to grind it for domestic use; there were, however, strict prohibitions about feeding it to animals.

Part of the frustration of these arrangements was that in post-war Britain there was, in other ways, a release from the austerity of war-time. While it is true that many local people, particularly ex-servicemen, were living in difficult circumstances, especially due to the shortage of housing, it is nevertheless the case that, for some people at least, post-war prosperity was beginning to become something to be enjoyed. Adverts in the local papers confirm that there was money about, for buying furs, or Ford

Flora Macdonald on her pedestal.

motor cars: in the summer of 1946 the middle classes were being invited to purchase a new Ford Prefect (10 hp) or Anglia (8 hp)— 'roomy enough to carry a family — and luggage — in comfort, their reliability, petrol economy and low maintenance cost make these cars ideal for holiday journeys'. But, even if you had the money to spend on a new car, you might have to wait: 'Your Ford dealer is doing his best with deliveries, so please be patient'.

Air Services

Invernessians with money, but unable to take delivery of a new car, could have started their holiday by travelling with Scottish Airways Limited, who on Monday October 7th 1946 announced the commencement of a new air service linking Aberdeen, Inverness and Stornoway. The future of aviation in the Highlands was something else for the Town Council to consider, and in December 1946 they put on record their strong support for the Longman Aerodrome to become the main airport for Inverness, rather than the RAF aerodrome at Dalcross. It was noted that the Longman aerodrome was within walking distance of the town, and so more convenient for business people, but they also wanted Dalcross to be used for landings 'if required and if available'.

Transport Services

Ordinary Invernessians, with less money to spend and little holiday leave to enjoy, would have welcomed the opportunity to take advantage of special transport arrangements for the mid-summer holiday, which in 1946 was observed on Monday 8th July. The *Inverness Courier* reported that 'offices and places of business (with the exception of public houses) were closed. Many people made a holiday weekend of it, departing in large numbers from the town for various destinations. The weather, it was said, 'was very propitious for holiday-making, and Inverness may be said to have been en fete, so many people left town'. The railway company, LMS, reported that they had carried nearly 5,000 passengers and that between two and three thousand had travelled by bus, in Alexander's coaches. Nevertheless, the streets of Inverness were busy over the weekend, 'for a large number of strangers were observed in Inverness and the neighbourhood'.

The location of a future bus station for Inverness exercised the Town Council in the summer of 1946 — should Farraline Park be a bus station? The Chief Constable thought it was an excellent idea, and would relieve congestion in the town centre. The proposal was to turn the buildings now occupied by the Public Library into offices for the bus company — originally built as Bell's School. The propect of income from the use of the land by bus companies was appealing, but the Council decided to postpone a decision until they could find out exactly what revenue and expenditure was involved.

A Visiting Golfer

Inverness golfers were glad to reclaim the Culcabock golf course in the summer of 1946 — five holes had been dug up and cultivated during the war. Their restoration was celebrated in July 1946 by a special exhibition match between Joe Kirkwood, 'the famous golfer from America', and the local professional, Tom Ainslie. Kirkwood duly won the match, and entertained the spectators with some of his trick shots, using strange and unusual clubs. One had a club head 'as big as a football'.

Why Joe Kirkwood? It transpired that his father was from Inverness, and had emigrated to Australia, where Joe Kirkwood was born. He had moved to America, and taken up American citizenship, because there were more opportunities there to employ and improve his golfing skills.

Squatters

Housing shortages were a big problem in post-war Britain, and in this regard Inverness was no exception. Ex-servicemen, especially those who had been wounded and disabled, were particularly aggrieved, and matters came to a head in the summer of 1946, in Inverness as in many other parts of the country. The principle manifestation of discontent was 'squatters' who occupied former War Department huts and buildings. About forty-one families in Inverness occupied sites at the Longman Aerodrome, Raigmore Wood, Annfield Road, Porterfield Road, and Muirtown. All were ex-servicemen. The largest 'squatter' colony was at the Longman site, where twenty families moved into huts recently vacated by the Air Ministry. Sanitary conditions there were poor.

At Raigmore, at the end of August, six families moved into huts owned by the Air Ministry, empty since November 1945, including ten children ranging in ages from fifteen months to nine years. One of the families had been waiting for a house for nine years. Not all of the empty huts were occupied at once, and some wrote their names and addresses on notices which were pinned to the doors, to reserve huts for future occupancy. One of the Porterfield huts was occupied by a family who had been living in a tent in the Haugh district because they could not get a house of their own from the Council.

The 'squatters' attracted a lot of sympathy throughout the town. Many thought that empty huts should have been used long before as a temporary remedy during the housing shortage, and Council employees were offered to make some of the huts more habitable, by connecting lighting and improving sanitation arrangements. Many of the 'squatters' let it be known that they were willing to pay rent, and they hoped that they would be allowed to stay, and that the government would find some way to legalise their position.

Housing Policy

Two years later they were still there. In December 1948, just before Christmas, the Secretary of State for Scotland was successful in getting eviction orders against six of the Raigmore 'squatters'. Meanwhile, the Town Council had been addressing the problem of housing and had made a start on two new housing 'schemes', at Dalneigh and Hilton. The Dalneigh Housing Site was the first to be started, and over the next five years was steadily extended. A feature of the new housing estate was the new 'Swedish' houses, purchased directly from Swedish suppliers in prefabricated form, and assembled in Inverness. At a sitting of the Inverness Dean of Guild Court (the planning authority) on 7th January 1946 permission was granted to the Scottish Special Housing Association to erect sixty-four permanent houses 'of the Swedish type' at Dalneigh, and at a meeting of the Housing Committee of the Town Council on the same night it was agreed to erect 'aluminium houses' at sites on Harrowden road, Coronation Park, Bruce Avenue, Ballifeary Road and Culduthel Road.

Public opinion was sceptical: a correspondent calling himself 'Hope Deferred' wrote to the *Courier* in June 1946 that local housing policy seemed to be 'in a stupid and foolish muddle'. The Council had started building twenty houses in Bruce Gardens in November 1944, but they would not be ready until November 1946, and perhaps not even then. In August 1946 the Inverness Trades and Labour Council protested to the Secretary of State in the strongest possible terms about the delay in providing housing.

The Burgh Surveyor, Mr I W Jack, reported in June 1946 that the total cost of schemes under construction was £657,250, which would provide 650 new houses. By January 1948 the Burgh Architect, Mr J Blackburn, was able to report progress: thirty-two houses rapidly approaching completion at Hilton, where at the end of 1946 no house-building at all had been commenced, and at Dalneigh, 64 Swedish houses finished. By mid-November 1948 Mr Blackburn was able to report the purchase of a further 100 Swedish houses, to be erected at Dalneigh beginning in the spring of 1949.

However, in November 1949 the Town Council's Housing Committee had to address the difficult question of housing

Army huts at Raigmore, occupied by squatters after the war.

allocation for the Swedish houses. The 'economic' rent for a Swedish house worked out at about £65 a year, and as one Councillor pointed out, there was no point in allocating such a house to an ordinary working man earning £5 a week if he would have to pay £2 a week in rent and rates. The proposed solution was to move council tenants who with a higher income into the newer houses, and allow those with a lower income to occupy existing housing. In due time, the names and addresses of the successful tenants for the new houses in the Hilton and Dalneigh schemes were published in the local press for all to see.

CHAPTER 10

INVERNESS AND THE MILLENNIUM, 1950–2000

The issue of public housing in Inverness continued to be an important one throughout the 1950s; despite the best efforts of the Council the demand for housing seemed insatiable. One of the features of the history of Inverness in the last half of the twentieth century has been the continuing and extensive growth of the town, both in population and in extent.

Population

1901	21,238
1911	22,216
1921	20, 944
1931	22,583
1951	28,107
1961	29,774

Thereafter, comparisons get a little tricky, but one thing is for sure, the population growth of Inverness since 1961 has been phenomenal — it is one of the fastest growing areas in Scotland. From 1861 to 1891 the population of Inverness grew by almost ten thousand, in the boom years caused by the coming of the Railway Age. From 1961 to 1991, the growth has, if anything, been greater. Changes in the way the Census Office publishes its figures, and changes in what is meant by 'Inverness', make it difficult to make direct comparisons, but by 1991 the population of 'Inverness Settlement Zone' was 41,766; this rises to 50,494 if including the new housing estates around Smithton, Culloden and Balloch. The projection for the area by the time of the next Census in 2001 is that the population of 'Inverness' will have risen to over 60,000.

Local Government Reform

One of the features of local life in Inverness in the last quarter of the twentieth century was the reform of local government — not once, but twice. In 1975 the Burgh of Inverness ceased to exist, and was replaced by a local government unit called Inverness

District Council, encompassing not only the boundaries of the former burgh but also a portion of the mainland part of what had previously been Inverness-shire. At the same time, Highland Region was created, under the control of Highland Regional Council, containing eight District Council areas: Inverness, Nairn, Caithness, Sutherland, Lochaber, Skye and Lochalsh, Ross and Cromarty, and Badenoch & Strathspey.

In April 1996 yet another reorganisation of local government in Scotland came into effect, with far-reaching consequences for Council employees and their families, who faced a major upheaval in their lives — in some cases, for the second time in their careers. Both Highland Regional Council and the eight District Councils created in 1975 were abolished, and replaced by the Highland Council, a new 'unitary authority' uniting the functions of its predecessors.

The reorganisation of local government in Scotland has a long history — in the last two hundred years there has scarcely been a generation which did not face the upheaval of changing old and familiar ways of doing things and learning new ways. Each time, the government of the day was persuaded that the reforms would make local government more efficient, more effective, more civilised, less of a threat, and less of a drain on central government. Each time, local government officials — the people who make the system work — complained at the innovations of far away bureaucrats, while the people they served, the people who over the years had to pay an increasing burden of local taxation, complained always at the changes being imposed upon them.

Until 1975 local government administration in Scotland was based around the burghs, first established by David I in the 12th century. By 1700 there were around three hundred of them throughout the country. Most powerful were the Royal Burghs, like Inverness, which were represented in the pre-1707 Scottish Parliament. Most burghs were towns which had been established in the neighbourhood of a mediaeval castle; they became centres of local administration and were often granted trading privileges, such as a market or fair. Burgh courts dealt with civil and petty criminal matters, while the Dean of Guild Court developed, with jurisdiction over buildings and public safety. After 1560, Kirk Sessions in burghs were given responsibility for education and poor relief, with the necessary money raised by a tax on local landowners — a system which evolved into the late and un-lamented rating system of local government finance.

After the Reform Act of 1832 it became possible for the people of a burgh to elect representatives to a Council. At the same time, Parliamentary Burghs were created, which could elect members of Parliament to Westminster. Sometimes smaller burghs were lumped together for parliamentary purposes. From 1833 to 1892 Inverness, like other Royal Burghs, was governed by a Provost, Bailies and Councillors. Other types of burghs, known as Police Burghs, and Burghs of Barony, were abolished under the Burgh Police (Scotland) Act of 1892, after which all burghs were administered under a uniform system, by the Town Councils (Scotland) Act of 1900.

The system was thus becoming increasingly democratic, though still falling far short of the standards of the present day. Scottish local government was fully democratic by 1914, and in 1929 there was new legislation which created three different categories of burghs: cities (4), large burghs (19) and small burghs (178), all with their own Provosts, Bailies and Councillors. This is the system which was swept away by the Local Government (Scotland) Act of 1973, which came into effect on 16th May 1975.

The counties of Scotland were administered under a completely different and separate system. County Councils evolved gradually out of mediaeval sheriffdoms by way of committees of landowners which took on various public duties from the 17th century onwards. Justices of the Peace — usually important local landowners — were made responsible for public order and highways, outwith burgh boundaries. The system of county councils developed in a somewhat haphazard way, with many local anomalies. In the north of Scotland county boundaries were often rather strange, with pockets of one county surrounded by the territory of a different county. After some tinkering, the system was standardised and formalised by the 1889 Local Government (Scotland) Act, and lasted until reorganisation in 1974.

The upheaval of the 1970s created a two-tier system of local government. Both the Burgh of Inverness and the County of Inverness-shire ceased to exist, and were absorbed into Highland Region and its District Councils. The population of Inverness-shire in 1971 was only 88,062, including Barra, Harris, North Uist, Benbecula and South Uist, which became part of a new Western

Isles Council — Comhairle nan Eilean. The remaining territory of the former county was then divided between four District Councils: Inverness, Badenoch and Strathspey (with part of Moray), Lochaber (with three areas from Argyll), and Skye and Lochalsh.

So, in 1975, Inverness District Council found itself responsible for a good deal less than the combined area of Inverness-shire and the former Burgh, but a good deal more than the area controlled by the former Town Council. Inverness District consisted of the town of Inverness, and a tract of land on either side of Loch Ness, extending as far south as Fort Augustus. To the west, it took in the villages of Beauly, Kirkhill and Kiltarlity, and to the east, the recently developed housing of Culloden, Smithton and Balloch, and the older villages of Croy and Ardersier. Inevitably, Inverness and its immediate surrounds became the focal point of the new Council's activities, and 'country members' sometimes had to struggle to ensure that their interests were represented too.

One of the abiding problems of Inverness District Council was that despite the fact that it was in existence for twenty-one years, many of the Inverness members continued to act as if they were still members of the old Town Council. Indeed, the District Council's decision to continue to use the term 'Provost' for the chairperson of the District Council served to perpetuate this antiquated and increasingly out-dated belief. Nevertheless, the District Council was able to accomplish much that was good for Inverness, due in no small measure to the imagination and innovation of council Officers. Ironically, although Council Members were firmly rooted in the past, with a sense of the history of their local burgh, the departmental Directors and other officials they employed to carry out their policies were often incomers, without any commitment to the past, or respect for it. The benefits of this were obvious: unfettered by local ties and without the historical baggage that had immobilised and incapacitated the Town Council in its latter years, council officials felt free to introduce new ideas and new ways of doing things, which, to their credit, the Councillors on the whole welcomed and encouraged.

Licensing Court

One of the darker episodes in the history of local government in Inverness reached the courts in 1977, when both the Provost and Chief Executive of Inverness District Council were charged with forming a criminal purpose to defeat the course of justice. It sounds fairly serious, and if they had been found guilty the consequences would have been very serious indeed for both men. What they were actually accused of was that they had deliberately altered the records of the Licensing Court, in order to accommodate the late application of a district and regional councillor — who happened to be the chairman of the Northern Police Committee.

The problem came to light in June 1977, when the two men appeared at Inverness Sheriff Court. Just a month before, the Provost had attended the Queen's Jubilee Thanksgiving Service in Glasgow Cathedral. The Police had noticed a discrepancy in the records of the Licensing Court and had carried out an investigation. The Procurator Fiscal agreed that there was a case to answer, and so the Provost and the Chief Executive appeared in chambers on petition where they were charged with 'having falsified and altered the records of the Inverness District Licensing Court, and having thereby defeated the course of justice. ' Both were fully committed and were released on bail. The Provost decided to step down temporarily until the matter was resolved, and the Chief Executive was suspended from his duties on full pay, 'pending and entirely without prejudice to, the determination of the charges against him'.

On the face of it, it seemed no more than that a simple clerical error had been committed, or at the worst, that the two men had tried to resolve problems created by an administrative muddle, had slightly bent the rules, and had been the victims of an overly zealous constabulary. There was never the slightest suggestion that either man had profited in any way from what they had done. At the trial in November, evidence was led that a clerkess in the Chief Executive's office had been ordered to alter the licensing register, the Provost was acquitted of all charges, and the Chief Executive secured a Not Proven verdict from the jury of eight men and seven women, by majority verdict in each case. The Provost resumed his duties and the Chief Executive's suspension was lifted. Everybody breathed a huge sigh of relief. In a cautious editorial, the *Inverness Courier* noted the verdicts, and warned the public that 'no matter what their opinion and feelings, the law has run its course, and an ordinary jury has reached its conclusions according to that law'. And there, it seemed, the matter would be allowed to rest. The editorial did go on to warn 'that those in public life must be extra careful about how they go about official business'.

But the police were not amused, and the Chief Constable let it be known that 'he was considering whether to make a further move' in the wake of the trial verdicts, according to a report in the *Highland News* of 1st December 1977:

> I am studying reports on the evidence of the whole court proceedings to see whether any further action is required by me…From the outset the police submission has been that the application was incompetent. That view has not altered. I want to see what the legal position is now, and what further steps may be open to me. I expect to take a decision in the next week or so.

No further action was taken.

The Labour Group on Inverness District Council were also not so willing to let matters rest. At the meeting of the council in December, the Provost was censured for his conduct by 15 votes to 9, but a motion to oust him from his office failed. Mr Dan Corbett, in typically combative mode, was uncompromising in his attack on the Provost, as reported in the *Inverness Courier* of 20th December 1977:

> You were elected chairman of this council to carry out your duties responsibly and honestly and you have failed miserably. You have adopted a domineering attitude and an arrogant manner in the way you have gone about things. And when members disagreed with you you have adopted or used ridiculous phrases such as 'witch-hunt' and 'personal vendettas', etc. You have destroyed morale in this council and the public's belief in it.

Mr Allan Sellar seconded Mr Corbett's motion of no confidence but proposed an amendment:

> That this council proposes a vote of censure on the Provost. It has become increasingly evident from recent events that he has employed unacceptable methods to influence events affecting the community and thus bringing Inverness District Council into disrepute. There must be an assurance that if he is to continue in office that this practice will cease and that business will proceed in a manner which the people of Inverness have a right to expect from their representatives.

This is the amended motion of censure that the council went on to vote for: when the result was announced the Provost stated briefly: 'I have taken note of your views'.

The Highland Council, 1996

In 1996, when the District Council was in its turn abolished, the new unitary authority, the Highland Council, gave an early commitment to decentralise its administration as much as possible, and to this end established 'Area Committees' in each of the eight former District Council areas. Thus, the area previously administered (for some services) by Inverness District Council now has its own Inverness Area Committee — and its chairperson, elected by the 19 Members from the Inverness Area, of whom 12 represent Inverness electoral wards, is still styled 'Provost'.

The new Highland Council has 72 members, first elected in April 1995. Under the old system, residents of Inverness and District were represented by 16 members elected to Highland Regional Council, as well as by their 28 District Councillors. Six District Councillors served also as Regional Councillors, so the people of Inverness District were represented by a total of 38 elected Councillors. Under the new regime, they have elected 19 representatives to the Highland Council. The increased workload for elected members is a cause of some concern — being a Highland Councillor is close to being a full-time job. And here, for the record, is a list of the Inverness Members of the Highland Council, elected to the new Council in May 1995:

THE HIGHLAND COUNCIL
Inverness Members
(elected in May 1995)

	Electoral Ward	Name
35	Strathnairn and Strathdearn	Mrs Kathleen G. Matheson
36	East Loch Ness	Mrs Ella MacRae
37	Fort Augustus	Patrick C Paterson
38	Drumnadrochit	Mrs Margaret C. Davidson
39	Beauly	James S. Munro
40	Kirkhill	Simon J Shiels
41	Scorguie	James T MacDonald
42	Merkinch	Alexander D MacLean
43	Muirtown	Mrs Christina M Cumming
44	Columba	James W A Thomson
45	Drummond	Mrs Margaret A MacLennan
46	Alt na Sgitheach	Clive L Goodman
47	Hilton	Ms Ann Darlington

48	Old Edinburgh	Allan G. Sellar
49	Canal	William J Smith
50	Raigmore	David R Munro
51	Inshes	Mrs Janet N Home
52	Culloden	John C Cole
53	Ardersier	Peter J Peacock

In October 1946 the *Inverness Courier* ran an editorial on 'Local Government' which, though it dates from a different era, contains sentiments which are still relevant today. The cause of their complaint was familiar — 'the loss of local control'. The immediate dispute had to do with education policy in the Highlands — a joint committee for Inverness-shire composed of County Councillors and Town Councillors got themselves into a bit of a muddle in trying to introduce a new administrative scheme. The details are now unimportant, but what rankled with the Town Councillors was that when they asked for the decision to be deferred until the Inverness Burgh representatives had had a chance to discuss it properly amongst themselves, they were outvoted. Burgh representatives made up only about one-third of the members of the Joint Committee, although they contributed nearly half the cost of the services it provided.

The *Courier* was incensed:

> One of the most disturbing features of public life in Scotland during the past decade has been the emphasis placed upon the centralisation of local government services by successive Secretaries of State for Scotland.

Suspecting the twin bogies of the Scottish Office at Whitehall and St Andrews House in Edinburgh of joint conspiracy, the Courier complained that:

> more than one Secretary of State has called for the amalgamation of public services previously carried out separately by the Town and County Councils, and while such amalgamations have probably suited the convenience of the Ministers and servants of the Crown it is highly questionable if they have served the public interest.

The *Courier* thought that if Mr Joseph Westwood, the Secretary of State — 'who evidently worships regionalisation as much as any of his predecessors' — had attended the education committee meetings in Inverness:

> he would have got an insight to the practical difficulties which are presenting themselves and to where centralisation is leading. The County Council, a local authority responsible for an area which is

173

geographically the largest in Great Britain, stretching from the Moray Firth to the Atlantic Ocean, has so many duties heaped upon it that membership is almost a full-time occupation...Experience has shown that centralisation and efficiency are not necessarily related, but experience is something which all too seldom guides those entrusted with public administration in Scotland.

The Golden Mile

As we have already noted, in the 1991 Census, the population of Inverness District was just under 63,000, with 41,766 (67%) living in the town of Inverness and a further 8,728 in Culloden, Smithton, Balloch and adjoining estates. It is one of the fastest growing areas in Britain. Comparisons with the 1981 Census showed that the population had increased by more than 6,000 in ten years, and that in the area under the jurisdiction of Inverness District Council was projected to reach 66,500 by the time of the next decennial Census in the year 2001.

Much of the future growth of the town will be along the area known locally as 'The Golden Mile' — the presently undeveloped stretch of road along the A96 towards Nairn. In November 1996 work will start on a new dual carriageway opening up the area for development; already property developers' signs along the existing road promise future delights. Inland from the A96, more housing is planned, and by the end of the first decade of the 21st century the area will have been transformed just as dramatically as other growth areas have been in former years. By then, Raigmore Hospital and the headquarters of the Northern Constabulary will be, geographically speaking, in the centre of 'Inverness'.

Developments continue in the Longman, already, through land reclamation, a much larger area than its eighteenth-century equivalent. The construction of a new football stadium at the south end of the Kessock Bridge is the biggest single project there in recent years. When opened in 1997 it will be a major new sporting venue, bringing thousands of visitors to the town. The 'new' football club, Inverness Caledonian Thistle, formed through the merger of two of the town's oldest sporting institutions, was elected to the Scottish Football League, Third Division, in 1995.

The approval of the financing of the new stadium and associated developments was one of the last acts of the old Councils before they were abolished in March 1996. There was much burning of midnight oil and scratching of financial brains before officials came up with a plan which would please everybody, would work, and was legal! With so much of the funds necessary for the stadium project contingent on other matching funds, nobody wanted to commit money before everybody else had, but eventually a formula was devised which made it possible.

However, some observers caution that it is by no means certain that the problems are over. The whole business of merging two football clubs and funding the new stadium was divisive and controversial from the start. Disenchanted supporters challenged the new arrangements vociferously, and within Inverness District Council there were serious divisions. Towards the end of 1995 there was a serious possibility that the District Council's contribution for the stadium might not be approved, but in the end it was, after a stormy Council meeting and some intensive lobbying behind the scenes.

Local Government Achievements

There is absolutely no doubt, despite the jaundiced view of local government reform for which there is good reason in the Highlands, that the standards of public services provided for Invernessians by Highland Region and Inverness District Council were immeasurably better than under the previous regime of the Town Council.

Nowhere is this seen more clearly than in the areas of leisure and recreation. Inverness District Council pumped millions of pounds into making the Bught area of Inverness the prime centre for leisure and sporting activities in the North of Scotland. The Floral Hall, the Sports Centre, the athletic stadium and running track, the Bught stadium and artificial pitch, the Whin Park recreation area and boating loch, and now, the state-of-the-art £10 million Aquadome — an outstanding legacy of achievement for the new Highland Council to carry forward into the next millennium.

The opening of the new Aquadome meant the closure of the existing swimming pool, located at the eastern end of the Friar's Street bridge. When opened in 1936 Inverness Baths was said to be 'the most up-to-date swimming baths in Scotland', 100 feet long and 40 feet wide, with Olympic size diving boards and traditional changing cubicles along the sides of the pool. Renovations and additions in 1984 included a toddler pool, sauna and jacuzzis, and a new reception area preserving and incorporating the original

175

facade. The new Aquatics Centre, when it opens in 1997, will once again be described as the most up-to-date swimming baths in Scotland — though with many more facilities available to members of the public of all ages.

Inverness Museum and Inverness Public Library, administratively separated for twenty-one years, are now together once again under the same bureaucratic roof as the responsibility of Highland Council's Cultural and Leisure Services. Once they shared the same buildings in Castle Wynd, as a result of the 1960s building boom, but in 1981 the library moved to Farraline Park. From 1975 to 1996 Inverness Library was part of the Highland Region Library Services, later renamed Highland Libraries, and although the library service generally suffered from inadequate resources, being at one time the worst-funded public library service in Scotland, there is no doubt that being part of a wider library system gave the public access to a much wider range of books and resources than had ever been possible when it was just a burgh library.

The buildings at Farraline Park were remodelled yet again in 1981, having been in their time a school, police station, theatre and social security office, and having narrowly avoided a fate as the headquarters of the local bus companies. The Reference Room at Inverness Library houses the best collection of books and pamphlets on the history and culture of the Highlands, including the library of the Victorian MP Charles Fraser-Mackintosh, housed on a purpose-built balcony.

Inverness Library serves an area of the Highlands extending far beyond Inverness — one-third of its readers live outside the town and people come from far and wide to make use of its facilities. There is a fine collection of local newspapers: the *Inverness Journal,* 1808–1849; the *Inverness Courier,* started in 1817 and still going strong as is the *Highland News,* started in 1883; the *Inverness Advertiser,* 1849–1885; the *Scottish Highlander,* 1885–1898; the *Northern Chronicle,* 1881–1962; and many other local and community newspapers from around the Highlands. There is a card index, covering both personal names and a wide range of subject entries, for the period 1809–1898. Microfilm copies of *The Times* of London, with indexes, cover the period from 1971 onwards for national and international issues.

Inverness Museum, situated beside the Town House, overlooking Bridge Street, is a good example of how professionalism and improved lighting and display can make all the difference; familiar material is enhanced, interpreted and presented to the public in an entertaining and informative way. The bookshop and cafe are welcome facilities for visitors. The ground floor is used for permanent natural history and archaeological displays; upstairs are exhibitions of Jacobite material, and a display space for art works and visiting exhibitions.

The parks and open spaces of Inverness have been a feature of the town for many years. Bellfield Park has attractive flower beds, a children's play area and paddling pool, tennis courts and a putting green. The Highland Council is responsible for Torvean golf course and for the former municipal bowling greens at Fraser park, Planefield road and Waterloo (Riverside Street).

One of the more controversial changes introduced by Inverness District Council during its regime came in 1993, when 'wheelie bins' replaced the previous system of kerbside plastic sacks and bins for domestic rubbish collection. This created some initial disquiet, especially in the areas of Inverness more densely populated, where the density of wheelie bins on some pavements on collection days proved to be a bit of an obstacle course, especially for elderly or visually disabled people. However, obvious improvements in service, and improved conditions of hygiene, were evident to most people, and after a year or so controversy and complaints died down. Certainly from the point of view of the work force wheelie bins cause fewer industrial accidents and are much easier to handle.

Another new, and controversial service introduced by Inverness District Council was the Crematorium at Kilvean on the western outskirts of Inverness, opened on 27th July 1995. Most of the religious leaders in the Highlands either supported it or maintained a certain detached neutrality; only Free Presbyterian Rev Donald Boyd campaigned against it. After twenty-three years on the drawing board it was finally built, at a cost of £1.4 million. Only Orthodox Jews and Muslims are completely against cremation, and most people, including Councillors, were prepared to accept the argument that it provided additional choice, and was widely accepted in other parts of Britain. With the nearest comparable facilities involving a round trip of hundreds of miles to Perth or Aberdeen, the new Inverness Crematorium was expected to serve a catchment area from Shetland in the north to Forres in the east, as well as the whole of the northern and western Highlands.

Many people commented favourably on the architecture of the new buildings, and their surroundings, as hundreds turned out for the inaugural open day. Many noticed an atmosphere of peace and serenity, enhanced by a Garden of Remembrance and a Book of Remembrance in which names are inscribed.

In the early 1980s some £10 million was spent upgrading the houses and physical environment of South Kessock. The 620 houses in the South Kessock housing estate were modernised. Built in the 1930s, the South Kessock houses had, by the 1950s, become run down, and the area was prone to vandalism. The situation was made worse by the policy of rehousing problem tenants there, and also homeless people, travelling people cleared off their encampments outside Inverness. Despite all the expenditure and effort, by local residents as well as Council planners, social problems in South Kessock continue, with rising anti-social behaviour, rising crime, problems of community safety, a high number of transfer requests, little demand for vacancies, and houses sitting empty for long periods. Almost a quarter of the housing stock changes tenants in the course of a year, with a destabilising effect on the community.

According to the 1991 Census, unemployment levels for Inverness were running at 9.1% of the economically active population, compared to 37.4% in South Kessock. Of the 16–24 age group, 39.8% were unemployed in South Kessock compared to 11.6% for Inverness as a whole.

As a first step to tackling these problems Inverness District Council applied to the Scottish Office in 1994 for additional resources to improve home security in the area, concentrating on improved doors and windows, new locks, security lighting at the rear and side of properties, and improved street lighting. The Council realised that this was only the first step; the current state of the area shows that public policy has failed, and a radical change of attitudes and approaches to the management of the area must take place. Since 1994 a group of tenants has been meeting with officials and have come up with their own proposals including road safety measures, improved lighting, safe play areas, a neighbourhood watch scheme, development of activities for adults and children and a local newsletter to improve community involvement. The aim is to make South Kessock a place where people will want to live, and want to remain.

The Town House

Before 1975, the Town House was the power centre of local government in the Burgh of Inverness, and it still houses some of the offices of the Highland Council, including its Inverness Area offices.

Completed in 1882, Inverness Town House is easily the most attractive public building in the town. It is basically an enlarged copy of Gilbert Scott's Albert Institute in Dundee (1864), modified by architects Matthews and Laurie. Under construction from 1876 to 1882, it cost £13,500, of which Duncan Grant of Bught (whose father had been Provost) donated £5000. In recognition of this gift the central windows in the Hall have a Grant crest (a burning rock) and a Macrae crest (a hand brandishing a short sword) — Mrs Grant was a Macrae.

Just outside the Town House are two of the town's oldest and most important symbols, the Market Cross and the Clach-na-cudain Stone, discussed in Chapter One. Inside, the most imposing feature of the building is the main staircase. Throughout, the walls are covered with portraits of former Provosts and local worthies. A portrait of Thomas Telford, builder of the Caledonian Canal, is at the top of the stairs.

The main Hall upstairs has nine marble busts and two oak panels commemorating the dead of two world wars. Next door is the Council Chamber, with more portraits and windows celebrating Queen Victoria's Diamond Jubilee of 1896 — she is flanked by the ten Prime Ministers of her reign. The British cabinet met in this Council Chamber on 7th September 1921, to discuss Irish affairs. At the time Prime Minister Lloyd George was on holiday at Gairloch and King George V was at Moy. A facsimile of a piece of paper signed by all those present is framed and on display; among the sixteen signatories were two future Prime Ministers, Stanley Baldwin and Winston Churchill.

The style of the Town House is described by architectural historian John Gifford as 'Flemish-Baronial, with *tourelles* at the corners and flanking the centre gablet'. (A gablet is simply a small gable.) *The Builder,* an architect's magazine, did not approve when it reviewed the building soon after its completion:

> The effect does not appear to us a successful one. The square corbelled angle-turrets are forced, and the gablets which flank the tower are apparently useless pieces of constructed decoration, which do not help the composition, merely introduced as tit-bits the designer could not part with.

Nevertheless, in today's townscape, it stands out as a work of creative imagination beside the squalid concrete of the 1960s and 1970s which now surround it. This was the hub of local government in Inverness, the place where all Town Council meetings were held, after 1882. After 1975 it became the headquarters of Inverness District Council, who held their meetings in the Council Chamber. The rest of the building was used for a variety of purposes from office accommodation for Council departments to venues for coffee mornings and public meetings.

Gallery 2000

What will become of the old town centre of Inverness, once the 'Golden Mile' is a reality? It looks as if there will still be shopping centres there, and that many of the service industries — banks, building societies, solicitors, estate agents, etc — will continue to operate there. More old buildings will be knocked down to make way for the 'improvements'. What about knocking down some 'new' buildings too?

As a reaction, if somewhat belated, to the depredations carried out in Inverness town centre during the 1960s, a group of concerned citizens put forward the project known as Gallery 2000 for consideration by the Millennium Commission, with the aim of redeveloping the concrete excrescences of Bridge Street and Castle Wynd and creating a cultural complex worthy of its prime setting. Perhaps the most eloquent piece of writing on this subject appeared in an article in the *Inverness Courier* of 26th September 1991 — 'Inverness — how not to protect its quality image'. Contributed by local writer and historian of churches and castles Leonella Longmore, this article dwelt first on a Report recently released by the development agency Highland and Islands Enterprise, predicting a 4% increase in population in the Highlands and Islands, and wondering if the arrival of so many 'white settlers' in the area was something to be welcomed, or not. But, she asked:

> It is easy to blame the incomers for spoiling the Highlands. But who are the real culprits — those who sell or those who buy, those who knock down or those who build?

The process of demolition began with the removal of the Suspension Bridge in 1959, and when the new concrete structure opened on a rainy day in September 1961, she wondered if this was a coincidence, or an omen. The 28th of September was

Only the 'Courier Office', seen here overlooking the river Ness and the 'new' bridge, survived the demolitions of the 1960s.

a sombre day of heavy rain — in mourning perhaps — it being the precise anniversary of the collapse of the main bridge over the Ness in 1664. In 1961, the demolition started of the cobbled street, narrow closes and historic, four-storeyed tenements in order to erect a concrete-panelled monstrosity. Did no eye foresee the incongruity of the grey blocks against the pink battlements of the castle?

Well, the local Chamber of Commerce did, and argued that the site should be left vacant as a grassy area leading up to the battlements of the castle. However, commercial considerations prevailed. In 1967 the other side of Bridge Street suffered the same fate, sweeping away the historic Queen Mary's house — how today's Tourist Board must wish that it could have been preserved, though one wonders if, from the concrete fastness of their headquarters across the road, they are aware of the irony of that location. Only Miss Barron stood in the way of progress:

> The towering facade of the new building which rose from the ashes succeeded in dwarfing its aged neighbour, the Courier office, and hid from view the face of the Steeple clock to those across the river.
>
> In 1966, the destruction mania had continued into Church Street — the oldest street in town — until it worked itself out, as illnesses tend to do. But not before slab-faced structures had appeared beside the Steeple; across the road where the Northern Meeting Rooms used to stand at the corner of Baron Taylor's Street; at the corner of Bank Lane where the Bank House...used to be; and at the site of the Caledonian Hotel.

Cutting through from Church Street to Queensgate, the bulldozers went to work on the Post Office and pulverised one of the most imposing Victorian buildings in the town. Academy Street was not spared when the Empire Theatre came down in 1971, thereby laying the ghosts of Harry Gordon and Dave Willis, comics of the war years.

And so it went on. The Clan Tartan Warehouse on the corner of High Street and Castle Street disappeared, and with it the 'Three Graces', the statue of Faith, Hope and Charity which surmounted its frontage. Unlamented locally, it was sold to an Orkney collector, whose gardens it now adorns. Recent attempts to recover it for the town seem unlikely to succeed in the short term, but perhaps one day the three ladies will return to their native town. The bulldozers crossed the river, knocking down half of Young Street and the closes between King Street and Huntly Street. Leonella Longmore was quite right to denigrate the result:

> The unimaginative tower block which sprang up still taunts the corbelled gables of Ness Walk — now a conservation area.

> But desecration went hand in hand. The face of Ardross Terrace designed by Dr Alexander Ross, 'the Christopher Wren of the North', to complement the Cathedral and Bishop's Palace, was sullied by the insert of a granite commercial frontage opposite the Cathedral. It is, as William Glashan, Inverness architect, said, '…a perfect example of bad manners'.

Even the Forbes Fountain, which had stood outside the Town House since 1882, did not survive. It was dismantled, and, 'minus its imposing, Gothic upper half', it was rebuilt in 'a morsel of park, beside the river'. In his *Old Inverness* column in the *Courier* of 14th June 1994, Tom Fraser comments that:

> a sadly truncated Fountain stands at the far end of Ladies Walk with no notice as to its origin — only an official injunction not to permit dogs to foul the footpath. I wonder how Doctor George Fiddes Forbes would have felt about such scurvy treatment of his fine gift to his native town.

This Dr Forbes was the son of the elderly doctor who had died during the cholera epidemic of 1832. He and his brother William, also a doctor, started up the Inverness Dispensary for the Poor, always known as the 'Forbes Dispensary', on the west side of the river — now occupied by the local headquarters of the Red Cross. George worked for the East India Company in India for about thirty years, and on his return to his native town offered to present a fountain to the town.

Inverness Museum on Bridge Street, in one of the concrete boxes replacing the traditional buildings swept away by the developers.

Returning to Leonella Longmore's article, she ends on a slightly optimistic note:

> For us there is hope for the future development of this fast-moving town. The predicted newcomers will not see the architectural beauty that was once an integral part of the Highland Capital, but they should be made aware of the Invernessians' desire for sensitive planning. Inverness is licking its wounds and slowly recovering.

It was in this context that the Gallery 2000 project emerged. The impetus came from the Arts world, in which it had long been recognised that Inverness needed an Art Gallery, a major piece of architecture to fill a cultural vacuum west of Aberdeen and north of Perth. A Steering Committee of luminaries and local enthusiasts was established, chaired by Mr Frank Spencer-Nairn; newsletters were produced, and when the government announced that it was setting up a Millennium Commission to distribute National Lottery funds for important community projects to celebrate the new century, optimism was unbounded.

In February 1996 the plans were unveiled to the public: a new cultural complex involving the complete redevelopment of both sides of Bridge Street, at a cost of nearly £30 million. As well as a showpiece art gallery there would be a new museum, increased

Concrete boxes occupied by the Crofters Commission and Inverness and Nairn Enterprise, ruining the approaches to the Castle Hill.

space and facilities for a new library, shops, offices, civic open space. Gallery 2000, the art gallery, would include an archive, studies and workshops, and a lecture theatre.

The plans attracted widespread support from community leaders, and from the general public. Existing tenants in the buildings which would be affected expressed their general support, and the prospect of a new library, releasing the present Farraline Park building for other use, was also welcomed; the existing library building, it was pointed out, is only one-third the recommended size for a town as big as Inverness. The bid was submitted to the Millennium Commission, who came to Inverness, assessed the merits of the bid — and rejected it.

The Steering Committee revised its plans, abandoned the Bridge Street dream, and started looking at other premises, including the Swimming Pool site on Glebe Street, soon to be closed when the new Aqua Centre in the Bught was finished, in 1997. Although the complete redevelopment of Bridge Street would be impossible without support from the Millennium Commission, other options could be considered if, for example, Highlands and Islands Enterprise were to move to a new location. Other sites in other parts of Inverness were also considered, and the possibilities of funding through the Scottish Arts Council's National Lottery Fund were being explored. The Gallery 2000 project still retains enormous goodwill in Inverness, and it seems likely that some positive result will emerge, eventually. It was unfortunate that the Millennium Commission did not share the Steering Committee's dream for Bridge Street — one reason why the application was turned down, it was surmised, was that the University of the Highlands and Islands Project was also applying for funds, and it was not likely that the Commission would support more than one Millennium Project in the Highlands.

The Good Old Days?

In 1841, in a Report prepared by George Anderson for the Poor Law Commissioners, in the aftermath of the cholera epidemics of 1832 and 1834, the full horrors of the public health crisis in Inverness were laid bare. Part of the Report is a contribution by Dr John Inglis Nicol, at the time the Provost of Inverness:

> Inverness is a nice town, situated in a most beautiful country, and with every facility for cleanliness and comfort. The people, are, generally speaking, a nice people, but their sufferance of nastiness is past endurance. Contagious fever is seldom or ever absent; but for many years it has seldom been rife in its pestiferous influence. The people owe this more to the kindness of Almighty God than to any means taken or observed for its prevention. There are very few houses in town which can boast of either water-closet or privy; and only two or three public privies in the better part of the place exist for the great bulk of the inhabitants. Hence there is not a street, lane, or approach to it that is not disgustingly defiled at all times, so much so as to render the whole place an absolute nuisance. The *midden* is the chief object of the humble; and though enough of water for purposes of cleanliness may be had by little trouble, still the ablutions are seldom — MUCK in doors and out of doors *must* be their portion. When cholera prevailed in Inverness, it was more fatal than in almost any other town of its population in Britain.

In the later years of the nineteenth century, much of the problem housing was swept away, and the infrastructure of sound public health provided: water and sewerage. In the town centre, in the 1860s, large-scale maps of the town show that behind the imposing facades were the remnants of former times, often converted to stables — the nineteenth-century equivalent of car parks. The mind boggles at the possibility of a multi-storey stables! Gradually these were cleared away, and with the redevelopment of the town centre from the 1860s onwards, eventually replaced completely by 'modern' buildings — there were no howls of protest from Victorian conservationists about the loss of

Drummond Street and Lombard Street, with a glimpse of the Music Hall on Union Street, venue for public meetings and concerts down the ages.

eighteenth-century buildings: all agreed that they could not be got rid of quickly enough.

The irony of the situation today, when conservationists strive to ensure the survival of buildings erected at the expense of the historic mediaeval and eighteenth-century buildings of Inverness, should serve as a warning that change is inevitable, and usually dictated by commercial considerations. The best we can often hope for is that wherever possible changes can incorporate the best of the past, by preserving the appearance of old buildings while reconstructing the interiors, as happened with the renovation of the Queensgate Hotel, gutted by fire in 1982.

What is inexcusable, is thoughtless change, the kind of architectural vandalism which ruined Bridge Street, Young Street, Church Street and Castle Street with unattractive, unimaginative, glass and concrete structures. Fortunately the Gallery 2000 project, while unlikely to be carried out by the millennium, has at least shown the community that architects are capable of designing appropriate and imaginative buildings which fit into the older townscape while providing the facilities required by modern Invernessians. So, the prospects are not entirely gloomy, though there are still battles to be fought.

CONCLUSION

All over Scotland, in the last ten years, there has been an explosion of local history publishing. In the nineteenth century, and for most of this century, history publishing was almost exclusively the preserve of the antiquarian, the Historiographer Royal, the retired lawyer. Always, in every corner of Scotland, there were honourable exceptions, often handicapped by lack of access to source materials, even to their local newspapers, which, as we have seen in this book, are the very life blood of local history in Scotland.

One reason for the proliferation of booklets and leaflets, books of all sizes, for all pockets, on Scottish history and local history, has been that publishing has never been so easy, and so economically within the grasp of the common man and woman, as it is today. The desk-top publishing revolution, making it possible for anybody with a personal computer to prepare text for a printer easily to convert to book form, has allowed local groups, local societies, local individuals, to burst forth into print. Highland bookshops are bulging with locally produced material, and of course it is also widely available in Highland post offices, craft shops, grocery stores, filling stations, tourist information centres, museums, ferries, hotels and B&B establishments.

Of course, some things have been published which might better have been left in somebody's bottom drawer, or hard disk, but on balance, the small-publishing revolution has been a tremendous boon to local history, bringing it back to the communities from whence it came.

On a more 'professional' level, many small but lively Scottish publishers have emerged in recent years and successfully republished ancient local history books, of great interest to communities which have changed so much in this century. But can we make a plea for these republications to include at least a brief introductory essay by a contemporary historian? Other more 'up-market', Scottish publishers have popularised Scottish history with their books on Scottish themes and Scottish landscapes. Dare we say it, even English publishers have contributed to the effloration of publishing on Scottish themes.

Which brings us on to perhaps the most impressive corpus of Scottish history publishing — 'academic' publishing, in books and journals. Here Scotland's universities have taken the lead, reclaiming Scottish history for the Scottish people.

For the north of Scotland, the books and journals published by Aberdeen University Press have provided other outlets for the labours of Ph.D. students to be made available to the general public. What is particularly gratifying is to see so many young Highland Scots returning to their roots, rediscovering their own history, the history of the people of the Highlands and Islands, in some cases admitting that they had gone through many years of formal education, at school, college and university, perhaps successfully completing a degree in history — perhaps even Scottish history — before turning their new skills and fresh thinking on the history of their own culture. The prospect of a new University of the Highlands and Islands, the recipient in 1996 of a large grant from the Millennium Commission, will surely ensure the continuation of this welcome trend.

So, whereas twenty years ago the oldest bookshop in Inverness had a shelf or two of books on all Scottish topics, including history, literature and poetry, now there are yards (or should we say *metres*) of 'Scottish' books, many of them relating to the history of the Highlands.

Many factors have combined at the present time to encourage an interest in local history in the Highlands, to give local people the self-belief they need to tackle local subjects and tell local stories: reforms in the secondary school curriculum; non-vocational evening classes and lectures on local history run by organisations like the WEA and Aberdeen University; a succession of anniversaries of crucial events in the crofting world in the last century; the 250th anniversary of the Battle of Culloden; increased access to local newspapers through the miracle of microfilm; increased access to the massive literature on the Highlands to be found in books and periodicals through the improvement of the public library service in the Highlands; an ever-increasing pool of ordinary people who have begun to realise that with their local knowledge and local contacts, and the historical skills they can learn and develop locally, they can research, understand and get published their own history; and, it has to be said, perhaps most of all because of the invention of the photocopier! — for all these reasons, local history has never been healthier.

On a national level, the Scottish Local History Forum has taken the lead in coordinating and stimulating the study of local history by local groups, and the establishment of an Inverness Branch has helped in developing local history networks in the Highlands. The Highland Council is committed to encouraging local communities, and has supported local history through the publishing programme of Highland Libraries, and in other ways. The Scottish Historical Society has not neglected the Highlands in its publications programme, and two of its recent annual volumes, on the Lords of the Isles, and on the abbey at Fearn, have proved important for historical research in the Highlands. Some important articles in *Scottish Historical Review* have initiated important reinterpretations of the history of Scottish burghs, and highlighted the pressing need for further research. There is so much to be done, but at least we can now be sure that there are sufficient historians around, amateur and professional, to carry the process forward.

In the field of archaeology, the growth of an Archaeology Service under first Highland Regional Council and now the Highland Council has ensured that the prehistoric culture of the Highlands is not neglected, in research and recording. In addition, Inverness Museum, run for twenty-one years by Inverness District Council but now with a much wider remit, has increased public awareness of archaeological issues and archaeological treasures through its programme of exhibitions.

Many outside groups, from English and Scottish universities, use Highland sites to train archaeology students, and a heightened awareness of the importance of our archaeological heritage, both on the part of the Highland Council and on the part of local societies and individuals, has ensured that some of the excesses of previous generations will not be repeated. In particular, there is much more contact now between visiting archaeologists and local people, to the great benefit of both, and much less arrogance and misunderstanding of local culture. One of the practical results of this change in attitude has been a greater readiness to publicise and publish the results of research, often in collaboration with local historical societies.

Scotland's literary renaissance has also contributed to greater awareness of historical issues, especially in the Highlands. The arts, drama, music and dance are all reinterpreting the past in new ways, sometimes rather disconcertingly, but always with an energy and enthusiasm sometimes lacking in the fairly recent past. The stories and novels of George Mackay Brown and Iain Crichton Smith have put the Highland imagination to work again, and Britain's greatest living poet, Sorley Maclean, with a background on Raasay and Skye, has the capacity to make your toes curl and the hairs on the back of your neck stand on end, even when you don't understand his native Gaelic!

The historical novelist Nigel Tranter is sometimes rather sneered at in academic circles, but has done more that a convention of academic historians to re-enthuse the people of Scotland with stories of their great historical figures. His style may sometimes be too unliterary for some tastes, but his books are always meticulously researched, and have proved a useful starting point for many Scots who have felt a desire to know more about their own history.

Even politics has encroached on the field of history in the Highlands: one of the most contentious local issues of recent years revolved around the infamous monument to the Duke of Sutherland that overlooks the Sutherland town of Golspie. The letters columns of all the Highland newspapers, including the *Inverness Courier,* have examined from every conceivable angle the proposition that the statue should be removed and replaced with — well, with something else.

In Inverness itself, the Culloden anniversary in 1996 provoked an interest in local history which unfortunately exposed the ignorance of the local population about a crucial event in the history of Scotland which took place literally on their doorstep, 250 years before. Culloden still evokes strong emotions, and on the day of the commemorative ceremony, conducted as always with quiet dignity by the Gaelic Society of Inverness, no less than 6,000 people, many of them Invernessians, congregated on Drummossie Muir to remember the events of 1746.

A recurring theme of this book has been to draw the reader's attention to the many large public gatherings which defined important events in the past and through which the community could, when gathered all together, share in celebrations, funerals, royal visits, unveiling of statues, dedications of new churches and buildings, in numbers which are rarely achieved today, despite the greatly increased population.

On 16th April 1996 the people of Inverness came close to

recreating this sense of community, and many of those who could not be present on the day took the opportunity to participate in many excellent programmes on radio and television, commemorating the battle and analysing the fate of Highland society as a result of its involvement in the Jacobite cause. Many in positions of authority in their communities were shocked by how little many people knew or understood of the events of 1745–6, and many expressed the view that more should be done to reclaim local history in the Highlands, which was good news for all of us with an interest in this issue.

In Inverness itself, a local history project calling itself the Inverness Remembered Project, has revitalised itself in recent years after a period of torpor and difficulty, and has been energetically collecting memories in the Inverness community, especially from the older members of the community. Such initiatives are to be much welcomed, and encouraged, and are deserving of more support from the local Council than hitherto.

The literature on Inverness, and the avenues of research remaining to be explored, will keep local historians occupied for the foreseeable future. Sometimes further light on the way of life of the people comes from unexpected sources. For example, the first editor of the *Inverness Courier* was John Johnstone — or was he the editor in name only? His wife, Christian Isobel Johnstone (1771–1851) was an established writer, the author of a novel, *Clan Albyn,* and the editor of the *Edinburgh Tales*. It is thought that she contributed extensively to the columns of the *Courier*.

However, Mrs Johnstone's main claim to fame, and the reason she is still remembered, was her popular cookbook, *The Cook and Housewife's Manual: a practical system of modern domestic cookery and family management* (1826). It went through many editions, and yet Christian Isobel Johnstone's name was completely unknown to its readership. On the title page, authorship is attributed to Mistress Margaret Dods, of the Cleikum Inn, St Ronan's. Readers of Sir Walter Scott will immediately recognise the reference to the cook in the hostelry described in *St Ronan's Well*.

The fourth edition of what rapidly came to be known as 'Meg Dods' Cookbook' was first published in 1829, and reprinted in 1988 for the enjoyment of modern gourmands. In a brief but interesting introduction, the travel writer and food expert Glynn Christian comments on the lasting reputation of a work which became as well known, and influential in Scotland as Mrs Beeton was to become in England:

> For me, Meg Dods helps regenerate the bridges between plate and palate, and stimulates interest in ingredients and what to do with them. She has the added and dual advantage of neatly illuminating the truth of the important cliches — that there is nothing new under the sun, and that we have forgotten far more than we have learned.

It is, says Glynn Christian, 'a real cookery book, a book for people who really like to eat'. There are no less than 1,180 recipes, or 'receipts' as they are called in the terminology of the early 19th century, with a marked international flavour — many French dishes, but also 'mulligatawny, or curry soup, as made in India'. Indian Burdwam, German onion beef, Provence brandade, Irish stew and China chile. However, it is in her domestic, indigenous preparations that Meg Dods excels, as in her recipe for Sheep's Head Broth, described as a 'national preparation...wont to be a favourite Sunday-dinner dish in many comfortable Scottish families'.

The complete recipe for Sheep's Head Broth is too long to quote in full here, but an extract will convey the flavour of Mrs Johnstone's style:

> Choose a large fat head. When carefully singed by the blacksmith, soak it...for a considerable time in lukewarm water. Take out the glassy part of the eyes, and scrape the head...and brush till perfectly clean and white; then split the head with a cleaver, and take out the brains, &c.; clean the nostrils and gristly parts; wash the head and...let blanch till wanted for the pot.

She is a great fan of the onion and quotes approvingly Sir John Sinclair's description of the diet of a Highlander, 'who, with a few of these and an oatcake, would travel an incredible distance, and live for days without other food'. She raves about onion soup:

> 'Soupe a l'oignon' is thought highly restorative by the French. It is considered peculiarly grateful, and gently stimulating to the stomach, after hard-drinking or night-watching, and holds among soups the place that champagne, soda-water, or ginger-beer, does among liquors.

Meg Dods' fish soups and fish dishes are marvellous and inspirational; her haggis recipes are, to modern sensitivities, disgusting. Her puddings melt in the mouth, even on the printed page — almond cheesecakes, lemon custards, syllabubs and trifles, apple fritters, even iced creams and jellies — a wonderful catalogue of delights.

The *Cook and Housewife's Manual* ends with practical advice on all manner of household routines — how to scour blankets, remove ink-spots, clean floor boards, make shoe-blacking and 'extinguish fire in female dresses' — the cause, it is said, of many fatal accidents. Meg Dods' advice to her mainly female readership reveals the nature of her audience: 'Give instant alarm by pulling the bell, (which is generally near the fireplace) by screaming, or by any other means'.

Meg Dods' Cookbook has only one or two passing references to Inverness and the north of Scotland, but it is difficult to think of a book written in the capital of the Highlands which has had a wider influence, or a more extensive readership. One thing is certain: in the middle of the nineteenth century a copy would have been found in all Inverness households with bell-pulls beside the fireplaces.

So, all things considered, the people of Inverness are in good heart when it comes to an interest in local history. They know that they live in a community with a long and interesting history, and that they now have an opportunity to know more about it than at any time in the past. Young and old, native and incomer, are taking full advantage of the many opportunities to learn more about the history of their community: there is great interest in the life and times of Inverness.

FURTHER READING

There is an extensive literature on various aspects of the history of Inverness; many of the items listed here contain references to other material. Gerald Pollitt's *Historic Inverness,* and the Inverness Field Club centenary volume, *The Hub of the Highlands,* both have excellent bibliographies and suggestions for further reading. Books listed here are published in Inverness unless otherwise noted.

Books

Acts of the Lords of the Isles, 1336–1493 (Scottish History Society: Edinburgh, 1986)

Anderson, George and Peter, *Guide to the Highlands* (Edinburgh, 1963)

Anderson, Isabel Harriet, *Inverness Before Railways* (1885; reprinted 1984)

Barron, Evan Macleod, *Inverness and the Macdonalds* (1930)

Barron, Evan Macleod, *Inverness in the Fifteenth Century* (1906)

Barron, Evan Macleod, *Inverness in the Middle Ages* (1907)

Barron, James, *The Northern Highlands in the Nineteenth Century* (1903-1913) 3 vols

Bond, Charles, *Miscellanies in Prose and Verse* (1842)

Burt, Edmund, *Letters from a Gentleman in the North of Scotland* (London, 1754; reprinted Edinburgh, 1974) 2 vols

Cameron, George A, A *History and Description of the Town of Inverness.* (1847)

Cook, Joseph, *Joseph Cook's Inverness* (1992)

Defoe, Daniel, *A Tour Thro' the Whole Island of Great Britain* (London, 1724–7) 3 vols

Fairrie, Angus, *The Northern Meeting,* 1788–1988 (Kippielaw, 1988)

Fraser, James, *Chronicles of the Frasers,* commonly known as the Wardlaw Manuscript (Edinburgh: Scottish History Society, 1905)

Fraser, John, *Reminiscences of Inverness: Its People and Places* (1905)

Fraser-Mackintosh, Charles, *Invernessiana* (1875)

Gourlay, Robert and Turner, Anne, *Historic Inverness: The Archaeological Implications of Development* (Scottish Burgh Survey, 1977)

Logue, Kenneth J, *Popular Disturbances in Scotland, 1780–1815* (Edinburgh, 1979)

MacDonald, Mairi A, *By the Banks of the Ness: Tales of Inverness and District* (Edinburgh, 1982)

Macintosh, Murdoch, *A History of Inverness* (1939)

Maclean, John, *Reminiscences of a Clachnacuddin Nonagenarian* (1886)

Mitchell, Joseph, *Reminiscences of My Life in the Highlands* (1883–1884; repr 1971) 2 vols.

Munro, Robert, *Recollections of Inverness by an Invernessian* (1863)

Noble, John, *Miscellanea Invernessiana* (Stirling, 1902)

Pollitt, A Gerald, *Historic Inverness* (Perth, 1981)

Records of Inverness (Aberdeen: New Spalding Club, 1911–1924) 2 vols. Vol. 1: *Burgh Court Books, 1556–86;* vol. 2: *Burgh Court Books, 1602–37; Minutes of Town Council,* 1637–88.

Suter, James, *Memorabilia of Inverness* (1887)

Inverness Field Club Publications

The Dark Ages in the Highlands (1971)

The Hub of the Highlands: The Book of Inverness and District (1975)

An Inverness Miscellany: No. 1 (1983)

An Inverness Miscellany: No. 2 (1987)

Loch Ness and Thereabouts (1991)

The Middle Ages in the Highlands (1981)

The Moray Firth Area Geological Studies (1978)

Old Inverness in Pictures (1981)

The Seventeenth Century in the Highlands (1986)

Newspapers

Highland News, 1883–

Inverness Advertiser, 1849–1885*

Inverness Courier, 1817–

Inverness Journal, 1807–1849*

Northern Chronicle, 1881–1969

Scottish Highlander, 1885–1898*

* Card indexes held in Inverness Library, arranged both by names and by subjects, are an invaluable aid to historical research.

Periodicals

These journals contain numerous articles relevant to the history of Inverness:

Celtic Magazine (1876–88)
Celtic Monthly (1892–1917)
Transactions of the Gaelic Society of Inverness (1871–)
Transactions of the Inverness Scientific Society and Field Club (1875–1925)

Statistical Accounts

These three inventories of all the parishes in Scotland give excellent summaries of social conditions, industries, education, trade, transport, civic institutions, geography, topography and antiquities. The first or Old Statistical Account was edited by Sir John Sinclair of Caithness and published in twenty-one volumes between 1790 and 1799. In the 1840s the exercise was repeated as the New Statistical Account of Scotland, and a third survey was completed in recent decades. The town of Inverness appears in the submissions for the parish of Inverness and Bona, and is described as follows, with the date of compilation in brackets:

Old Statistical Account (1791)
New Statistical Account of Scotland (1835)
Third Statistical Account of Scotland (1951; revised 1970)

Schools Library Resource Service: H.E.L.P. Publications

A series of booklets has been produced by the Highland Environmental Link Project aimed at the pupils in Highland schools, on historical topics. These should be available in the libraries of all secondary schools in the Highlands, and in addition, a set is kept on file in the Reference Room at Inverness Library. A Catalogue produced by the Schools Library Resource Service lists forty-nine publications, of which the following are relevant to the history of Inverness:

Timber Extraction in the Highlands
Education in the Highlands, 1800–1939
Emigration from the Highlands
The Great Highland Famine
Highland Economy, 1750–1900
Potato Famine in the Highlands, 1846–1849

Scottish Poor Law in the Highlands
Caledonian Canal: Resource Handbook
Chapel Yard Cemetery, Inverness
Early Ecclesiastical Buildings in Inverness
Muirtown Basin of the Caledonian Canal
Port of Inverness
The River Ness (4 booklets)
Photographic Collections
From Drover to Driver (6 booklets on the history of road
    transport)
Highland Ferries
*The Highland Transport Revolution: Growth of the Highland
    Railway Network, 1855–1930* (3 booklets)
*Highland Transport Revolution: Growth of the Highland Road
    Network, 1725–1920*
Nineteenth Century Rail Travel
Queen Victoria in the Highlands
Royal Events in the Highlands
The Highlands at War, 1939–1945
The Highlands During the First World War
Inverness During the Second World War

INDEX

Aberdeen University viii, 188
Adam, John 83–87
Adomnan 6–7
AI Welders 155–156
Air services 161–162
American influence 158–159
Anderson, Isabel Harriet 92–93
Antiquarians vii–viii
Aquadome 175–176,184
Archaeology 1–8, 11–13, 189
Assynt murder 71–79
Atrocities 45–47

Benyon, Harry 156
Bomb explosion, 156–158
Bond of manrent 20
Brahan Seer 138–141
Bught leisure facilities 175–176
Burgh Police Court 98–100
Burt, Captain Edmund 49–52

Caledonian Canal 65–66, 68, 94–95, 148
Caledonian Hotel 116
Cameron Monument 133–135, 154–155
Census records 148–149
Charters 13–16
Chisholm, Grizell, 61–62
Cholera 80–83, 182, 185
Christmas 89–90
Clachnacuddin stone 49–51, 108, 179
Cook, Joseph 135
Craig Phadrig 3–6, 8
Crematorium 177–178
Cromarty 82–93
Culcabock golf course 162–163
Culloden, battle of 44–46, 53, 56–57, 146, 190–191
Cunningham, Robert 107

Davidson, Andrew 136
Defoe, Daniel 47–49
Dogs 41, 52
Dunghills 40

Economy 53–55, 5–59, 65
Edmond's Menagerie 97
Emigrations, 66
Fairs 16, 22–23

Ferguson, Robert, 70
Fires 63–64
Food rationing 160–161
Forbes, Dr George 81
Forbes fountain 182
Fraser, Charles
    see Mackintosh, Charles Fraser-
Fraser, Rev James 18–19, 24–37
Fraser, John 92
Fraser-Mackintosh, Charles
    see Mackintosh, Charles Fraser-

Gaelic Society of Inverness 44, 190
Gallery 2000 180, 183–185
Geology 1
Gifford, John 130, 179
Golden Mile 174
Grant, Charles MP 90–91
Grant's Clan Tartan Warehouse 127
Gunpowder explosion 63–64

Hangings 38–39, 68–70, 74–71, 85–86
Highland Archives ix, 37, 148
Highland Council 172–173, 179
Hogmanay 89–90
Horse-races 34–35
Housing policy 164–165, 178

Inverness
    bridges 19, 25, 27–29, 41–42, 64, 138–141, 180–181
    Burgh Court 37–39
    Castle 9, 13, 11, 26, 50, 53–54, 136–137, 184
    Common Good Fund 15
    charters 13–16
    Cromwell's Fort 30–33, 48, 54
    Great Charter 15–16
    hospitals 55
    mercat cross 40, 52, 179
    population 53, 60, 110, 148, 166, 174
    seal 9
    Town Council minutes 37, 39–43
Inverness Caledonian Thistle 174–175
Inverness District Council 169, 175–180
Inverness English 32–33, 40, 64–65
Inverness Field Club viii–ix, 3, 11, 49, 93, 135
Inverness Library ii, ix, 55, 96, 99, 107, 120–122, 149, 176, 189

Inverness Local History Forum 189
Inverness Museum 46, 176–177, 183, 189
Inverness Remembered Project viii, 191

Jacobite occupation 46–47
Jacobite Exhibition 146–147
Jacobites 44–47, 117
Johnson, Dr Samuel 32, 57–58
Johnstone, Christian Isobel 191–192

Licensing Court 169–171
Local Government 166–169,172–178
Longmore, Leonella 180–193
Lords of the Isles 10, 17–21

MacBeth 8–9
MacDonald, Flora 135–138, 157–158, 161
Macdonald, Sir Murdoch 153–154
MacDougalls' Tartan Warehouse 126
Mackintosh, Charles Fraser 112–115, 117–122, 146–147
Mackenzie, Alexander 138–140
Maclean, John 92
Macleod, Hugh 71–79
Macpherson, John 130
Major, John 16–19
Maps 51, 147–148
Matheson, Sir Alexander 114–115, 123–125, 128–129
Meg Dods' cook book 191–192
Meldrum, Edward viii, 133
Middle Ages 11–23
Millennium celebrations 141–143
Miller, Hugh 81–83
Mitchell, Joseph 94–96
Montrose, Marquis of 24–29

Napier Commission, 118–119
Nessie 7–8, 33, 66, 152–155
New Statistical Account 45–46
Newspapers vii, 105, 154, 176, 190
Nicol, Dr John Inglis 185

Old Statistical Account 52–53, 58–60
Parkhurst, Emmeline 151–152
Pennant, Thomas 53–57
Picts 5–6
Pillory 38
Place-names 130–133
PLUTO Project 155–156

Pollitt, Gerald 130
Population 53, 60, 110, 148, 166, 174

Rag, Rev David 22
Railways 63, 93–96, 114–115
Records of Inverness vii, 37–43
Religion 103–110
Reminiscences viii, 92
Revivalism 103–110
Riot Act, 62
Riots 36–37, 60–62, 70–71
Ross, Donald 74, 87–89
Royal visits 100–103

St Columba 6–8, 152
Scottish Local History Forum 189
South Kessock 178
Squatters 163–165
Station Square 154–155
Steuart, Bailie John 46–47
Street names 124, 130–133
Strother, Alexander 122
Sturgeon 33
Suffragists 150–152

Taylor, John 122–123
Taylour, Jane 150–151
Three Graces 127
Tolbooth 1, 38, 67
Tomnahurich 34–35, 54
Tourists 47–49, 56, 64–68, 96, 153
Town House 105, 179–190
Trade 13, 20–21, 53–54, 58–59, 64–65
Transport 78, 162

University of the Highlands and Islands Project 185, 188

Vandalism 70–71
Victoria, Queen 100–103, 143–145, 179
Vikings 9–10

Wardlaw Manuscript 18–19, 24–37
Watson, William J 130
Weather 36
Wheelie bins 177
Women 48–49, 150–152
Workers' Educational Association viii–ix, 188
World War II 155–161

Young, Colin 108–110